The Best Plants for Midwest Gardens

Flowers, vegetables, shrubs, and trees for spectacular low-maintenance gardens season after season

Written and illustrated by Laara K. Duggan

CHICAGO
REVIEW
PRESS

D1455973

Library of Congress Cataloging-in-Publication Data

Duggan, Laara K.
    The best plants for Midwest gardens / Laara K. Duggan. — 1st ed.
        p. cm.
    Includes index.
    ISBN 1-55652-284-3 (alk. paper)
    1. Gardening—Middle West.   2. Low maintenance gardening—Middle West.
I. Title.
    SB453.2.M53D84   1998
    635'.0977—dc21   97-52710
                                                                    CIP

Text and illustrations ©1998 by Laara K. Duggan
All rights reserved
First Edition
Published by Chicago Review Press, Incorporated
814 North Franklin Street
Chicago, IL 60610
ISBN 1-55652-284-3

For fellow gardeners past, present, and future.

Contents

Acknowledgments

Special thanks to Linda Matthews and Cynthia Sherry
of Chicago Review Press; to the Waterloo-Cedar Rapids
Branch of the National League of American Pen Women; to
the Garden Writers Association of America; to the Authors
Guild; to all my gardening friends, neighbors, and family; to
R. Tarz and the guys; to Beverly for knowing; and most of
all to my husband, researcher, and best friend, Desi Duggan.

A Note from the Author

In one hundred years we have gone from lamplight to electric light and from quill pen to computer. We have increased our travel capabilities from a few miles per day to thousands of mile per hour. In the midst of this unbelievably rapid material and mechanical progress, many of us feel that we have lost track of ourselves and our lives. We just don't have enough time.

Gardening offers each of us the chance to take a deep breath and get down to something that is understandable. A chance to mark the seasons as gardeners have always marked the seasons. A chance to work with life on an intimate level, to be surprised and experience wonder before nature slips away.

Gardeners are special people. They feed the hungry, create beauty where none existed, raise property values, and transform communities. The more we garden, the better our gardens are, and the more we want to garden.

This book about low-maintenance, site-specific plants and techniques is written in response to questions from fellow gardeners I met touring with my first book, *The Best Flowers for Midwest Gardens*. This book's information and format came from these and other conversations with master gardeners, garden center gurus, naturalists, growers, and my own gardening journals about what really works and what doesn't in our regional gardens.

Life moves very quickly. Through it all, seeds sprout. Birds sing. Butterflies visit. In the garden, it is easy to feel the great spiritual energy ticking away, keeping a steady beat of seasons and life. More than any other gardeners, midwesterners are double blessed, with rich soil and definite seasons that produce incredible vegetables, tall trees, and acres of flowers. These blessings and the plants and techniques in this book will help you create the garden of your dreams in the sunny, snowy, ever-changing weather of the great Midwest.

Happy gardening!

—Laara Duggan
www.process.com

Fundamentals

Great Gardens Start Here

Gardening Calendar

Winter

Early Spring

Spring

Late Summer

Autumn

Great Gardens Start Here

Today's gardeners, no matter how enthusiastic, have so many demands on their time that they need to achieve the best possible results with minimum labor. Good soil and fertilizing and mulching at the right time are the first steps in that direction.

Soil

Soil is the foundation of a successful garden. Soil anchors plants and provides nourishment. Without good soil everything else in the garden is a struggle.

There are thousands of individual types of soils, each differing in amounts of sand, silt, clay, and organic content. A few soils have special problems that may need correcting before general planting. Some are too wet, others are too hard, and a few dry out too quickly. All types of soil will grow some type of plant.

Sandy soil is well-drained and crumbly. Soil with a high sand content feels gritty when wet. A ball made by squeezing this soil will easily break apart when dry. Sandy soil warms up early in the spring, but water passes quickly through it, stripping the soil of nutrients. To make sandy soil water retentive and fertile, add organic matter.

Clay soils are heavy and difficult to work. Soil with a high proportion of clay feels smooth and sticky when wet. A ball made by squeezing this soil will retain its shape and set hard when dry. Roots have a hard time penetrating this type of soil. Clay soil is slow to warm up in the spring and drains poorly. Sand and organic matter help the texture of this soil. If the soil is very dense, you might consider growing plants in raised beds filled with good loam.

Loam is the ideal proportion of clay, sand, and organic matter. It feels slightly gritty and holds together when dry. Since it is moist, drains well, and is rich in nutrients, this is considered a good garden soil. Loam is usually a rich, dark color and contains an abundance of earthworms.

The deeper the topsoil, the better. The desirable depth for good root growth is two feet; it should never be less than one foot. Most plants grow best in a soil with a neutral 7.0 pH balance. To find your rating, have your soil tested.

Soil Tests

Soil testing will save you time and money. The least expensive and most accurate way is to contact your county extension agent. A soil test costs less than dinner for two at a fast-food restaurant. Your county extension office has free shipping boxes, directions for taking samples, and information sheets to be mailed with soil samples. The general soil test includes soil pH, phosphorus, and potassium, plus recommendations of nutrients you might need to add to your garden when growing specific plants.

On your soil test, the pH will be shown on a scale from 0 to 14 that measures the acidity or alkalinity of soil. Acid is 0 to 6.9. Neutral is 7.0. Alkaline is 7.1 to 14. Soil pH affects how plants grow by determining the availability of soil nutrients. Different plants have different requirements of nutrients and pH. Favorable conditions equal great plants. Unfavorable pH causes problems in growth and health. To adjust the pH for the plants you are growing, use sulphur or lime. Lime will raise pH, making soil more alkaline. Sulphur will lower pH, making soil more acidic.

Next look at the other ratings in your soil test—phosphorus (P), potassium (K), magnesium, and calcium. Phosphorus encourages healthy roots and flowers, potassium promotes vigor, magnesium helps photosynthesis, and calcium builds strong cell walls. Under each nutrient on your soil test you will find a rating. A rating of very high or extremely high indicates overfertilization. High is ideal. Low or medium generally suggests fertilizing or adding the low-rated nutrient.

Topsoil and Subsoil

Topsoil is a rich layer of organic matter that is usually two to twenty-four inches deep. The deeper your topsoil, the happier your plants. On new construction, some contractors will scrape off this layer and sell it to offset their costs. When starting your landscape, make sure that this soil has been replaced and is at least six inches deep. No matter what assurances contractors give you, plants will not be healthy in subsoil.

Subsoil is low in organic matter. It will not grow landscaping plants or lawn. It will, however, grow some very aggressive weeds. Subsoil is usually light in color with a heavy, thick, claylike feel to it. It can also be full of broken rocks. Subsoil can be six feet deep or more. If the roots of your new plants will be growing into subsoil, take a spike and punch holes in the subsoil at the bottom of your planting hole to help roots penetrate. Fill these with topsoil or sand.

Bedrock is a solid layer of rock. Even tree roots have a hard time penetrating bedrock. While bedrock is good for foundations, it is not good for plants.

As a general rule, whatever you see above the soil is mirrored below the soil. A plant's roots are as wide and as tall below the surface as its

How Deep Do Plant Roots Go?

Lawn grass: roots averages four to six inches

Annual vegetables: roots average six to eight inches

Annual flowers: roots average six to ten inches

Perennial flowers: roots average twelve inches or more

Shrubs: roots average twenty-four to forty-eight inches

Climbing vines: roots average thirty-six inches

Trees: roots can go down for a long, long way

leaves and trunk are above. Your garden soil has distinct levels that change according to where you live.

Fertilizer

Somewhere along the way you will have to decide whether to be an organic gardener, using only natural products to fertilize and protect; a traditional gardener, using chemical technology; or a practical gardener, using the best of both worlds. Organic fertilizers and commercial fertilizers are both effective and both can be misused.

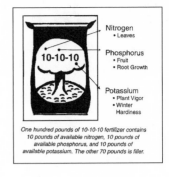

One hundred pounds of 10-10-10 fertilizer contains 10 pounds of available nitrogen, 10 pounds of available phosphorus, and 10 pounds of available potassium. The other 70 pounds is filler.

By law, all fertilizers, both organic and chemical, must state the guaranteed analysis on the container, always in the same order: nitrogen, phosphorus, potassium. Sometimes they are abbreviated by their chemical symbols: N (N) + P (P2O5) + K (K2O).

The first number listed is always nitrogen (N). Nitrogen stimulates green leaf and stem growth. Too much nitrogen causes heavy leaf growth and delayed flowering. Small doses of nitrogen should be applied every spring and throughout the summer months to ensure that plants and soil bacteria have all the fuel they need for growth.

The second number listed is always phosphorus (P). Phosphorus increases root growth. Too little phosphorus cause leaves to become a dull blue-green glazed with purple. The third number is always potassium (K). Potassium increases plant vigor and hardiness. Too little potassium results in stunted growth. Phosphorus and potassium should only be added to your garden after your soil has been tested.

One hundred pounds of a 10-10-10 fertilizer contains 10 pounds of available nitrogen, 10 pounds of available phosphorus, and 10 pounds of available potassium. The other seventy pounds are fillers. Higher analysis fertilizers, those containing thirty percent or more of nitrogen, phosphorus, and potassium, are more economical, but carry the danger of overfertilizing and chemically burning garden plants.

Animal manure, the standby of pioneer gardeners, is harder and harder to find. When you can find composted, weed-free manure, mix it with wood chips or compost and spread on the garden in place of nitrogen. Most organic fertilizers become available to plants slowly. Before nutrients can be absorbed, they first have to be broken down. Cottonseed meal, fish meal, and alfalfa meal also can be used as nitrogen sources. These should be dug into the soil.

It is easiest to work with "complete" fertilizers such as 10-10-10 with slow-release nitrogen to keep the soil elements balanced. Applying a spray of liquid fertilizer once a month works just as well for some gardens and usually does not affect soil balance.

Stop fertilizing perennials, trees, and shrubs at the end of July. In August, you might want to try a light dusting of potash to help with winter hardiness. Annuals and lawns can be feed through the first killing frost.

If, after your soil test, you decide to apply soil supplements, the following are readily available through local garden centers.

Chemicals

Ammonium nitrate (33% N)

Ammonium sulfate (21% N): soil acidifying

Sodium nitrate (16% N): soil sweetener

Calcium nitrate (15% N): soil sweetener

Urea (45% N): very strong; mostly agricultural use

Rock phosphate (30: 36% P): insoluble in soil above pH 6.0

Concentrated triple superphosphate (46% P): available to all soil pHs

Normal superphosphate (20% P): available to all soil pHs

Muriate of potash (Potassium: 60% K)

Magnesium sulfate (Epsom salts: 10% magnesium and 14% sulfur)

Animal Manures

Poultry	(N) 1.3%	(P) 1.2%	(K) .5%
Cow	(N) 1.0%	(P) 1.2%	(K) 1.5%
Horse	(N) .7%	(P) .3%	(K) .6%
Rabbit	(N) 1.1%	(P) 1.5%	(K) .5%

Application Methods

Broadcasting: spreading uniformly over an area

Top dressing: hand application in a ring around plant

Liquid feeding: applying with hose attachment or water can

Foliar feeding: spraying liquid solution on leaves, useful as an emergency supplement, does not affect soil

The Benefits of Mulch

WITHOUT MULCH — More Weeds, Evaporation

WITH MULCH — Less Watering, Less Weeding

Mulch

The healthiest plants in the garden are those that can quickly establish their root systems. Growth depends on two conditions: water and nutrition. When the Midwest sun beats down, soils begin to crack and water is lost through surface evaporation. As the soil dries, plants lose their ability to absorb nutrients. Over a long period of drought in warm or cold weather, a plant without water actually starves to death.

Applying a layer of summer mulch will conserve soil moisture and cut down on weeds. Remember to keep mulches away from plant crowns where roots and stems join. Mulching is a low-maintenance, proven tool that really works. Mulching material costs are offset by better yields, less plant loss, and less disease.

Natural, organic mulches become part of the garden, slowly decomposing and enriching the texture of the soil. A very successful mulch for home gardens is a mixture of wood chips and grass clippings. Man-made nonorganic mulches, such as plastics, act as specialty mulches that can increase produce yields. Field tests with colored mulches have shown increased crop yields: cucumbers, 18% with red mulch; peppers, 22% with yellow mulch; squash, 14% with red or blue mulch.

Ideally, mulch should be applied to the garden in mid-June after the soil warms and removed the following year for spring planting. Once a mulch is down, however, it is usually easier to simply pull the mulch away from plants after the danger of spring frost is past and push it back in place after the soil has warmed. If left in place, plants may mature and flower later due to slow soil warming.

If the soil has been properly prepared and a layer of mulch applied, watering should only be necessary during drought. Moisture helps plants absorb nutrients. Always check for moisture in the soil under the mulch before watering.

Soil soaker hoses buried under garden mulch and left in place are the easiest and most effective way to water. Frequent shallow watering produces shallow roots close to the soil surface. Deep watering encourages deep roots. Deep roots need less water to survive.

Summer mulches keep weeds out, the soil cool, and moisture in. Winter mulches protect plants by stabilizing the soil and prevent plant heaving caused by thawing and freezing. Mulches should be at least three inches and at the most six inches thick. Remove winter mulch when tulips bloom to allow the soil to warm. Begin summer mulching as weather warms for water retention and weed control.

Mulch with whatever is available in your local area, including compost, grass clippings, evergreen branches, leaves, peat moss, pine needles, corn cobs, seedless straw and hay, spent brewery hops, sawdust, wood chips and shavings, or shredded bark. As mulches interact with the soil, they will decompose at different rates and tie up soil nutrients. If you see the leaves on your plants turn yellow, apply a light application of nitrogen to offset the chemical reaction of the mulch breakdown.

Traditionally, vegetable gardens are stripped in the fall and tilled under in the spring. Newer conservation methods encourage tilling organic summer mulches under in the fall, seeding with a "green manure" crop such as annual rye, then tilling the green manure crop under in the spring. This method improves soil texture, adds nutrients to the soil, and protects plants.

Whichever method you use, do not use flowers to mulch flowers or vegetables to mulch vegetables. Sometimes fungus spores and insect pests hide in foliage and will cycle from the ground to the foliage and back again. Burn all infested foliage.

Plants need protection in winter too. Shredded leaves and snow are the best protection from drying winds. Christmas tree branches spread over the garden help trap snow and act as a windbreak.

Ground covers form a living green mulch and are a key element in easy-care gardens. Hardy perennial ground covers to grow as a living mulch are profiled in Ground Covers and Vines, in Section Four.

Natural Mulches and Soil Conditioners to Try

To use any of the mulches listed below, kill all weeds and grasses in the bed area, fertilize, and add mulch around the plants up to, but not over, their crowns. An important advantage of natural mulches is that they decompose and condition the soil. A disadvantage is that they can deplete the nitrogen supply in the garden. If leaves turn a pale green, add several light applications of nitrogen over the next few weeks. Apply these mulches to the depths suggested here.

two inches deep	three inches deep	four inches deep
Crushed corncobs	Grass clippings	Compost
Pine needles	Sawdust	Spoiled hay (up to six inches)
Wood chips and bark (up to four inches)	Soybean straw	
	Shredded leaves (up to four inches)	

Man-made Mulches and Weed Barriers to Try

To use any of the mulches listed below, kill weeds and grasses in the bed area, fertilize, water, and lay down the mulch, cutting holes for the plants to grow through. A major advantage of these artificial mulches is their low cost. Disadvantages are that these mulches become a nuisance as they wear out and need to be removed. Also, weed seeds blow in and grow on the surface of the barrier as dirt or soils collect there over time. Further advantages or disadvantages to individual mulches are given in parentheses.

- Cardboard (attracts sowbugs that eat young plants)
- Carpet (deer will not walk on carpet)
- Black plastic (prevents weed growth)
- Clear plastic (raises soil temperature; herbicide may be needed to control weeds)
- Colored plastic (colors may enhance crop production)
- Landscape fabric (expensive but easy to use)

The No-Dig Back-Saving Plan

Digging is hard work and takes too much effort. To start a new garden, mark out your garden area using a garden hose. Take samples of soil for testing. Spray area with glyphosate, sold as Roundup. You can mulch and plant in twenty-four hours or wait ten days and respray if necessary. Amend soil as noted in your soil test. Then mulch. Pull mulch apart and dig holes for plants as needed.

(Please note that glyphosate is a man-made chemical and should be used with discretion and according to label directions.)

MULCH AND TOPSOIL COVERAGE

Bags hold 3 cubic feet; areas are expressed in square feet.

Bags		Yards	1 in. deep	2 in. deep	4 in. deep
4.5	=	.5	160	80	40
9	=	1	320	160	80
18	=	2	640	320	160
27	=	3	960	480	240
36	=	4	1280	640	320
45	=	5	1600	800	400
54	=	6	1920	960	480
63	=	7	2240	1120	560
72	=	8	2560	1280	640
81	=	9	2880	1440	720
90	=	10	3200	1600	800

Ten Steps to a New Garden

1. Make a site plan of your home and property on graph paper or your computer. Make note of:

   Scale (one inch = one foot, one square = ten feet, etc.)

   North, south, east, and west

   Buildings

   Windows and doors

   Sidewalks, paths, driveways, streets, and roads

   Fences

   Good and bad views

   Trees and type—deciduous, leaves fall off; evergreen, leaves stay on

   Bushes and hedges

   Slopes

   Established gardens

2. Photocopy your plan to experiment with different sizes, shapes, and locations of proposed gardens.

3. Note the amount of sunlight each garden area receives.

4. Take photos of each garden area, enlarge on a photocopier, and draw in the basic shapes and sizes of plants you would like to use.

5. Drawing on the plant profiles given in this book, use tracing paper, graph paper, and colored pencils to sketch your ideas.

6. Pick garden color schemes. Use paint chips from the hardware store or colored pencils to play with color choices.

7. Prioritize the gardens. Set your budget and plant choices. Make a plant shopping list.

8. Locate plants through the catalogs and nurseries listed in Section Six.

Nature's Tillers

Earthworms improve your garden by eating their weight in soil each day. Worms mix layers of soil and compost while digging tunnels. These thin tunnels help air and water reach plant roots. While worms need moisture to survive, too much moisture will drown them. In rainstorms, when the soil gets flooded, worms come to the surface. Once on dry ground, they can get disoriented and die when the sun comes out. Smart gardeners find new homes for refugee worms in their gardens.

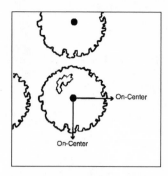

On-Center

On-Center

Rejuvenating Old Gardens

Established beds should be cleared of decaying vegetation. Wonderful new things can happen in old gardens if you follow the steps outlined above. Just draw in that favorite rosebush and mark the existing daffodils on your plan, and you are ready to go.

9. To make the garden functional, lay out the new garden with a garden hose and mark the edges with spray paint or sand. Before beginning any physical work, run the lawn mower along the lawn edge to check for ease of mowing and adjust garden edges as necessary.

10. Lift your shovel and move your garden from an idea into reality.

HOW MANY PLANTS DO YOU NEED?

Use your plant's size and garden square footage (width x length) to figure how many plants you will need for your garden project.

Plant Size	Plants Per Square Foot
On 6-in. centers or 12 in. across	4
On 8-in. centers or 16 in. across	2.25
On 9-in. centers or 18 in. across	1.75
On 10-in. centers or 20 in. across	1.50
On 12-in. centers or 24 in. across	1
On 18-in. centers or 36 in. across	.50
On 24-in. centers or 48 in. across	.25

Gardening Calendar

When people first realized that seasons repeated themselves, they devised systems for recording these repetitions. At first, the sun and the moon were used to measure changes. Days were marked by sunrise and sunset. Calendars tracked lunation—the period from one new moon to the next. Even our word for these lunar cycles, month, is a derivative of the word moon. And our weeks are based on the phases of the moon—new moon, first quarter, full moon, and last quarter.

Today the Western world uses a calendar system that was devised by Pope Gregory XIII in the 1850s and is based upon the birth of Jesus Christ. This "Gregorian" calendar uses both solar and lunar influences to mark the passage of time.

Gardeners borrow a little from both systems, keeping one eye on the calendar and another on the seasons to know when to do what.

Winter

It's cold. Sometimes there's snow and there is always wind. Most of us have an intense desire to be somewhere warm. Officially winter begins December 21, but watch for juncos at your feeders and flower catalogs in the mail to know when the season really begins.

Flower Gardens

- Go over your garden notes and photographs to see what plants you need to fill the holes in your garden's design. Use small envelopes to package flowers seeds saved from your garden to give as gifts. Use catalog pictures to decorate the envelopes.

- Check perennials for heaving—that is, being pushed out of the soil by freezing temperatures. If heaving occurs, cover exposed roots with mulch to protect them from winter winds.

Kitchen Gardens

- Prune grapes and other small fruits before the sap rises.

- Plan next spring's vegetable crop. Order seeds from catalogs. If a plant description includes "runners," run. This is an invasive choice that can take over your garden.

- Check small fruit-bearing plants like raspberries and currants for rodent damage.

Unplanted Bulbs

Place unplanted spring-flowering bulbs in a plastic bag filled with damp potting soil and store in the refrigerator at 35 degrees. Plant as the ground thaws in early spring.

Landscaping
- Brush heavy snows off evergreens.
- Prune evergreens and use the trimmings as holiday decorations.

Wildlife Gardens
- Christmas bird count time is here. Call your local seed store or bird club to join in the fun.
- Continue watching for rare birds at your feeders.
- Remember that songbirds need to eat their weight in seeds every twelve hours to survive.
- Add chicken grit to the ground near your feeders.
- Scented clothes-dryer sheets and deodorant bath soap have both been effective in keeping deer away from shrubs and trees. Mothballs help discourage rabbits.

Early Spring

Early spring in our area is an event. Everything and everyone is ready to begin the new year. Our days are streaked with hail, blown by wind, and warmed by crisp sunshine. Officially spring begins March 20, but watch your garden for budding crocus and the roadsides for red-winged blackbirds.

Cut Christmas Trees

Commercial Christmas trees are raised on farms. They are harvested when the weather turns cold and before the needles change to their winter colors, usually in early November. Try these Christmas trees for good needle retention and wonderful fragrance:

Fir: balsam, Douglas, Fraser
Pine: red, Scotch, white

Flower Gardens
- Sow meadows and prairies with wildflower seed.
- Order bareroot roses.
- Spray iris for borers and add mothballs to protect the plants from them.
- Start flowering annuals inside.
- Check beds and borders for heaving. Cover exposed roots with mulch to prevent them from drying. As the ground thaws, these plants will settle back in without damage.
- If the season is dry and the ground thawed, consider watering.
- Remember to check any seedlings you have in cold frames.
- When shopping for perennials locally, check under leaves and in soil for hitchhiking bugs and diseases.
- Remove buckets and other windbreaks from roses but leave mounded soil and mulch until tulips bloom.
- Begin feeding peonies with liquid fertilizer as they emerge from the ground.
- Deadhead early tulips and daffodils as they finish flowering to direct the plant's activity to bulb building.
- Look for extra-large leaves on tulips that do not bud. Dig out these bulbs and toss, as they won't ever bloom again.
- Mark new plants and seeds as they are planted to protect from weeding them out by mistake.

❧ As the temperature at night stays above freezing, pull winter mulch from around perennials to allow surrounding soil to warm up.

❧ Pull dead leaves from hostas.

Kitchen Gardens

❧ Now is the time to start new gardens and amend soil in established beds. If the soil is wet and can be formed into a soggy ball, wait a few sunny days until it dries out before beginning work.

❧ Soak dormant mail-order plants for forty-five minutes before planting. Use plant starter food to help with transplant shock. If the ground is wet, dormant plants can stay wrapped on the back porch out of the sun until planting time.

❧ As crocus flower, plant your choice of the very hardy vegetables listed in Section Three, Table Vegetables A to Z.

❧ Start warm-season vegetable seeds inside.

❧ Hoe young weed seedlings as they appear.

❧ Plant any leftover spring bulbs: dig a hole three times deeper than height of the bulb; add sand, compost, and bulb food; then cover with soil.

Landscaping

❧ Start spring early by cutting branches from flowering shrubs and bringing them inside to flower.

❧ Feed lawns, trees, shrubs, and gardens.

❧ Seed any bare spots in your lawn.

❧ Spray dormant oil on deciduous shrubs and trees per directions on bottle.

❧ Prune deciduous trees and shrubs before they leaf out. Remember that spring-flowering plants are full of flower buds. These should be pruned after they bloom.

❧ Plant trees and shrubs.

Wildlife Gardens

❧ Birds begin returning. Watch for robins and red-winged blackbirds along roadsides. As the insect population increases, courtship and nest building will begin in earnest.

❧ Watch for hunting owls and hawks as mice, shrews, and voles begin moving about. Predators will begin their families as food becomes more plentiful.

❧ Goldfinches turn bright gold.

❧ Watch for chipmunks to come out of hibernation on warm days.

❧ Continue feeding birds with suet, peanut butter, and sunflower seeds. If there is not enough food, the weakest nestling will starve.

❧ Watch for migratory birds at your feeder.

❧ Clean out birdhouses and set up.

❧ Set up hummingbird and oriole feeders.

Early Spring Precipitation

MIST
Very small, irregular cloud droplets from stratus clouds; beneficial in the garden.

DRIZZLE
Small uniform cloud droplets from stratus clouds; soaks into ground immediately with little soil erosion.

RAIN
Large drops from nimbostratus or stratus-cumulus cloud combinations; heavy storms can cause soil erosion or flooding.

FREEZING MIST
Supercooled mist that can coat trees, bushes, and plants, causing branches and stems to break.

FREEZING RAIN AND SLEET
Partially frozen droplets from a storm produced by a warming trend; can cause serious damage in the garden.

GRAUPEL
Frozen cloud droplets found in early spring thunderstorms; messy but too soft to cause much damage in the garden.

HAIL
Ice stones from cumulonimbus clouds; damage caused by hailstones is multiplied by accompanying wind.

Forcing Cut Branches

Most spring-flowering trees and shrubs set their blossoms in the fall. Any time after January, these branches can be encouraged to flower by pruning exterior twelve-inch-long branch tips and bringing them inside. Soak the entire branch in a bucket of warm water for at least twelve hours before arranging in a vase. The closer to spring you pick your branches, the quicker the branches will bloom. Often, branches that are forced will also set roots and can be replanted in the garden. Forcing can take anywhere from one to six weeks. Rinse branches weekly. Plants for forcing include apple, beautybush, cherry, crabapple, forsythia, quince, lilac, redbud, serviceberry, wisteria, and witch hazel.

Spring

Spring makes us forget all about Midwest winters. With the birds singing love songs to each other, peonies budding, and our garden centers stuffed with new plants, anything outdoors seems possible.

Flower Gardens

- Watch for yearly garden-club sales.
- Remember to photograph garden areas as flowers bloom.
- Order new perennials.
- Feed flowers.
- Good bugs as well as bad bugs enter the garden at this time of year. Know your bugs before spraying or killing anything. Chemical sprays are expensive and environmentally unsound. Try using liquid dish soap mixed with water or natural insecticidal soap with pyrethrum, a distillation of painted daisy (botanical name: *Chrysanthemum coccineum,* also known as *Pyrethrum roseum*).
- Hoe weed seedlings before they flower and seed.
- Make sure flowers have one inch of water per week if the weather has been dry.
- This is a wonderful time to visit local gardens; see Section Six for listings of public gardens in your area.
- Deadhead spring bulbs as they finish flowering to direct the plant's activity to bulb building.
- Throw away any tulip bulbs that produce large leaves and no flowers.
- Tuck yellow ripening spring bulb foliage into ground cover.
- Give perennials three to six inches of mulch. Don't mulch annuals until summer, they need heated soil for a quick start to the growing season.
- Fill in empty holes in flower beds with annuals from garden centers. Plant seeds of annuals around new plants to replace bedding plants as they die back in late summer.
- Divide perennials as their flowers fade.
- Watch for perennial weeds and dig them out by the roots.

Kitchen Gardens

- Plant your choice of the hardy, frost-tolerant vegetables listed in Section Three, Table Vegetables A to Z.
- Feed rhubarb and other perennials in vegetable and fruit gardens.
- Pull winter mulch into rows for walking on and allow soil to warm.
- Purchase vegetable plants from garden centers.

🐾 To keep birds at your feeders and off your garden, attach a string to two stakes and stretch the string across the row. For some reason, this seems to scare birds.

🐾 Last cutting of asparagus.

🐾 Snap flower heads off of rhubarb.

Landscaping

🐾 Plant new trees, shrubs, ground covers, lawns, and vines.

🐾 Sow seeds of annual vines indoors.

🐾 Finish pruning shrubs and trees and vines.

🐾 Rake, trim back, and fertilize ground covers.

🐾 Hold off mowing meadows and prairies—many birds nest during this period.

🐾 Fertilize lawns with spring formulas. Crabgrass seeds start growing the first to the middle of May.

🐾 Prune trees and shrubs.

🐾 Mow lawn at low settings.

Wildlife Gardens

🐾 Orioles and hummingbirds are busy at feeders.

🐾 Look for mating behavior at feeders.

🐾 Consider offering oyster shells at feeders to help with eggshell strength.

🐾 Many goldfinches will migrate north.

🐾 Look for southern and northern migrators passing each other at your feeders.

🐾 Set broken clay flower pots in the garden for toad houses. One toad will eat up to ten thousand insects in three months. Toads will need access to water.

🐾 Hang birdhouses as summer visitors begin to arrive in the garden—swallows, wrens, swifts, and flycatchers.

🐾 Monarch butterfly eggs can be found on milkweed.

🐾 Continue feeding peanut butter, suet, and sunflower seeds to nesting birds.

🐾 Encourage butterflies and bees by planting native plants, which have a sweeter scent than hybrids.

Summer

Summer is deep blue with sailing cloud skies, pristine mornings, and soft evenings, all rich with floating butterflies, blooming flowers, and nesting birds. Officially summer begins June 21.

Flower Gardens

🐾 Buy bagged topsoil as it goes on sale at garden centers and save to mound over roses in autumn.

🐾 Remember to photograph gardens for winter planning.

Arbor Day

On March 31, 1874, Nebraska governor Robert Furnas, prompted by newspaperman J. Sterling Morton, set aside the second Wednesday of April to celebrate trees. Other states, and even foreign countries, soon followed Nebraska in adopting this tree-planting day. The Morton Arboretum in Lisle, Illinois has a memorial monument at Arbor Lodge dedicated by former President Grover Cleveland in 1905 and inscribed with a quote from Morton: "Other Holidays Repose upon the Past . . . Arbor Day Proposes for the Future."

Bug Zappers

There have been several articles in gardening journals stating that neon bug zappers kill more beneficial insects than pests. Check the dead bugs at the bottom of your zapper to see if that's true in your garden.

Stormy Weather

Birds fly less and perch more just before storms. The lighter, low-pressure air that brings weather changes makes it harder for birds to fly. Large groups of birds in trees or on the ground may mean that rain is on the way.

- Perennials go on sale locally in July. If they're in bad shape, cut back and water faithfully until recovered.
- This is a wonderful time to visit local gardens—see Section Six for listings of public gardens in your area.
- Bulb catalogs begin to arrive. Check garden photos and notes for garden areas that need new spring- or fall-flowering bulbs.
- For medium-sized plants that topple over, use short bushy branches to prop up flowers. For taller plants, use stakes and twine for support.
- Water young plants regularly until they are established.
- Pinch back phlox, asters, and mums to make them bushier.
- Cut spent rose blossoms back after blooming to the first set of five leaves. Watch for aphids and fungus. Aphids can be washed off and left on the ground. Leaves with fungus should be cut off and burned.
- Feed roses.
- Apply applications of diluted liquid fertilizer to perennial and annual foliage.
- Make sure garden has one inch of water per week.
- Deadhead perennials to encourage plant to build a strong root system.
- Use grass clippings to mulch around flowers.
- Trim back gangly annual bedding plants, then water every week with liquid fertilizer to encourage strong second bloom.
- Hoe annual weeds before they go to seed.
- This is last period to safely transplant and divide perennials.

Kitchen Gardens
- Plant tender vegetables listed in Section Three, Table Vegetables A to Z.
- Mulch vegetable garden to slow weed growth and conserve water.
- Start a second series of hardy vegetable crops.
- Fertilize in June but not July.
- Harvest vegetables and herbs.
- Mulch, mulch, mulch.

Landscaping
- Transplant annual vines into garden.
- Prune arbor vitae, junipers, and yews.
- Mow grass on high setting.
- Make sure lawn and garden gets one inch of water per week.

Wildlife Gardens
- Fireflies appear.
- Watch for ladybugs on warm walls and at your birdbaths.
- In early morning it is possible to catch glimpses of night predators. Watch for foxes, owls, bats, opossum, and raccoons.
- Check birdhouses for unwanted tenants.

❧ Continue feeding seeds to resident birds.

❧ Consider a birdbath outside the kitchen window.

❧ Baby birds are everywhere.

Late Summer

Late summer is lazy before it falls into autumn. Enjoy our warm days and cool nights as fledglings practice at feeders and gardening is easy. Watch for late-summer lilies and butterflies.

Flower Gardens

❧ Remember to photograph gardens for winter planning.

❧ Shop for spring bulbs.

❧ This is a wonderful time to visit local gardens—see Section Six for listings of public gardens in your area.

❧ Cut flowers for dried winter bouquets in the morning and hang upside down to dry in the shade.

❧ If you planted butterfly weed for monarch butterflies, cut off seed-pods before they open and spread seeds into neighborhood gardens or farmers' fields. Closed pods and stems hung upside down will ripen and open as they dry.

❧ Check for mildew on leaves in perennial beds. Remove infected leaves and burn, or spray with soapy water mixed with one table-spoon of baking powder.

❧ Stop fertilizing perennials and allow plants to prepare for winter.

❧ Continue fertilizing annuals for increased show.

❧ Prevent perennial and annual weeds from going to seed.

❧ Leave the last rose blossoms of summer on plants to encourage dormancy.

❧ Make sure garden has one inch of water per week. Keep water off plant leaves to prevent mildew.

❧ Use grass clippings to mulch around flowers.

❧ Deadhead perennials.

❧ Begin planting fall bulbs. Use synthetic fertilizers. Animal manures can spread underground diseases throughout bulb colonies. Add a scoop of sand, topsoil or compost, gravel, and bulb food to each hole.

❧ Plant rooted cuttings in beds and borders.

Kitchen Gardens

❧ Berries are ripening.

❧ Rake up dropped fruit to control pests.

❧ Harvest vegetables.

❧ Seed quick-growing vegetables for a second crop.

Landscaping

❧ Mow lawn at high setting.

❧ Make sure yard and gardens have one inch of water per week.

Garden Folklore

Crickets act as living thermometers, chirping faster as the temperature rises. Try counting the number of chirps in fifteen seconds, add thirty-seven, and you have the temperature.

Out-Think Those Pests

Use your child-rearing skills to out-think garden pests. Usually you can distract rabbits, deer, squirrels, and even bugs by covering plants with nets or cloths. Soapy sprays can make plants taste unappealing. Wood ashes discourage snails. Slugs and grasshoppers are irresistibly drawn to bowls of beer or water and molasses mixes.

Wildlife Gardens

🐾 Increase seed variety at the feeder as birds begin to gather in flocks for migration. Young birds can be distinguished from older birds by their neutral "baby" feathers and confused behavior.

🐾 Birds gather around farmlands during harvest to feed on mice and rodents.

🐾 Pile fallen pinecones for the squirrels around a tree trunk visible from the window.

🐾 Butterflies start grouping together for migration.

Dog Days

The "dog days" of late summer do not refer to dogs at all. Ancient Romans believed that the Dog Star, Sirius, had an disrupting influence on people. Egyptians used the Dog Star as an indicator of when the River Nile would flood and irrigate their crops. In the Midwest, the rising of Sirius precedes the uncomfortable sticky weather we call "dog days."

Autumn

What can midwesterners expect? Who knows? Perhaps a heat wave, perhaps a thunderstorm, perhaps some snow, maybe a little of everything. It's hard to say. Autumn separates the hardy from the not-so-hardy. Officially autumn begins September 22, but watch for turning maples and goldfinches dressed in winter colors to know when the season really begins.

Flower Gardens

🐾 Sow meadows and prairies with wildflower seeds.

🐾 Remember to photograph autumn gardens for winter planning.

🐾 Enjoy the second flush of roses. After the first hard frost, cut back canes to twelve inches and cover roses with a mixture of topsoil, shredded leaves, and mothballs. As the ground freezes, cover mounded roses with something that will act as a windbreak. Large groups of roses can be protected by covering with leaves and a portable windbreak.

🐾 Make sure your perennials and bulbs have one inch of water per week.

🐾 After the first hard frost, cut spent perennials back, leaving six inches of stalk.

🐾 Leave mums as they are until spring.

🐾 Remove mulch from pinks.

🐾 Use grass clippings mixed with shredded leaves to mulch around flowers. Mulch right up to plant crowns—where the roots meet the stems—but not over the top of the crown.

🐾 Save one or two bags of shredded leaves for mulch touch-up in February.

🐾 Winter-mulch perennials with evergreen branches and leaves.

🐾 Lily bulbils (offsets) produced along stems can be replanted either directly into beds or separated into nursery beds. They will have one leaf the first year and produce flowers in the second or third year.

🐾 Purchase chrysanthemums at nurseries and markets.

🐾 All hardy bulbs can be planted until the ground is frozen. Mulch heavily until February.

Kitchen Gardens

- Plant lettuce in cold frames.
- Enjoy berries and grapes fresh off the vine.
- Prune raspberries.
- Gather precious tomatoes from their vines.
- Clean up garden and till debris under the soil. Cover with a light mulch of shredded leaves mixed with a nitrogen fertilizer to offset wind erosion.
- Mulch and protect small fruits.
- Have your soil tested every three years at a county extension service office.

Landscaping

- Spray evergreens with an anti-transpirant such as Wiltpruf to reduce moisture loss. Anti-transpirants are nontoxic sealants designed to reduce moisture loss through the leaves.
- Keep lawns short, mowing as needed.
- Apply broad-leaf weed killers if necessary.
- Use "winter" lawn fertilizers.
- Aerate lawns as needed.
- After ground freezes, add extra mulch to vines and ground covers.
- Make sure your lawn, trees, and shrubs have one inch of rain or water per week until the ground freezes.
- Sod or seed bare spots in lawn.
- Add trees and shrubs.
- Protect young tree trunks from rabbits and deer with wrapping or other barriers.
- Shield tender evergreen conifers with burlap to prevent winter sunburn.
- Use any leftover garden fertilizers on the lawn.

Wildlife Gardens

- Watch for unusual birds at feeders and birdbaths as migrants stop in for refreshment on their way south.
- Consider joining your area's Christmas bird count either as an active participant or as part of the feeder watch. Check with your local feed outlet for information.
- After collecting seeds for next year, allow flower seed heads of dormant plants to remain standing as fresh food for the birds.
- Watch for garden wildlife to change into their winter coats.
- Restock the birdfeeder to include high-energy foods like suet and peanut butter.
- In rural areas, flocks of gulls and crows will begin following harvesting machines and ploughs, seeking food.

Shine on, Harvest Moon

In the Midwest, during the full moon nearest the autumnal equinox, there is a period of several days when the moon rises soon after sunset. This annual phenomenon gives farmers and gardeners extra hours of light in which to complete harvesting.

Fall Color

Fall color begins in the upper Midwest during September or October and sweeps south in a tide of color as shorter days and longer nights trigger a chemical reaction that causes leaves to change color.

Weather influences the timing of these changes. A heavy frost can kill leaf cells before they can change color. Strong winds or heavy rains can strip trees of their leaves too soon. The most brilliant fall colors occur when weather conditions are clear, dry, and cool. Watch your local weather forecasts to time your leaf-viewing trips.

For weekly updates on the best fall foliage locations, check with your state's Department of Natural Resources Forests and Forestry Division. For national color updates, call the National Leaf Hotline at 1-800-354-4595.

The Mother of Thanksgiving

During the Civil War, Sarah Hale, author of *Mary Had a Little Lamb*, used her influence to urge President Abraham Lincoln to declare Thanksgiving a national celebration. In 1864, she became known as the Mother of Thanksgiving.

The Best Hardy Bulbs to Plant in Perennial Gardens

Allium

Camassia

Crocus

Daffodils

Grape Hyacinth

Lily

Siberian Squill

🦋 Bats, snakes, frogs, toads, opossums, chipmunks, and ground squirrels all go into hibernation as the insects they feed on disappear.

🦋 Rabbits, raccoons, and squirrels will sleep deeply during cold spells, but will be out foraging during winter warmups.

· 🦋 As freezing weather covers the Midwest, water becomes as important as food. Consider setting out fresh water daily.

Fall Colors of Familiar Leaves

YELLOW	PURPLE	BURGUNDY	RED	BRONZE
Green Ash	White Ash	Silver Maple	Bur Oak	Red Oak
Elm	Frontier Elm		White Oak	
Ginkgo	Serviceberry		Sumac	
Hickory			Virginia Creeper	
Hard Maple				
Honey Locust				
Pin Oak				
Walnut				

Flower Gardens

Domesticated Wildflowers

Favorite Perennials

Hardy Bulbs

The beautiful shapes, colors, and fragrances of flowers bring a smile to people's faces, brighten our holidays, and honor our romances and celebrations. In our gardens, they increase property values, beautify our neighborhoods, and make our communities better places to live.

As much as we love flowers, they are more than just beautiful ornaments for our enjoyment. The reality is that each flower blossom is created to attract ants, bats, beetles, gnats, bees, moths, butterflies, birds, mice, and men for pollination and seed production. The closer a flower is to its natural cousins, the more appeal it seems to have to pollinators. Light, white flowers are often adapted to night pollination. Bright red flowers are especially attractive to hummingbirds. In summer and fall, yellow and purple flowers attract butterflies.

When and how long a flower blooms depends on when its pollinators are active and when it is pollinated. You can use these traits to have gardens that bloom spectacularly from the last frost of spring to first killing frost of winter. The flowers in this section are gardener-tested and preapproved for low-maintenance beauty.

Domesticated Wildflowers

Domesticated wildflowers are wild flowers that have become entwined with history and tamed into garden settings. Some domesticated wildflowers still retain close relatives in woodland and wildlife refuges. Others are the last of their kind, saved from extinction because of their beauty or usefulness. Some of our favorite wildflowers were already part of the Midwest before the first human appeared. Others came hidden as stowaways in agricultural seeds, in the stuffing of household furniture, or in the wool of sheep. Native or introduced, wildflowers are one of the Earth's greatest gifts to those swayed by natural beauty.

The twelve domesticated wildflowers in this section are one hybridized step away from their wild relatives. When hybridizing these flowers, growers have made them bloom longer, brighter, and bigger. Because they are hybrids, they will not breed true from seeds, so deadhead (remove spent flower heads) to encourage the plant to reinvest its energy in its own growth.

Please note: The drawings of flowers, fruit, foliage, and butterflies in this book are scaled at thirty-five percent; images appear at about one-third their actual size.

Successful wildflower gardens start here:

S Select healthy, nutrient-rich soil. Have a soil sample tested by your county extension office to find out if your soil needs any additives to grow flowers. Bed preparation is the most important step to beautiful flowers. See Great Gardens Start Here in Section One for more information on mulches and soil. As always, the work you do at the beginning stages of gardening will pay off later on.

T Think about how your young plants will look when they reach full maturity. Place accordingly. Some wildlflowers are taller in their second year and others will spread. Some need dividing and replanting every two or three years; others go on indefinitely without fuss.

A Always plant wildflowers in bunches or clumps rather than neat rows, and choose types that will bloom at different times of the year for frost-to-frost color.

R Rake or hoe to control early spring weeds. Mulch with untreated grass clippings to improve soil or add wood chips to give your beds a tidy, clean look.

T Thin and share with neighbors as wildflowers mature and fill up their allocated garden space.

Want to Know More About Flowers?

For profiles of 202 flowering plants that love living in the sunny, snowy, ever-changing weather of your state, order *The Best Flowers for Midwest Gardens,* Laara Duggan (ISBN 1-55652-263-0) from your favorite bookseller.

Weeds

Weeds are plants that are in the wrong place at the wrong time. One person's unwanted and unloved weed is another person's prized wildflower.

Aster

Asters are both native and introduced wildflowers that have been hybridized in European gardens since the early 1600s. There are over two hundred species of aster in the world, of which one or more will be perfect for your garden.

BOTANICAL NAME: *Aster*

HYBRIDS TO TRY: 'Wonder of Staffa', 'Alert', 'Dark Beauty', 'Calico', 'Alma Potschke', 'Hella Lacy', 'Purple Dome', 'Red Star', 'September Ruby', 'Professor Anton Kippenberg', 'Rose Serenade', 'Nanus', 'Bonny Blue', 'Snow Cushion', 'Eventide', 'Purple Glory'

COMMON NAME: starflower

FLOWERS: purple, white, or pink stars

FOLIAGE: tall stems with alternating leaves

SIZE: 12 to 48 inches tall × proportional

SEASON: autumn

LIGHT: sun to partial shade

CULTURAL NEEDS: average; water if autumn is dry

PROPAGATION: purchase plants

WINTER HARDINESS: −40°

Columbine

Columbine are native wildflowers with airy, graceful flowers that belong in every garden. In cool weather, they will bloom for a month if given adequate water. In the late 1600s plant hunters took specimens of columbine from Virginia to England, where the plant was extensively hybridized and then returned to America.

BOTANICAL NAME: *Aquilegia*

HYBRIDS TO TRY: 'Nora Barlow', 'Harlequin', 'McKana', 'Biedermeier', 'Dragonfly'

COMMON NAME: granny bonnets

FLOWERS: petals curving up into spurs in all colors

FOLIAGE: small gray-green hands; some have variegated leaves

SIZE: 12 to 48 inches tall × proportional

SEASON: spring

LIGHT: partial shade to shade

CULTURAL NEEDS: humus-rich soil

PROPAGATION: purchase plants

WINTER HARDINESS: −40°

Coreopsis

The Coreopsis family includes more than one hundred species. Twelve are native to our area. Coreopsis love to grow in open fields and along roadsides wherever the soil has been disturbed.

BOTANICAL NAME: *Coreopsis*

HYBRIDS TO TRY: 'Goldfink', 'Early Sunrise', 'Moonbeam', 'Rosea', 'Zagreb'

COMMON NAME: golden wave, tickseed, golden daisy, calliopsis

FLOWERS: small daisies in pink and various yellows

FOLIAGE: narrow leaves

SIZE: 12 to 36 inches tall × 12 inches across

SEASON: summer

LIGHT: sun

CULTURAL NEEDS: average soil, drought-tolerant once established

PROPAGATION: purchase plants

WINTER HARDINESS: −40°

Coneflower

Coneflowers are wonderful native plants that are popular hybridized additions to flower borders all over the world. They begin blooming in summer and continue till frost.

BOTANICAL NAME: *Echinacea*

HYBRIDS TO TRY: 'Bravado', 'Purpurea', 'White Lustre', 'Leuchtstern', 'Magnus'

COMMON NAME: black sampson, red sunflower

FLOWERS: purple, pink, or white daisies

FOLIAGE: large, fuzzy leaves

SIZE: 24 to 36 inches tall × 18 inches across

SEASON: summer to autumn

LIGHT: sun to partial shade

CULTURAL NEEDS: average soil; drought tolerant once established

PROPAGATION: purchase plants

WINTER HARDINESS: −40°

Gaillardia

A native of the high plains, this is a bright, happy, easy-care flower to fill whole beds. Its common name, Indian blanket, refers to its jagged flower edges. New hybrids will bloom from spring to frost.

BOTANICAL NAME: *Gaillardia*

HYBRIDS TO TRY: 'Baby Cole', 'Golden Goblin', 'Kobold', 'Monarch'

COMMON NAME: blanket flower, Indian blanket

FLOWERS: showy daisies of red, yellow, red and yellow, and wine red

FOLIAGE: gray-green

SIZE: 24 inches tall × 12 inches across

SEASON: summer through autumn

LIGHT: sun

CULTURAL NEEDS: well-drained soil

PROPAGATION: purchase plants

WINTER HARDINESS: −40°

Liatris

Liatris are prairie natives that bloom from the top down. They are valuable garden perennials hybridized in European and American gardens. At last count, there were over twenty-five species with different traits and blooming times. Easy to grow and long-lasting in the garden and as cut flowers.

BOTANICAL NAME: *Liatris*

HYBRIDS TO TRY: 'Floristan Violett', 'Floristan Weiss', 'Kobold'

COMMON NAME: blazing star, gayfeather, button snakeroot

FLOWERS: tall spikes in white and purple

FOLIAGE: tuft of small narrow leaves surrounding flower spikes, thin straps at base

SIZE: 24 to 48 inches tall × 18 inches wide

SEASON: late summer

LIGHT: sun

CULTURAL NEEDS: well-drained soil; wet heavy soil in winter is fatal

PROPAGATION: purchase plants

WINTER HARDINESS: −40°

Bee Balm

Bee balm is a North American native with a patriot history. After the Boston Tea Party in 1773, Americans stopped drinking black tea and switched to a tea made from *Monarda* leaves and blossoms. The British stationed in America tried the new tea and liked it. Refusing to abandon black tea altogether, the English added bee balm to black tea and named the blend Earl Grey.

BOTANICAL NAME: *Monarda*

HYBRIDS TO TRY: 'Alba', 'Aquarius', 'Cambridge Scarlet', 'Croftway Pink', 'Marshall's Delight', 'Violet Queen', 'Mahogany'

COMMON NAME: wild bergamot, horsemint

FLOWERS: ragged red, pink, white, or purple heads

FOLIAGE: hairy, gray-green, mintlike

SIZE: 24 to 36 inches tall × 24 inches across

SEASON: late summer

LIGHT: sun to partial shade

CULTURAL NEEDS: moist, humus-rich soil

PROPAGATION: purchase plants or take stem cuttings; will naturalize by offshoots

WINTER HARDINESS: −40°

Sundrop

Native sundrops were heralded by European garden writers as early as the 1600s. The original species plant is very aggressive, hybrids are less so. Those that open during the day are called sundrops. Those that open during the evening are called evening primrose.

BOTANICAL NAME: *Oenothera*

HYBRIDS TO TRY: 'Aurea', 'Summer Solstice', 'Fremontii'

COMMON NAME: evening primrose, Missouri primrose, sand lily

FLOWERS: yellow with orange buds, pink, white

FOLIAGE: dark green

SIZE: 20 inches tall × 24 inches across

SEASON: summer

LIGHT: sun to partial shade

CULTURAL NEEDS: any soil; once established will survive drought

PROPAGATION: purchase plants

WINTER HARDINESS: −40°

Phlox

Phlox is a native of Texas and one of the earliest plants to migrate with plant hunters to Europe, where it was hybridized for gardens. In the language of flowers, phlox is a proposal of love and a wish for sweet dreams.

BOTANICAL NAME: *Phlox*

HYBRIDS TO TRY: 'Anja', 'Miss Lingard', 'London Grove', 'Louisiana Blue', 'Alpha', 'Natascha', 'Omega', 'Rosalinde', 'David', 'Fairest One', 'Fairy's Petticoat', 'Norah Leigh', 'Orange Perfection', 'Prime Minister', 'Starfire', 'Spring Delight', 'Doddo Hanbury Forbes', 'Charles Curtis', 'Bright Eyes', 'Blue Boy', 'Mt. Fuji'

COMMON NAME: garden phlox

FLOWERS: pink, white, purple, or red-domed clusters

FOLIAGE: long and narrow

SIZE: 36 inches tall × 30 inches wide

SEASON: late summer, autumn

LIGHT: sun

CULTURAL NEEDS: humus-rich moist soil; good air circulation

PROPAGATION: purchase plants

WINTER HARDINESS: −40°

Obedient Plant

Obedient plant is one of the more important fall blooming natives of Midwest gardening, too often overlooked. Hybrids have varied flower colors and original plant traits. This is a great flowering plant.

BOTANICAL NAME: *Physostegia*

HYBRIDS TO TRY: 'Alba', 'Summer Snow', 'Vivid'

COMMON NAME: false dragonhead

FLOWERS: spikes of pink, purple, or white

FOLIAGE: narrow mintlike leaves; some hybrids are variegated

SIZE: 24 to 48 inches tall × 18 inches across

SEASON: autumn

LIGHT: sun to partial shade

CULTURAL NEEDS: average

PROPAGATION: purchase plants

WINTER HARDINESS: −40°

Black-Eyed Susan

Native to the Midwest and state flower of Maryland, the annual, *Rudbeckia hirta,* is a very aggressive spreader. Hybridization has created wonderful perennials, taking this plant's good points and toning down its bad points.

BOTANICAL NAME: *Rudbeckia*

HYBRIDS TO TRY: 'Goldsturm', 'Gold Drop', 'Goldilocks', 'Indian Summer', 'Gloriosa Daisy'

COMMON NAME: brown-eyed Susan

FLOWERS: gold daisies

FOLIAGE: gray-green, narrow

SIZE: 24 inches tall × 15 inches across

SEASON: late summer

LIGHT: sun to partial shade

CULTURAL NEEDS: average soil

PROPAGATION: purchase plants

WINTER HARDINESS: −40°

Goldenrod

Goldenrod's Latin name, *Solidago,* comes from the root word *solido,* "to strengthen." There are eighty-five species of goldenrods native to the United States. A popular garden plant everywhere but in America, where it was believed for many years to cause hay fever. Experts have since shown that ragweed, which blooms at the same time, is the real culprit.

BOTANICAL NAME: *Solidago*

HYBRIDS TO TRY: 'Golden Baby', 'Cloth of Gold', 'Crown of Rays', 'Golden Fleece', 'Peter Pan', 'Fireworks'

COMMON NAME: Aaron's rod

FLOWERS: yellow clusters

FOLIAGE: narrow lances up stem

SIZE: 18 to 60 inches tall × 10 to 20 inches across

SEASON: autumn

LIGHT: sun

CULTURAL NEEDS: average soil; in rich soil leaves will overdevelop; once established will survive drought

PROPAGATION: purchase plants

WINTER HARDINESS: −40°

What Wildflowers Need

Wildflowers are easier to grow than other flowers. They are less demanding and actually happier in poor to average soil. Once established, they need less water and will flourish where fussy special-needs plants fail. Be sure to check Midwest Gardens to Visit in Section Six for a listing of Midwest gardens with wildflower displays.

Free Materials from Your Department of Transportation

The Department of Transportation (DOT) in many states has wonderful four-color foldout brochures of the wildflowers that they have planted along our highways. These brochures are free just for the asking. You can find them at rest stops or call to request that they be sent to you. Two favorites: *Discover Iowa's Roadside Flowering Plants and Grasses* and *Wildflowers and Grasses along Nebraska Roadsides.*

Plant Groups and Associations

Illinois Native Plant Society
Forest Glen Preserve
20301 East 900 North Road
Westville, IL 61883

Annual membership dues of $15 for a quarterly newsletter, *The Harbinger;* an annual scientific journal, *Erigenia;* an annual meeting; and participation on local and state levels.

National Wildflower Research Center
4801 LaCrosse Avenue
Austin, TX 78739

Founded fifteen years ago by Lady Bird Johnson and a group of volunteers, its mission is "the preservation and re-establishment of native North American wildflowers, grasses, shrubs, vines, and trees in planned and natural landscapes." This group has a membership of twenty-five thousand and responds annually to fifteen thousand requests for information. Annual dues are $25 and include benefits similar to those of botanical gardens: newsletter, gift shop discounts, library, and reciprocal privileges at other gardens.

Ohio Native Plant Society
6 Louise Drive
Chagrin Falls, OH 44022

Annual membership dues of $10 for classes, field trips, and a newsletter. Chapters throughout Ohio.

Wildflower Association of Michigan
PO Box 27032
Lansing, MI 48909-7032

Annual membership dues are $15 and include a quarterly newsletter, discounts on conferences and wildflower prints, and roadside planting expeditions.

Purchasing Wildflower Plants and Seeds from Local Garden Centers

This is a reliable but usually rather expensive way to buy new plants and seeds. Local nurseries stand behind their products but have a limited selection. Plants here will be larger and healthier than those from other sources. Always ask if the nursery grew the plant or purchased it, and if the plant is guaranteed to winter over. If so, keep your receipt and packaging materials.

Harvesting Wildflowers

A word of caution—wildflowers are protected in most states. It is punishable by law to collect plants or seeds in public areas or along roadsides. On private land, you will need the owner's permission.

Purchasing Wildflower Plants and Seeds from Mail-Order Sources

Local selection of plants is often limited, and sometimes plant labels are switched. Shopping for plants by mail is a way to increase variety in your garden and ensure plant type. When shopping by mail, gardeners must be on their toes. Some nurseries grow their own plants and sell them through catalogs. Many mail-order companies buy plants from all over the country and sell them through catalogs. Many catalogs show pictures of mature plants in all their glory, and then fill your order with seedlings or two-inch pieces of roots. Choice plants will be more expensive and will give you quicker satisfaction. Most plants you receive will be in dormant condition. It will take at least two years for these new plants to flourish.

Check each catalog's warranty policy and allow each new plant time to acclimatize. If plants do not show growth in three weeks, contact the mail-order company and ask for new plants.

For the backbone of your garden, it is best to buy plants raised in the Midwest. Once you find a mail-order nursery that you like, tell your friends and other Midwest gardeners about it.

For Midwest sources of wildflower plants and seeds, see Midwest Mail-Order Plant and Seed Sources in Section Six.

Favorite Perennials

Perennials are flowering garden plants that return year after year after year. Favorite perennials are popular for both practical and inspirational reasons. Those listed here can boast their own fan clubs. Whether you live in the city or have a rolling acreage on some rural lane, you can use these perennials to create an easy-care do-it-yourself flower garden that reflects your tastes and lifestyle.

When planning your flower garden consider the size, habit, leaf form, color, shape, and texture of each plant. If you wash dishes in front of your kitchen window, plan a garden that you can enjoy while you clean up. If you entertain in the evening, choose pale flowers that glow in the sunset—whites, yellows, and pinks. Place tall things in the middle or back, then tier down to the edges. Contrast will make or break your garden design. Place light flowers against dark backgrounds, and dark flowers against light backgrounds. It is better to plant an odd-numbered group of the same plant, rather than one of this and two of that. A few flowers planted in a group will be more pleasing to the eye and easier to maintain. Time of flower bloom is also an element to consider. Something should in bloom each season to keep your garden full of color.

Whichever perennials become your favorite, remember each spring to feed with a pelleted complete fertilizer such as 10-10-10, to mulch, and to shower plant leaves each June and July with a diluted liquid fertilizer.

Flower gardening is easy with the low-maintenance perennial flowers in this section that will multiply and spread in your garden with a minimum amount of time and effort on your part.

Successful perennial gardens start here:

S Select healthy, nutrient-rich soil. Have a soil sample tested by your county extension office to find out if your soil needs any additives to grow flowers. Perennial bed preparation is the most important step to beautiful flowers. See Great Gardens Start Here in Section One for more information on mulches and soil. The work you do at the beginning stages of gardening will pay off later on.

T Think about how your young plants will look when they reach full size and place them accordingly. Some perennials are taller in their second year, and others will spread. Some need dividing and replanting every two or three years; others go on indefinitely without fuss.

A Add a diluted liquid starter fertilizer when transplanting young plants, and water frequently.

R Rake or hoe to control early spring weeds. Mulch with untreated grass clippings to improve soil or add wood chips to give your beds a tidy, unified look.

T Thin and share with neighbors as plants mature and fill up their allocated garden space.

Chrysanthemum

Chrysanthemums are popular hybrid plants that can be purchased in late summer and autumn as flowering plants or in the spring as small rooted cuttings. Native to Asia, Europe, and North America, chrysanthemums have been cultivated for over two thousand years.

Just when other flowers are gearing down for their winter nap, mums light up the gardens around the Midwest with glowing golds, luminous lavenders, pearly pinks, and burnished burgundies. Mums bloom in the fall, rather than the spring, because shorter days and longer nights trigger flowering and pollination. Some varieties of mums react more quickly to seasonal changes than others. Late-season varieties bloom too late for Midwest winters and often freeze before they can flower. By mixing early and mid-season varieties, the mum season can be extended well past October or until our first killing frost. Many special colors and styles can be ordered from nursery catalogs listing hybrid colors and traits.

BOTANICAL NAME: *Chrysanthemum*

COMMON NAME: mums

FLOWERS: buttons, pompons, spiders, and daisies in every shape and color except blue

FOLIAGE: jagged-edged and pungent in tall or mounded shapes

SIZE: 10 to 24 inches tall × proportional

LIGHT: sun

CULTURAL NEEDS: well-drained soil; water regularly; heavy feeders; cleanup and pruning of dead stems and leaves should wait until spring growth begins

PROPAGATION: purchase plants; easy stem cuttings

WINTER HARDINESS: −40°

Mums are easy to grow and are happy in any garden that offers full sun, well-drained soil, mulch, monthly feedings, and one inch of water weekly throughout the growing season. Gardening folklore tells us to pinch the top third of each plant off on the fourth of July. Unpinched plants will have weak stems that need to be staked when they bloom. Trimmed plants will be stockier with more flowers. To produce huge blooms, remove all the flower buds in each cluster except one. If you dip the pinched-off plant top into a hormone rooting powder and then plant it, you can make new mums that will often bloom that same fall. After July fourth, any trimming or fertilizing should wait until spring to allow the plant time to prepare for flowering. In spring, when new growth shows from the roots, cut off the old flower stems and fertilize.

ORGANIZATION:

National Chrysanthemum Society
Galen Goss, Secretary
10107 Homar Pond Drive
Fairfax Station, VA 22039-1650

The $12.50 general annual membership dues include the quarterly *Journal of the National Chrysanthemum Society* and a copy of the *Beginner's Handbook*.

Perennials, Biennials, Annuals

Perennials usually take two to three seasons to come into their own and can be mixed with annual bedding plants and seasonal bulbs for first-season satisfaction. Perennials, biennials, annuals, and bulbs are the main categories of flowering plants. A perennial is a plant that will survive for longer than two years. A biennial will last for only two years, and, an annual will last for only one growing season.

If You Have More Time than Money . . .

Each summer start seeds of new perennials in trays. Store seedlings in a sheltered location and plant in the garden next spring. Extra seedlings and established garden plants can be traded with neighbors to expand your flower collection.

If You Have More Money than Time . . .

Throughout the spring, summer, and late summer buy two-year-old blooming plants from garden centers in one-gallon pots for an instant garden.

Daylily

When most people think of daylilies they remember wild ditch lilies and long, hot summers. But daylilies are much more than that. Because they are easy to hybridize and change, new daylilies have been created that bloom in early summer, late summer, and fall. They can be found in every color and new shapes with long narrow petals, wide ruffled petals, double petals, contrasting petal and eye zones, watermarks, and much more.

BOTANICAL NAME: *Hemerocallis*

FLOWERS: trumpets in all colors except true blue and pure white

FOLIAGE: green straps

SIZE: 11 to 48 inches tall × proportional

LIGHT: sun to partial shade

CULTURAL NEEDS: damp or dry soils; adaptable to most conditions

PROPAGATION: purchase roots

WINTER HARDINESS: −40°

Daylilies are not only beautiful, they are also a very practical choice for most garden situations. Daylilies make a great ground cover in areas where the soil is washing away, under trees, or on a slope that is too hard to mow. Daylilies prefer full sun for as much of the day as possible, but will tolerate partial shade. To plant, make a mound of soil in the center of the hole for the daylily to sit on. Spread the roots out in a circle with the crown of the plant on top of the mound. Replace the soil and water thoroughly.

ORGANIZATION:

The American Hemerocallis Society
Elly Launius, AHS Executive Secretary
1454 Rebel Drive
Jackson, MS 39211-6334

The American Hemerocallis Society is a national society devoted to daylilies. Its publication, *The Daylily Journal,* is included in its $18 annual membership dues. An annual national convention offers garden tours, speakers, and plants. An eighty-page handbook, *Daylilies—The Beginner's Handbook,* is available for $6 from Bill Reinke, Route 1, Box 136-H, Bells, TN 38006.

Dianthus

Dianthus are charming flowers filling late spring and summer gardens with a spicy fragrance that butterflies and people love. They received their botanical name, meaning "divine flower," from the great eighteenth-century Swedish botanist, Carolus Linnaeus. Native to the Far East, they first came to America via Europe with the earliest settlers.

There are six classes of dianthus suitable for home gardens: *Dianthus caryophyllus,* or carnations; *D. plumarius,* or cottage pinks; *D. alpinus* and *D. gratianopolitanus,* rockery pinks; *D. barbatus,* or sweet Williams; *D. chinensis,* or annual pinks; and a group of miscellaneous species. The nickname "pink" is thought to be derived from the German word Pinksten, or Pentecost, the period in which dianthus bloom. Rewarding and easy to grow, dianthus are ideal for flower arrangements.

BOTANICAL NAME: *Dianthus*

COMMON NAME: garden pink, pinks

FLOWERS: fragrant and fringed pinks and whites

FOLIAGE: blue-green spiky mats

SIZE: 12 inches tall × 12 inches across

LIGHT: sun

CULTURAL NEEDS: alkaline, well-drained soil; remove all mulch in winter to prevent crown rot; frequent picking encourages new flowers

PROPAGATION: purchase plants and seeds; easy stem cuttings

WINTER HARDINESS: −40°

These are easy plants that flower into great pink and red carpets in perennial beds and rose gardens. The key to successful pinks is to encourage new growth by fertilizing and shearing after blooming. Mulch should cover the root area during summer's heat and then be removed during winter to prevent rot root.

ORGANIZATION:

American Dianthus Society
P.O. Box 22232
Santa Fe, NM 87502-2232

This group encourages the enjoyment and cultivation of dianthus in North American gardens. Annual dues of $15 include four issues of their newsletter and involvement in the annual members-only seed distribution program.

Hosta

Hosta is the backbone plant of Midwest gardens and landscapes. There is a hosta for almost every design and garden area. Try some of the smaller ones for ground covers and add larger ones as foundation coverings. Traditionally hosta are shade plants, but many of the newer hybrids can be grown in full sun. In either sun or shade they are versatile, easy to grow, low-maintenance plants with bold leaves and blooming spires that work where other plants fail.

BOTANICAL NAME: *Hosta*

HYBRIDS TO TRY: *H. plantaginea* 'Aphrodite', 'August Moon', 'Francee', 'Frances Williams', 'Ginkgo Craig', 'Gold Standard', 'Golden Tiara', 'Halcyon', 'Krossa Regal', 'Piedmont Gold', 'Royal Standard'; *H. sieboldiana* 'Elegans', 'Shade Fanfare', 'Sun Power', 'Sum and Substance'; *H. ventricosa* 'Aureomarginata', 'Wide Brim'

COMMON NAME: plantain lily

FLOWERS: lavender or white bells on long stems

FOLIAGE: grown for mounds of variegated, blues, golds, or greens; heart-shaped leaves

SIZE: 6 to 36 inches × proportional

LIGHT: sun to shade

CULTURAL NEEDS: moist soil; heavy feeders; love mulch; hate snails

PROPAGATION: purchase plants; easy root cuttings

WINTER HARDINESS: −40°

Slugs and snails can attack leaves, but they are easy to bait or even ignore. And, although hosta flourish with fertilizer, it is not essential. As clumps grow bigger, they grow more attractive. Many gardeners plant young plants too closely together and when these reach their mature size, they look crowded. Hosta combine well with other plants. Try Japanese painted fern, Solomon's seal, toad lily, and coral bells in shaded gardens.

ORGANIZATION:

The American Hosta Society
7802 NE 63rd Street
Vancouver, WA 98662

Founded in 1968, The American Hosta Society's annual dues of $19 a year include the twice-yearly *Hosta Journal* and a hosta yearbook plus an annual convention and auction of new and rare varieties.

Iris

Irises belong to one of the oldest plant families. A large and diverse group of over twelve hundred species, it was named after the Greek goddess of the rainbow. Iris was Juno's attendant and a messenger of the gods. In stories, the rainbow was the road that Iris used to carry messages to the earth. Records of these beautiful flowers have been found in paintings on Egyptian tombs, on the walls of the great palaces of ancient Crete, and in the writings of a Greek physician who served in the armies of the Roman Emperor, Nero.

Iris grow wild all over the world in temperate regions north of the equator. They are easily hybridized into different forms and colors, and there are many specialty nurseries for iris throughout North America.

BOTANICAL NAME: *Iris*

FLOWERS: all colors including breathtaking two-tones; various petal formations and blooming sequences

FOLIAGE: traditional sword-shaped

SIZE: tall, from 30 to 40 inches; intermediate, from 15 to 30 inches; dwarf, 5 to 15 inches

LIGHT: sun to partial shade

CULTURAL NEEDS: well-drained soil; water in dry spells

PROPAGATION: tuberous roots called rhizomes; purchase roots to ensure desired colors

WINTER HARDINESS: −40°

German iris (*I. germanica*) is the old-fashioned showy iris with fuzzy-throated petals that is a mainstay of Midwest gardens. To plant this iris, choose a well-drained site and work the soil to a depth of six inches, adding sand and compost if necessary. Place the root, or rhizome, so that it floats in the top level of the soil and is partially but not completely covered with soil . . . like a duck sitting in water. Point the green leaves in the direction you want the plant to grow. Space rhizomes eight to twelve inches apart. Iris rhizomes can be cut into two-inch sections with a leaf for propagation. Mulch up to and around the rhizome to retain moisture and discourage weeds. Plan to divide plants every third year after blooming. While the rhizomes are out of the ground, wash the dirt off and check for borers. These are small larvae of a fly that bores into the bulbs and turns the inside to mush. If the rhizome feels mushy, burn or discard it. Replanted rhizomes will need to be watered until the green leaves begin to grow. Each fall cut foliage down and toss into the compost pile. Fertilize each spring with 10-10-10.

Two other iris are good bets for Midwest gardens: Siberian iris (*Iris sibirica*) and Japanese iris (*Iris kaempferi* or *I. ensata*). Siberian iris are hardy. They bloom in June and continue for about two weeks. Their blue, purple, white, and yellow flowers are flatter than those of the German iris and smaller than Japanese iris blooms. Siberian iris stand two feet tall and have beautiful arching, bright green foliage that is a strong addition to any garden.

Siberian iris prefer acid to neutral soil in sun to partial shade. When planting, add peat moss and sand to heavy clay soils. Place clumps twelve inches apart with the leaves pointing in the direction you want the plants to grow. Plan to divide clumps every three years or when flower production dwindles. Use a sharp shovel or knife to cut the clumps into eight-inch sections. Mulch to conserve water and discourage weeds. Water until new growth starts and during droughts. Each fall cut foliage down and toss into the compost pile. Feed with 10-10-10 each spring.

Japanese iris bloom after the first delphiniums and before our summer phlox. This is the most exotic iris of all, with large flowers six to ten inches across in wonderful rich blues, purples, and cool whites. Plants stand three feet tall and should be spaced two feet apart.

Japanese iris need peat moss and steady moisture in a well-drained site to be really happy in the garden. Standing winter water or cold, heavy clay soil will rot these roots. If you find a place to keep them happy, it will be well worth your effort. Divide when the blossoms decrease in size, usually every three years. To divide, separate each clump into two or three sections. If you get the sections too small, the plant will need to rebuild its root system before using energy to flower. Mulch heavily and water regularly. Each fall cut the foliage down and toss into the compost pile. Feed with 10-10-10 in the spring.

ORGANIZATION:

American Iris Society
PO Box 8455
San Jose, CA 95155

The members of this organization include iris specialists, gardening experts, and amateur gardeners. These folks have wonderful fund-raising plant sales and many local chapters. Yearly dues of $18 include a copy of their quarterly bulletin.

Peony

Peonies are gracious plants that live incredibly long lives and come in every color of white and red. Garden peonies are hybrids of two species, *Paeonia officinalis,* a European native, and the Chinese peony, *Paeonia lactiflora.* Peonies were first mentioned in American gardening literature in the 1800s and have become a staple of flower gardens. The peony is the state flower of Indiana.

Many gardeners have peonies that have been passed on through generations. If you don't, ask your neighbors or order one of the new hybrids and start your own multigenerational plant. Autumn is the best time to divide plants or add new peonies to your garden.

BOTANICAL NAME: *Paeonia*

HYBRIDS TO TRY: *Paeonia lactiflora* 'Duchesse de Nemours', introduced in 1856, double blossoms, early blooming, white, fragrant; 'Karl Rosenfield', introduced in 1908, double blossoms, midseason flowering, deep red; 'Sarah Bernhardt', introduced in 1906, double blossoms, late flowering, deep pink

FLOWERS: fragrant pinks, whites, or reds

FOLIAGE: large glossy leaves that emerge each spring and die back to the ground with autumn's first frost

SIZE: 24 to 48 inches tall × 36 to 48 inches across

LIGHT: sun

CULTURAL NEEDS: average soil; heavy feeders; weather conditions have to be "just so" for peonies to emerge; ants love peonies

PROPAGATION: purchase plants or ask friends and family; eight weeks of bloom can be achieved by planting early-, middle-, and late-blooming varieties

WINTER HARDINESS: −40°

Peonies thrive in the Midwest as long as they are planted at the correct depth—their red eyes must face upward one to two inches below the soil, and they must be topped off with a light mulch. As spring-flowering plants, peonies are equipped with a natural antifreeze that enables them to endure cold snaps and bloom safely at the correct time. Use peonies next to foundations, along a walk, in a border with other perennials, against a fence, or massed in front of shrubs or at the edge of the lawn.

Double-flowered forms often get so top-heavy from the weight of their flowers that they bend over and sometimes even break off. These should be staked with a short wire fence or other removable support.

Peonies make excellent cut flowers. Cut the stems early in the morning or late in the evening. Choose stems with flower buds that are just beginning to show color. These flower buds are loaded with fragrance and will have a sticky sap to help attract pollinating insects. Unfortunately, this stickiness also feeds ants who protect the peony from bud-nibbling pests. To remove the ants, rinse each flower with a garden hose or dip in a bucket of water before bringing inside.

ORGANIZATION:

Nichols Arboretum
University of Michigan
School of Natural Resources and Environment
3012D Dana Building
Ann Arbor, MI 48109-1115
(313) 763-5832

The Peony Garden at the Nichols Arboretum was established in 1927 and is one of the outstanding historic collections in the Midwest. It contains over seven hundred plants of 260 varieties introduced between 1807 and 1948. A $25 membership to their Friends of the Arboretum group brings you their newsletter, a peony guide with alphabetized names, dates, blooming season, characteristics, and coloring of the varieties in their collections, plus an invitation to their annual Peony Garden Party.

Rose

The rose is the national floral emblem of the United States. With over four hundred million dollars in sales every year, roses are the most popular flower grown in American gardens. The history of roses has been traced back to 2300 B.C. Roses have been referred to in every period of recorded history including Egyptian texts and ancient Chinese writings. As a symbol of love and tenderness, nothing rivals the rose for grace and fragrance, and no other flower brings such a delightful sense of romance to the garden. Today there are fifty classifications of roses and each has its own unique characteristics.

BOTANICAL NAME: *Rosa*

FLOWERS: single, double, or ruffled in every color except blue

FOLIAGE: consistent compound leaves and a variety of thorns

LIGHT: sun five to six hours a day

CULTURAL NEEDS: rich, loose well-drained soil; heavy feeders; trickle irrigation needed to keep soil moist and leaves dry; mound with soil and cover canes to protect from winter winds; plant chives around roses to repel aphids

PROPAGATION: may be purchased as dormant bareroot plants or in containers; when buying look for smooth canes that are plump and green; the best plants have three canes each; avoid plants with canes that are shriveled or brown

It is difficult to grow roses in many parts of the Midwest, especially root-grafted hybrid teas, climbers, and floribundas, because of our winter winds. But if you have a sheltered corner next to your house, especially one with a clothes dryer vent that creates a warmer microclimate, you can grow these wonderful hybrids successfully. Roses grown on their own wood are hardier. These do very well here in winter with a shovelful of compost and topsoil covering the crowns and burlap-wrapped canes. The newer landscape and ground cover roses survive with just year-round mulch. Rose hardiness reports are often contradictory. The care given before, during, and after the growing season are major factors in determining winter hardiness. Feeding roses regularly through July and leaving the last flush of flowers to mature into hips will encourage deeper dormancy and hardier bushes.

ORGANIZATIONS:

The Heritage Rose Foundation
Beverly Dobson, Secretary
1034 Taylor Avenue
Alameda, CA 94501

This group is dedicated to preserving and studying old garden roses. Great for rose networking. Annual dues of $6 brings a quarterly newsletter with cultural information and listings of meetings and events.

American Rose Society
PO Box 30,000
Shreveport, LA 71130-0030

With 485 chapters throughout the United States, the American Rose Society answers questions, lists mail-order sources, offers a lending library, has national conventions, and publishes a monthly magazine, *American Rose*. Annual dues $32.

Rose Hybridizers Association
Larry D. Peterson
21 South Wheaton Road
Horseheads, NY 14845

Organized in 1969 by thirteen amateur rose lovers, the Rose Hybridizers Association has grown to over four hundred members. Members have introduced more than five hundred new roses to the commercial market, and in 1996, one of its members was awarded the coveted All-America Rose Selection Award for 'St. Patrick'. Annual dues are $10 and bring a quarterly newsletter and contact with knowledgeable people who love roses.

All-America Rose Selections (AARS)

This group represents commercial rose growers and sponsors 138 rose test gardens in forty-three states, where each year's winners are in bloom when their names are announced each June. When shopping for

Just For Cut Roses

Try one of these homemade formulas for freshly cut roses that are circulating around garden-club meetings. For three cups of water, add one aspirin, one teaspoon vinegar, and one tablespoon sugar. Or for three cups of water, add two teaspoons bleach and one tablespoon of sugar.

roses, look for the round metal tag with the AARS logo that tells you if it has been tested and recommended by this group. Midwest AARS test gardens to visit are listed in Section Six.

Other Prize-Winning Perennials to Try

Beautiful low-maintenance gardens are always the result of planning based upon informed choices. Since 1990, the Perennial Plant Association has been helping gardeners by testing and evaluating perennial flowers for home gardens. The plants they choose as "Perennial Plant of the Year" flower longer, bigger, and better and are more resistant to disease than most. These plants can be found at reputable nursery centers. They will cost just a little more than other plants, but will give you more for your gardening dollar. All "Perennial Plants of the Year" are hybrids and will not reproduce true from seed, but they can be divided after they bloom for additional plants.

1997 Perennial Plant of the Year

Summer Sage

BOTANICAL NAME: *Salvia* x 'May Night'

SIZE: 18 inches tall × 18 inches across

FLOWERS: summer; dark blue spikes on narrow, coarse foliage

LIGHT: sun to partial shade

CULTURAL NEEDS: average well-drained soil; deadhead as flowers fade

1996 Perennial Plant of the Year

Beard Tongue

BOTANICAL NAME: *Penstemon digitalis* 'Husker Red'

SIZE: 24 inches tall × 12 inches across

FLOWERS: summer; white flower stalks on burgundy foliage

LIGHT: sun to partial shade

CULTURAL NEEDS: average well-drained soil; deadhead as flowers fade

Extending the Vase Life of Fresh Cut Flowers

1. Before placing in vase, trim flower stems with an angled cut.
2. Remove any foliage that will stand below the water line.
3. Use warm water in the vase.
4. Add a commercial floral preservative. Or make your own preservative with equal amounts of warm water and lemonade or lemon-lime soft drink mixed with a teaspoon of chlorine bleach. The sugar in this mixture acts as an energy source, citric acid acts as a preservative, and the bleach prevents bacteria from forming. Change water mixture every four days.
5. Place vase in a cool area away from direct sunlight, heaters, air-conditioning vents, and the ethylene gas released by ripening fruits or vegetables.

1995 Perennial Plant of the Year

Russian Sage

BOTANICAL NAME: *Perovskia atriplicifolia*

SIZE: 36 inches tall × 24 inches across

LIGHT: sun

FLOWERS: late summer, long spikes of silver-blue complement silver-gray foliage

CULTURAL NEEDS: average well-drained soil; deadhead as flowers fade

1994 Perennial Plant of the Year

Perennial Spirea

BOTANICAL NAME: *Astilbe* x 'Sprite'

SIZE: 12 inches tall × 12 inches across

LIGHT: partial to full shade

FLOWERS: late summer; short pink plumes and bronze foliage

CULTURAL NEEDS: partial to full shade; rich soil; damp in summer; dry in winter; deadhead as flowers fade

1993 Perennial Plant of the Year

Golden Daisy

BOTANICAL NAME: *Coreopsis verticillata* 'Moonbeam'

SIZE: 18 inches tall × 24 inches across

LIGHT: sun

FLOWERS: summer through fall; pale yellow flowers and threadlike leaves

CULTURAL NEEDS: average soil; divide plant every other year; deadhead as flowers fade

1992 Perennial Plant of the Year

Summer Speedwell

BOTANICAL NAME: *Veronica* x 'Sunny Border Blue'

SIZE: 24 inches tall × 18 inches across

LIGHT: sun to partial shade

FLOWERS: summer until frost; navy blue flowers and coarse leaves

CULTURAL NEEDS: well-drained soil; deadhead as flowers fade

1991 Perennial Plant of the Year

Purple-leaf Coral Bell

BOTANICAL NAME: *Heuchera micrantha* 'Purple Palace'

SIZE: 12 inches tall × 12 inches across

LIGHT: partial shade to shade

FLOWERS: summer, sprays of white bells dangle above burgundy leaves

CULTURAL NEEDS: rich, well-drained soil; deadhead as flowers fade. The old blossoms can be dried and used in winter arrangements.

1990 Perennial Plant of the Year

Woodland Phlox

BOTANICAL NAME: *Phlox divericata*

SIZE: 12 inches tall × 8 inches across

LIGHT: partial shade to shade

FLOWERS: spring, mixed blue or white star-shaped flowers

CULTURAL NEEDS: damp shade; allow to die back to the ground naturally

What Perennials Need

A low-maintenance garden is a healthy garden. Like people, perennials have basic needs, their own part of the American dream—a nice home (soil), good food (fertilizer), and shelter from the storm (mulches). Flowering plants are disease-resistant, long-lasting, and easy to care for if they have their basic needs met, if old flower heads and yellow leaves are removed and destroyed, and if they have enough water. Be sure to check Midwest Gardens to Visit in Section Six for a listing of Midwest gardens with perennial displays.

Plant Groups and Associations

American Horticultural Society
7931 East Boulevard Drive
Alexandria, VA 22308-1300
1-800-777-7931

The American Horticultural Society offers seeds, books, a help line, and a reciprocal admissions program to many botanical gardens and arboretums throughout the country. Annual membership is $35.

Center for Northern Gardening
1755 Prior Avenue North
Falcon Heights, MN 55113

Annual dues are $25 and include a subscription to *Minnesota Horticulturist;* use of a gardening library; discounts on tours, classes, and special events; and the "Spring Green Card," good for fifteen-percent discounts at participating nurseries.

Hardy Bulbs

Few sights are as wonderful as the crocus, daffodils, and tulips of spring and the exotic lilies of summer. Once planted, these hardy bulbs come up year after year with little care. Bulbs produce among the most popular and best-loved flowers in the world. Hardy bulbs are the stars of the garden, and these stars love Midwest gardens.

Bulbs are underground flower factories that allow plants to sprout and flower at the appropriate time. All these remarkable factories need are well-drained soil, fertilizer in the spring and fall, mulch, and water.

Spring-flowering crocus, daffodils, and tulips are the first to bring life back to a barren winter landscape. Lilies bring variety, texture, and warm colors to summer gardens. Planted with care and planning, bulbs can keep a garden alive with color from the last snows of winter through the first frosts of fall.

Successful bulb gardens start here:

S Shopping list. Use photos from catalogs and magazines to find the plants you want.

T The bigger the bulb, the bigger the flower. Consider "bargains" carefully. Less expensive bulbs often are smaller and will produce smaller flowers. Once in the garden, most bulbs will not increase in size and may actually get smaller as they adjust to garden conditions.

A Avoid soft, mushy, or moldy bulbs and those that are heavily bruised. Bulbs have an outer papery skin tunic that may become loose or torn. This condition does not damage the bulbs and may actually promote faster rooting after the bulb is planted.

R Read labels and check botanical names. Prepackaged bulbs provide planting information on their labels. Bulbs purchased from garden centers come with information slips. Mail-order firms list information in their catalogs and include instructions with the bulbs when shipped.

T Try different sources. Bulbs are sold in many places—garden centers and nurseries, mail-order catalogs, supermarkets, home centers, mass merchandisers, hardware stores, other specialty stores, and even on the Internet.

Bulbs, Corms, Rhizomes, and Tubers

"Bulb" is a generic term used for most fall-planted spring- and summer-blooming plants. Many popular "bulb" flowers are not produced from bulbs at all. Crocus grow from corms, dahlias from tubers, and iris from rhizomes.

Bulbs and corms look very similar. The difference is the plant's method of storing food. In corms, most of the food is stored in the enlarged basal plate rather than in the scales, which in corms are small. Bulbs tend to be round; corms squat and flat. Tubers, rhizomes, and roots are easily distinguished from bulbs and corms. They have no protective tunic and are really just enlarged stem tissue.

Whether they are called bulbs, corms, tubers, or rhizomes, these underground storage units contain large amounts of carbohydrates that are used up during the blooming period and are replenished by the bulbs' leaves before they turn yellow or are killed by frost in the fall.

Crocus

At the end of the grey months of winter, when the last patches of snow linger in shady corners, few sights are as welcome as the first flowers of early spring. Crocus open with the arrival of our returning robins and bloom until they are fertilized by small bees. Depending upon the weather, crocus can bloom a week or several weeks.

In ancient cultures, crocus flower petals were scattered on the ground during parties and on matrimonial beds after weddings. A flower of ritual and ornament, the crocus was also used in medicine, as a perfume, as food, and as a source of dye.

A flower so popular inspired many myths. A favorite myth involves young love. Crocus was a shepherd boy of fine and noble spirit who fell deeply in love with the lovely nymph Smilax. So impressed were the ancient gods with the depth of his devotion that they granted him immortality and turned him into a flower. To ensure that they could be forever together, Smilax turned into an evergreen—the yew. Romantic and practical gardeners always plant this perfect duo together.

BOTANICAL NAME: *Crocus*

HYBRIDS TO TRY: *C. ancyrensis* 'Golden Bunch', orange-yellow; *C. chrysanthus* 'Blue Bird', violet-blue; 'Blue Pearl', blue with yellow; 'Cream Beauty', ivory; *C. vernus* 'Jeanne d'Arc', white; 'Pickwick', white, lilac; 'Remembrance', blue, purple; *C. tommasinianus* 'Ruby Giant', lilac; 'Whitewell Purple', red-purple; 'Golden Yellow', yellow

FLOWERS: cups and stars

FOLIAGE: grasslike from a central base appearing before, with, or after flowers

SIZE: 3 to 8 inches high × 3 to 6 inches across

LIGHT: sun to partial shade

CULTURAL NEEDS: gritty, well-drained soil; plant twice as deep as bulb is wide; water after planting; use cayenne pepper or other coverings to distract squirrels until the ground freezes; needs 8 weeks in the ground to prepare for winter

WINTER HARDINESS: −40°

Planning for a blanket of spring color starts in the fall garden. Planting crocus takes a smidgen of effort and a leap of faith. Crocus bulbs are about the same size as seed onions. It is hard to believe, holding a handful of crocus corms, that something so wonderful could possibly grow from them. Because they are so small and easy to grow, crocus corms are very inexpensive—fifty bulbs for about the price of a fast-food meal. Corms are available through local nurseries, garden centers, and nursery catalogs. For rich color, plan on fifteen bulbs per square foot. Planting drifts of crocus is as easy as clearing an area two inches deep, amending the soil with chicken grit or other coarse sand to discourage moles, and adding cayenne pepper to discourage squirrels, then tossing the corms across the ground, uprighting them, and pulling back the soil to cover them. Crocus will come up each year, seed themselves, and spread into larger colonies.

Once in the ground, each little corm will send out roots gathering food that it needs for a quick start next spring. As the ground freezes, the corm will stop growing. Then as the soil thaws, bright flowering cups of yellow, purple, or white will burst from the ground overnight. Narrow, grasslike leaves follow about two weeks later and then the whole plant returns to the ground as the days become longer and hotter.

Freezing mist and pelting sleet will not hurt these little plants but will damage their flowers. So plant a mixed handful of any of the twenty different varieties for constant flowers and forget the Midwest's erratic spring weather. Crocus are a sure sign that the frozen soil is warming and spring is on its way.

Daffodil

Daffodils say "spring is on its way." Plant some along warm south walls for extra-early blooms as well as in beds or borders. Daffodils are among the easiest plants to grow and a great garden bargain. They flower year after year and multiply freely if you allow the leaves to ripen and die back to the ground.

BOTANICAL NAME: *Narcissus*

FLOWERS: trumpets and cups

FOLIAGE: green straps

SIZE: 6 to 20 inches tall × 3 to 6 inches across

LIGHT: sun to partial shade; flower will face the sun

CULTURAL NEEDS: well-drained soil; dry in summer until autumn rains signal a new growth cycle; heavy feeders; allow foliage to ripen and die back to ground; plant 6 inches deep and mulch; water after planting

WINTER HARDINESS: –40°

There are over one hundred daffodil species, subspecies, and varieties of species in a huge array of sizes and patterns. Most Americans know narcissi as daffodils, though in the South they are traditionally called jonquils. Daffodil is the correct common name for all *Narcissus*. Jonquil is the common name for a hybrid from a specific group, *Narcissus jonquilla*. The botanical name for the entire daffodil family, *Narcissus*, comes from a Greek myth about Echo, a young wood nymph, and Narcissus, a young man who was given the gift of beauty by the gods. His gift came with one qualification—that his beauty and youth would never fade, provided he never looked upon his own reflection. When poor Echo fell hopelessly in love with Narcissus, he did not even notice her.

Echo was literally consumed by love until all that was left of her was her voice. The goddess Nemesis decided to get even. She led the clueless Narcissus to a shimmering lake where he was dazzled by his own reflection. Unable to turn away, he too was consumed by passion and faded away. Some of the gods thought that Nemesis might have played a bit rough and commuted Narcissus's sentence to eternity as a flower. In the language of flowers, the narcissus stands for vanity and egoism. In psychoanalysis, narcissism is, of course, excessive self-love.

ORGANIZATION:

American Daffodil Society
1686 Grey Fox Trails
Milford, OH 45150-1521

These folks will help you "grow better daffodils, in more colors and sizes than you ever dreamed . . . for a longer blooming season. . . and grow special friendships." Their $20 annual membership dues include the quarterly *Daffodil Journal,* conventions, and shows.

FAVORITE DAFFODILS

Name	Group	Colors
'Barret Browning'	Small-cupped	white petals, orange cup
'Fortissimo'	Trumpet	white petals, yellow cup
'Ice Follies'	Large-cupped	white petals and cup
'King Alfred'	Trumpet	yellow petals and cup
'Las Vegas'	Trumpet	white petals, yellow cup
'Minnow'	Tazetta	yellow petals and cup
'Mount Hood'	Trumpet	white petals and cup
'Salome'	Large-cupped	white petals, pink or yellow cup
'Tahiti'	Double group	red petals, yellow cup
'Tête à Tête'	Cyclamineus group	yellow petals and cup

Lily

If you would like to have a beautiful garden, plant lilies, one of the greatest garden choices of all time. Historians, poets, and artists have all admired lilies and immortalized them in their work. The lily family consists of over two hundred types, many native to our area and all outstanding for ease and beauty. Mixing different lily varieties in your garden will guarantee a breathtaking show from summer through the late days of autumn.

BOTANICAL NAME: *Lilium*

FLOWERS: creams, yellows, oranges, golds, pinks, and reds that smell like sweet warmed vanilla

FOLIAGE: straight leaves that climb stem

SIZE: 12 to 48 inches tall × 8 inches wide

LIGHT: sun to partial shade; like clematis, lilies like "their feet in the shade and their heads in the sun"

CULTURAL NEEDS: dry, gritty soil—wet soils will rot bulbs; heavy feeders; allow foliage to ripen before cutting back to 12 inches after blooming; plant 6 inches deep and mulch; water after planting

WINTER HARDINESS: −40°

Some of the most wonderful lilies love life in the Midwest. Listed below are three types that will thrive during our hot summer months and reward any attention that you give them with incredibly beautiful, fragrant blossoms.

Asiatic lilies are the first to bloom. They are quick to establish themselves and put on a glorious show through summer's heat. They have straight stems and grow two to three feet tall with upward-facing, backward-curving petals. Not only beautiful, Asiatic lilies are also fun to grow. Each August, along the matured stem, small bulblets form. If scattered in the garden, these small bulbs will each produce another stalk of flowers in two to three years.

Trumpet lilies are next to bloom. The most famous of these, the Easter lily, or *Lilium longiflorum* 'Nellie White', is grown in vast fields in California, Michigan, Ohio, and Pennsylvania. Each fall over eleven million bulbs are harvested and shipped to greenhouses, where they are forced into early bloom in time for Easter. For many, this flower symbolizes the spiritual essence of the Easter season. You can plant your potted Easter lily outside if you separate it from other lilies. Greenhouse bulbs often carry a virus that is fatal in the garden.

Other lesser known but equally beautiful trumpet lilies range in height from three to six feet and bloom in warm, deep colors that will revive a tired summer border. Introduced in 1992, the recently developed LA hybrid lily (named for its parentage, not for the city in California) combines the signature trumpet shape of the longiflorum species lily with the warm colors of the Asiatic hybrids. Trumpet lily bulbs multiply underground and should be divided when the plant stems seem crowded, usually every three to four years.

Oriental lilies are the last to bloom, in late summer. They have open flat faces and back-curving petals. The various hybrids grow twelve to forty-eight inches tall. These are not as winter-hardy as trumpet and Asiatic lilies and will need an extra blanket of winter mulch. Oriental lily bulbs also multiply underground and can be divided in the fall along with the trumpet lilies.

Lilies return each year, multiplying and spreading as they go. Bulbs look like a white artichoke or a rosebud and should be tipped so that they lie toward either side rather than upright. This will prevent water from collecting inside the cupped bulb petals.

Lilies are favored by florists as cut flowers. To bring lilies into your home, cut the flower when fully formed, making sure that two-thirds of the plant stem is left to feed the lily bulb. Then remove the yellow anthers to prevent pollen from staining your furniture or clothes.

ORGANIZATION:

The North American Lily Society
3556 Oakwood
Ann Arbor, MI 48104

This group includes a quarterly bulletin in their $12.50-a-year membership, and an introductory publication, *Let's Grow Lilies,* for $3.50 additional.

Tulip

Tulips have a rich history of folklore and fact. Originating in central Asia close to the borders of Russia and China, tulips spread through China, Mongolia, and then outward to far-flung parts of Europe. In 1593, an elderly botanist named Carolus Clusius planted a handful of tulip bulbs from Turkey in a small garden at the University of Leiden in the Netherlands. This act is considered by the Dutch as the birth of their famous flower business. By the early 1700s, it was Turkey that was importing bulbs from Holland.

Today the tulip remains the national flower of modern Turkey, and nearly half of Holland's farms are planted with tulip bulbs. Every year about three billion tulip bulbs are produced in Holland. Of these, approximately two billion are exported to the United States, Japan, and Germany. Tulips are also grown in Washington state and sold all over the West Coast.

BOTANICAL NAME: *Tulipa*

FLOWERS: cups of warm dark and pastel colors, some fragrant

FOLIAGE: wide straps

SIZE: 6 to 24 inches tall × 6 inches across

LIGHT: sun

CULTURAL NEEDS: dry, gritty soil—damp shade will rot bulbs; heavy feeders; allow foliage to ripen and die back to ground; plant 6 inches deep and mulch; water after planting

WINTER HARDINESS: −40°

FAVORITE FRAGRANT TULIPS

Name	Group	Colors	Bloom Time
'Bellona'	Single early	golden yellow	early
'Christmas Marvel'	Single early	cherry-pink	early
'Couleur Cardinal'	Single early	dark red or violet	early
'General de Wet'	Single early	orange	early
'Keizerskroon'	Single early	red and yellow	early
'Mr. van der Hoef'	Double early	yellow	early
'Monte Carlo'	Double early	sulphur yellow	early
'Schoonoord'	Double early	white	early
'Prinses Irene'	Triumph	orange	midseason
T. tarda	Species	yellow and white	late

Favorite Tulips for Naturalizing

Most hybrid tulip bulbs will only bloom for one season. Some will naturalize—that is, reproduce and spread. Others will perennialize, or come up for at least three seasons. Species tulips are those that have not been bred or hybridized and remain essentially as they are found in nature. Botanical tulips are hybrids, but hybrids that remain very close to the original species. Neither of these terms refers to "wild" tulips. Species and botanical tulips are generally smaller than other tulips. They are prized for growing in rock gardens and woodlands.

Name	Group	Colors
'Apeldoorn'	Darwin hybrids	red
'Apeldoorn's Elite'		red, yellow
'Beauty of Apeldoorn'		yellow
'Golden Apeldoorn'		yellow
'Hollands Glorie'		red
'Oxford'		red, yellow
'Candela'	Fosteriana botanicals	yellow
'Easter Moon'		yellow
'Juan'		orange, yellow
'Orange Emperor'		orange
'Purissima'		white, yellow
'Red Emperor'		red
'Solva'		red, pink, orange
'Sweetheart'		yellow
'Yellow Empress'		yellow
'Zombie'		red, yellow
'Corsage'	Greigii botanicals	coral, yellow
'Czaar Peter'		red, white
'Golden Yellow'		yellow
'Oratorio'		red
'Plaisir'		red, white edges
'Red Riding Hood'		red
Sweet Lady'		pink, coral, red
'Toronto'		salmon pink, red
'Ancilla'	Kaufmanniana botanicals	red, yellow
'Stresa'		yellow, red
'Weber's Parrot'		white, purple
'White Parrot'		white
'Ballade'	Lily-flowering hybrids	violet, white edges
'Maytime'		violet, white edges
'Red Shine'		red
'West Point'		yellow
'White Triumphator'		ivory
'Burgundy Lace'	Fringed hybrid	deep red
'Charles'	Single Early hybrids	deep red

'Couleur Cardinal'		violet-red
T. praestans	Multiflowering species	orange, red
T. tarda		yellow, white edges
T. turkestanica		white, cream

FLOWERING TIMES FOR TULIPS

Early Spring	Spring	Early Summer
Single Early	Triumph	Single Late
Double Early	Darwin hybrids	Lily-flowered
Fosteriana	Species:	Fringed
Greigii	*T. acuminata*	Viridiflora
Kaufmanniana	*T. bakeri*	Rembrandt
Species:	*T. chrysantha*	Parrot
T. eichleri	*T. clusiana*	Double Late
T. pulchella violacea	*T. kolpakowskiana*	Species:
T. saxatilis	*T. praestans*	*T. batalinii*
T. turkestanica	*T. tarda*	*T. eichleri*
		T. linifolia
		T. marjoletti
		T. urumiensis

What Bulbs Need

Bulbs are sold by size. Larger bulbs bring a higher price than the smaller ones. For big showy displays, large bulbs are worth the price. However, some excellent bargains are to be had by buying lots of smaller bulbs for grouping together and brightening up a spot in the spring yard.

Hardy Bulb Tips

1. Unpack the bulbs as soon as you get them home or when they arrive. If they can't be planted immediately, store them in a cool, dry place with good air circulation.

2. Bulbs don't like wet feet. Plant in areas that drain well. Add medium chicken grit or rough sand to soil for drainage and as mole repellent. Standing water rots bulbs.

3. Bulbs often do well in shady areas where grass won't grow, such as wooded areas with open deciduous tree canopies in early spring. Overplant with one of the groundcovers listed in Ground Covers and Vines in Section Four.

4. Plant tulips and daffodils eight inches deep. A planting depth equal to twice the height of the bulb is a good rule of thumb for other bulbs. Planting deep slows spring flowering, but helps bulbs perennialize. Mulch counts as part of soil depth.

5. The ideal time to plant bulbs is eight weeks before the ground freezes. Root growth is optimal at 50°. A thick layer of mulch, four to six inches, will keep the soil warm longer and give bulbs extra time to establish themselves.

6. Bulbs planted in grass need at least six weeks to die back before grass can be mowed.

7. Bulbs are very sensitive to lawn and garden herbicides.

8. Deadhead spent flowers after blooming and allow foliage to mature and wither.

9. Every few years, remove mulches and renew the upper layer of soil with compost and a complete slow-release (9-9-6) fertilizer.

10. Cluster-forming bulbs, such as daffodils and tulips, can be split after three seasons to make more plants.

HOW MANY SPRING-FLOWERING BULBS DO YOU NEED?

Garden Area in Square Feet (width x length)	Number of Bulbs Needed
1	9
90	10
450	50
900	100
1350	150
1800	200
2700	300

METRIC EQUIVALENTS TO USE WHEN BUYING BULBS

Centimeters are one-hundredth of a meter, equivalent to .3937 inch.

2.5 cm	=	1 in.
5.1 cm	=	2 in.
7.6 cm	=	3 in.
10.2 cm	=	4 in.
12.7 cm	=	5 in.
15.2 cm	=	6 in.

If You Have More Money than Time . . .

In early spring, look for potted spring flowering bulbs in nursery centers to fill any blank spaces that need something extra.

The Permanent One-Time Quick-Planting Method
for Spring Bulbs

- Mark off the area where you want to establish your permanent bulb garden. Remove the sod or ground cover and place out of the sun on plywood or a tarp.

- Digging down seven inches, place the topsoil in a garden cart, on plywood, or on the driveway. If your topsoil is heavy or clay, add sand up to thirty percent of the mix.

- In the hole, add one inch of chicken grit or sharp pebbles as a mole and rodent repellent.

- Then place an inch of sand, the topsoil you removed, and a slow-release bulb fertilizer over the pebbles.

- Add another thin layer of sand, topsoil, and bulb fertilizer.

- Broadcast the larger bulbs. Then position them so that the points are up and the root plate is nestled into the topsoil.

- Cover them with more topsoil, sand, chicken grit, and bulb food mixture.

- Toss in the smaller bulbs, positioning them upright in the soil mix.

- Fill the hole to ground level with topsoil, sand, chicken grit, and bulb food mix. Mound soil lightly to allow for natural settling.

- Sprinkle the soil with cayenne pepper and mothballs to repel squirrels for the first season.

- Cover with a layer of mulch and water well.

- Be sure to check Midwest Gardens to Visit in Section Six for a listing of Midwest gardens with displays of hardy bulbs.

Purchasing Bulbs

Bulbs are available everywhere each fall. Since ninety-five percent of the bulbs available in the United States are raised in Holland, almost every bulb you find will come from there. Your task will be to find the colors, types, and sizes you want at the best prices. Look in local stores, garden centers, home centers, and mail-order catalogs.

Kitchen Gardens

Culinary Herbs

Edible Flowers and Ferns

Popular Vegetables

Table Vegetables A to Z

Small Fruits

G ardeners have been tending kitchen gardens for over ten thousand years, and kitchen gardening has evolved from a survival strategy into a craft that has become one of America's tastiest hobbies.

Eating five servings of fruits and vegetables a day is one of the healthiest choices you can make. One serving is considered one-half cup of fruit or vegetable, three-fourths cup of juice or herbal tea, or one cup of leafy greens. Fruit and vegetables fresh from the garden make these choices easier and much more fun than constant grocery shopping.

In the grocery store, market vegetables and fruits are grown to standard sizes, flavors, and types. In the kitchen garden, you can nibble produce while it's young and tender or mature and sweet. Your garden is your very own produce stand, where you are the boss and can concentrate on flavor and beauty.

A kitchen garden can be as simple as pots on your porch or as involved as neat raised rows of carefully labeled produce. All of the herbs, flowers, ferns, vegetables, and small fruits listed in this section can be used to tease your tastebuds and to help maintain your health.

Culinary Herbs

In cooking, there is a distinction between spices and herbs. Spices generally come from tropical trees and bushes. Herbs are the leaves of garden plants valued for their flavor and fragrance. Fresh herbs may be used as sprigs, chopped fine, or dried or frozen for later use. Dried herb leaves and seeds are approximately three times as strong as those fresh from the garden. Frozen herbs have the same value as fresh herbs.

An astonishing amount has already been written about herbs—so much, in fact, that it would seem easier to put off planting herbs and just buy them in little, incredibly expensive packets from the experts. But before you do, ask yourself why you might want to grow herbs.

If your answer has anything to do with a steady supply of fresh seasonings, then consider this group of herbal plants that have been grown by cooks for hundreds and hundreds of years. They are easy to plant, easy to grow, easy to harvest, and easy to use.

Successful herb gardens start here:

S Sun. Most herbs need full, hot sun. A few can be grown with four to six hours of sun per day.

T Taste tells. Only grow what you like to eat.

A Always use organic or natural, chemical-free products to care for herbs.

R Remember to harvest herbs early in the morning before the leaves release their aromatic oils in the sun.

T Tell your friends which herbs you are growing in your garden. Swapping plants, seeds, and fresh herbs can be half the fun of herb gardening.

Using Herbs in the Kitchen

Garden herbs can be mixed and matched to turn an ordinary dish into a taste sensation. Here are a few ideas for how to use the herbs from your garden.

	Crushed Seeds	Chopped Leaves
Baked Goods	anise caraway coriander	basil dill
Casseroles	caraway fennel	chervil dill marjoram parsley sage savory thyme
Dips		chervil chives cilantro dill garlic chives parsley
Marinades		chervil chives cilantro dill garlic chives parsley rosemary sage thyme
Roasts		marjoram mint oregano rosemary sage thyme
Salad Dressings	caraway coriander dill fennel	celery chervil chives dill fennel garlic chives marjoram

Perennials, Biennials, Annuals

Perennials, biennials, and annuals are the main categories of herbal plants. A perennial is a plant that will survive for longer than two years. A biennial will last for two years, flowering and setting seed in its second year. An annual will last for only one growing season.

	Crushed Seeds	Chopped Leaves
		mint
		parsley
		sage
		thyme
Sauces	fennel	basil
		celery
		chervil
		cilantro
		dill
		fennel
		garlic chives
		marjoram
		mint
		oregano
		parsley
		sage
		tarragon
		thyme
Soups	fennel	anise
		basil
		celery
		chervil
		cilantro
		dill
		fennel
		marjoram
		parsley
		sage
		savory
		thyme
Spreads		celery
		chives
		cilantro
		dill
		garlic chives
		parsley
Stuffings	coriander	celery
		dill
		marjoram
		parsley
		rosemary
		sage

	Crushed Seeds	Chopped Leaves
		savory
		thyme
Vegetables	fennel	anise
		basil
		celery
		chervil
		cilantro
		dill
		fennel
		marjoram
		parsley
		rosemary
		sage
		savory
		thyme
Vinegars	caraway	basil
	coriander	chives
	dill	garlic chives
	fennel	savory
		tarragon

Midwest Garden Herbs

Anise

BOTANICAL NAME: *Pimpinella ansium*

OTHER COMMON NAME: aniseed

PLANT TYPE: annual

CULTIVATION: every 6 inches, in rows 24 inches apart; directly sow seed in early spring; cover seeds lightly with soil; does not transplant well

SEED GERMINATION: tends to be poor

HARVESTING: cut leaves as needed; seeds are ready when they turn brown

IN YOUR KITCHEN: seeds and leaves

FLAVORS: licorice flavor enhances cheese, rye bread, onion bread, cakes, cookies, apple anything, beef, lamb, veal, vegetables, soups

Basil

BOTANICAL NAME: *Ocimum basilicum*

OTHER COMMON NAME: sweet basil

PLANT TYPE: annual

CULTIVATION: every 10 inches, in rows 24 inches apart; pinch for fuller plants

SEED GERMINATION: easy, late spring

HARVESTING: cut fresh leaves as needed; harvest entire plant before flowering; consider potting a trimmed plant for winter use; make pesto and freeze in small quantities; can be pureed with water in blender and frozen in ice-cube trays

IN YOUR KITCHEN: leaves

FLAVORS: clove flavor enhances anything with tomatoes, eggs, eggplant, fish, cheese, beef, poultry, venison, breads

Basil with its clovelike taste is the most popular herb in the world. Not just a pretty plant that tastes good, it is also rumored to chase bad luck away.

Caraway

BOTANICAL NAME: *Carum carvi*

OTHER COMMON NAME: caraway seed

PLANT TYPE: biennial

CULTIVATION: plant 6 inches apart, in rows 24 inches apart; the first year caraway will form a rosette of finely cut leaves; the second year it will send up a seed stalk in midsummer

SEED GERMINATION: fair

HARVESTING: harvest seed heads just before they turn brown and store in paper bags until dry

IN YOUR KITCHEN: seeds

FLAVORS: breads, cakes, cookies, apple pie, vinegars

Celery

BOTANICAL NAME: *Apium graveolens*

OTHER COMMON NAME: cutting celery, wild celery

PLANT TYPE: annual

CULTIVATION: bred for leaf production instead of stems

SEED GERMINATION: good

HARVESTING: cut fresh leaves as needed

IN YOUR KITCHEN: leaves

FLAVORS: cheese, tomatoes, seafood, ham, beef, lamb, pork, veal, vegetables, French dressing

Chervil

BOTANICAL NAME: *Anthriscus cerefolium*

PLANT TYPE: annual

CULTIVATION: transplants poorly; direct seed on top of soil in spring and cover with light mulch or sow in fall

SEED GERMINATION: needs moisture and light to germinate

HARVESTING: cut fresh leaves as needed; harvest before flowering, leaving bottom 50% for regrowth

IN YOUR KITCHEN: leaves

FLAVORS: delicate parsley flavor enhances cottage cheese, eggs, beef, lamb, pork, veal, vegetables, sauces, soup, butter sauce

Chives

BOTANICAL NAME: *Allium schoenoprasum*

PLANT TYPE: perennial

CULTIVATION: buy potted plant to start; divide every three years

SEED GERMINATION: slow

HARVESTING: cut fresh leaves to ground; can be dried or pureed with water in blender and frozen in ice-cube trays; can be potted in fall and set on the windowsill

IN YOUR KITCHEN: leaves

FLAVORS: mild onion flavor enhances anything with potatoes, vegetables, dips, sauces, vinegars

Cilantro, Coriander

BOTANICAL NAME: *Coriandrum sativum*

OTHER COMMON NAME: Mexican parsley, Chinese parsley

PLANT TYPE: annual

CULTIVATION: plant seeds in early spring 1 inch apart, rows 20 inches apart

SEED GERMINATION: fair

HARVESTING: cilantro is the leaf; begin harvesting when 4 inches high, pick and dry leaves as needed; coriander is the seed; clip brown seed heads and dry in paper bag; fresh leaves can be dried or pureed with water in blender and frozen in ice-cube trays

IN YOUR KITCHEN: seeds and leaves

FLAVORS: coffee, tea, steamed milk, apples, pears, fish, poultry, pork, salsa, beans, baked goods, dressings

Dill

BOTANICAL NAME: *Anethum graveolens*

OTHER COMMON NAME: dill weed, dill seed

PLANT TYPE: annual

CULTIVATION: plant away from fennel

SEED GERMINATION: easy, will self-seed

HARVESTING: cut fresh leaves as needed; harvest seeds when light brown

IN YOUR KITCHEN: seeds and leaves

FLAVORS: lamb, fish, poultry, cheese, pickles, apple pie, salad dressings, soups, vegetables

Fennel

BOTANICAL NAME: *Foeniculum vulgare*

OTHER COMMON NAME: florence fennel

PLANT TYPE: tender perennial that might winter over if mulched

CULTIVATION: grow from seed

SEED GERMINATION: easy

HARVESTING: cut fresh leaves as needed; dry brown seed heads in paper bag

IN YOUR KITCHEN: seeds and leaves

FLAVORS: licorice flavor enhances breads, cakes, cookies, cheese, fish, seafood, apple anything, rice, salad dressings, sauerkraut

Garlic Chives

BOTANICAL NAME: *Allium tuberosum*

PLANT TYPE: perennial

CULTIVATION: buy potted plant to start; divide every 3 years

SEED GERMINATION: slow

HARVESTING: cut fresh leaves to the ground; can be dried or pureed with water in blender and frozen in ice-cube trays; garden plants can be potted in fall and set inside on the windowsill

IN YOUR KITCHEN: leaves

FLAVORS: potato anything, vegetables, dips, sauces, vinegars

Marjoram

BOTANICAL NAME: *Origanum majorana*

OTHER COMMON NAME: sweet marjoram

PLANT TYPE: annual

CULTIVATION: purchase potted plants

SEED GERMINATION: difficult

HARVESTING: cut fresh leaves as needed; harvest after buds form but before flowering, leaving half of plant for regrowth

IN YOUR KITCHEN: leaves

FLAVORS: egg, fish, lamb, veal, beef, seafood, vegetables, stuffing

Mint

BOTANICAL NAME: *Mentha* spp.

PLANT TYPE: perennial

CULTIVATION: easy plants in moist areas; can be invasive—plant in buried containers to control roots

SEED GERMINATION: buy plants to ensure smell and taste of leaves

HARVESTING: cut fresh leaves as needed; harvest new growth before flowering

IN YOUR KITCHEN: leaves

FLAVORS: teas, jelly, salads, sauces, vinegars, lamb

Oregano

BOTANICAL NAME: *Origanum vulgare* sp. *hirtum*

OTHER COMMON NAME: winter marjoram, wild marjoram

PLANT TYPE: tender perennial that might winter over if mulched

CULTIVATION: watch your botanical names when buying oregano plants—smell the leaves, nibble on a leaf. If it tastes peppery, it's the good stuff.

SEED GERMINATION: buy plants to ensure quality of herb

HARVESTING: cut fresh leaves as needed; harvest top 30% of plant before flowering

IN YOUR KITCHEN: leaves

FLAVORS: beef, lamb, seafood, veal, pork, tomato anything, salsa, beans, salad dressings, green pea soup, bean soup, butter sauces

Chervil, parsley, thyme, and tarragon are a flavorful quartet often used as "fines herbes" in French cooking. These herbal bouquets are traditionally added at the last minute to soups and sauces, probably because chervil becomes bitter with lengthy cooking.

Parsley

BOTANICAL NAME: *Petroselinum crispum* var. *crispum*

OTHER COMMON NAME: flat-leaf parsley, Italian parsley

PLANT TYPE: biennial grown as an annual

CULTIVATION: difficult to start from seed, consider potted plants

SEED GERMINATION: soak seeds overnight and direct sow into garden; cover lightly with soil

HARVESTING: cut fresh leaves as needed, roots edible; harvest before flowering leaving half of plant for regrowth; spread out to dry, does not dry well hanging in bunches; puree with water in blender and freeze in ice-cube trays

IN YOUR KITCHEN: leaves

FLAVORS: a "green" flavor that adds sparkle to eggs, all meats, all fish, all vegetables

Rosemary is native to the Mediterranean. Its Latin botanical name translates to "dew of the sea." In the language of flowers, rosemary is the traditional symbol of remembrance.

Rosemary

BOTANICAL NAME: *Rosmarinus officinalis*

PLANT TYPE: tender perennial that might winter over if mulched

CULTIVATION: buy potted plants

SEED GERMINATION: very slow

HARVESTING: cut fresh leaves as needed; harvest top 30% of plant before flowering

IN YOUR KITCHEN: leaves

FLAVORS: fruit punches, eggs, poultry, fish, lamb, pork, potato soup

Sage

BOTANICAL NAME: *Salvia officinalis*

OTHER COMMON NAME: garden sage

PLANT TYPE: perennial; mulch to winter over

CULTIVATION: plant 18 inches apart

SEED GERMINATION: easy, start inside for early crop

HARVESTING: cut fresh leaves as needed; harvest top 30% of plant just before flowering

IN YOUR KITCHEN: leaves

FLAVORS: corn bread, cream cheese, cottage cheese, marinades, salad dressings, sausage, fish, pork, poultry, cheese spreads, butter sauces

Savory

BOTANICAL NAME: *Satureja hortensis*

OTHER COMMON NAME: summer savory

PLANT TYPE: annual

CULTIVATION: cover seeds lightly with soil

SEED GERMINATION: easy

HARVESTING: cut fresh leaves as needed; harvest before flowering, leaving half of plant for regrowth; woody stems should be removed after drying

IN YOUR KITCHEN: leaves

FLAVORS: similar to sage, but its subtler flavor enhances eggs, chicken, beef, lamb, pork, green beans, vegetables, seafood, stuffing

Tarragon

BOTANICAL NAME: *Artemisia dracunculus* var. *sativa*

OTHER COMMON NAME: French tarragon

PLANT TYPE: perennial; mulch to winter over

CULTIVATION: watch your botanical names when buying tarragon plants—if the leaves don't smell like licorice, the plant might be mis-marked or an inferior seed strain

SEED GERMINATION: only buy potted plants; seeds unreliable

HARVESTING: cut fresh leaves as needed; harvest new growth in early summer for vinegars; harvest top 30% of plant before flowering

IN YOUR KITCHEN: leaves

FLAVORS: pungent flavor used sparingly to enhance vegetables, eggs, fish, chicken, pork, cabbage, vinegars

Thyme

BOTANICAL NAME: *Thymus vulgaris*

PLANT TYPE: perennial, mulch to winter over

CULTIVATION: plant 12 inches apart

SEED GERMINATION: good, start from seed

HARVESTING: cut fresh leaves as needed; harvest top 30% of leafy stem ends when budding, remove stems after drying

IN YOUR KITCHEN: leaves

FLAVORS: fish, cheese, seafood, poultry, lamb, stuffing, vegetables

What Herbs Need

During the summer, herbs need average soil, mulch, and one inch of water per week. Perennial herbs should be planted around the outside or at one end of your garden. Annuals can be left until autumn's first frost, when all dead and dying material should be removed and added to your compost pile or used to mulch flowers. The soil should be turned over to expose insect eggs and larvae to the birds. After the ground freezes, perennials should be mulched with shredded leaves to protect them from frost heaves. In the spring, pull the mulch aside and lay between rows to keep the mud off your shoes.

Be sure to check Section Six for a listing of public gardens in the Midwest that offer plantings of herbs.

Potted Herb Garden

For smaller families or limited spaces, consider a strawberry pot with pockets full of herbs. For a great gift, consider planting theme gardens—pizza herbs or herbal teas. This potted garden works well with strawberry plants, too (see later in this section under Small Fruits).

Project Supplies
- A strawberry pot with pockets
- Top quality potting-soil mix
- As many different herb plants as you have pockets
- Small stones
- A long cardboard wrapping-paper tube, long enough to protrude from the top of the strawberry pot when stood on the pot bottom

Here's How
1. Add three inches of soil mix to bottom of pot.
2. Stand tube upright in the center of the pot.
3. Add soil mix up to the first tier of pockets.
4. Plant herbs.
5. Repeat steps 3 and 4 until you reach the rim. Do not remove the tube.
6. Plant parsley, chives, cilantro, or other upright plants around the cardboard tube on top.
7. Fill the cardboard tube with small stones.
8. Carefully remove the tube.
9. Water the herbs through the column of stones.
10. Place in full sun, water daily, and feed with a weak solution of natural fertilizer weekly.

Harvesting Herbs

Optimum harvest times for herbs are determined by weather conditions. Plants are at their most flavorful and ready to harvest just before blooming. Gather them early in the morning when the dew in the garden has evaporated but before the plant begins releasing its oil in the sun. Once cut, wash the leaves under running water. Then use your microwave, food dehydrator, or the old-fashioned method of wrapping a handful of stems in a paper bag and hanging them in a warm, sunless spot to dry for two weeks. To freeze herbs, dip them in boiling water, then in a bowl of water and ice cubes, shake dry, and store in plastic freezer bags.

Keeping Cut Herbs Fresh

Fresh herbs can be a snip away if you take a tip from florists and store cut herbs in the refrigerator. Place stems in a container of water and loosely cover leaves with a plastic bag. Change the water when it looks cloudy and expect herbs to last at least one week.

Herb Vinegars

Herb vinegars are fun to use and easy to make.
1. Rinse herb leaves and stems in running water.
2. Place in a glass jar and cover with white, wine, or apple cider vinegar.
3. Place a small plastic bag over the mouth of the jar and then cover with the lid.
4. Steep for a month.
5. Strain to remove herbs.
6. Pour into smaller bottles and add fresh herbs for decoration.
7. Refrigerate until needed.

Plant Groups and Associations

American Herb Association
PO Box 1673
Nevada City, CA 95959

The American Herb Association is dedicated to reeducating the public about herbs and rekindling the art of growing herbs for both health and pleasure. Their quarterly newsletter is written by professional herbalists. Annual dues are $20.

The Herb Society of America
9019 Kirtland Chardon Road
Kirtland, OH 44094

This twenty-five-hundred-member group was founded in 1933. The Herb Society provides funds to support the National Herb Garden at the National Arboretum in Washington, D.C. Annual dues of $35 include a quarterly newsletter, seed exchange program, and lending library.

Purchasing Herb Plants and Seeds from Local Garden Centers

When buying potted seedlings from your garden center, if you don't like the smell of a potted herb, try another pot or another store. The aroma and flavor of an herb can vary from plant to plant and with the quality of seed used. When you find an herb that you like, buy two or three. Remember, your nose knows!

Purchasing Herb Plants and Seeds from Mail-Order Sources

Shopping for plants and seeds by mail is a way to increase variety in your garden. Many mail-order companies buy plants from all over the country and sell them through catalogs. A few nurseries specialize in growing and selling herbs.

Check each catalog's guarantee policy and allow each new plant time to acclimatize. If plants do not show growth in three weeks, contact the catalog company and ask for new plants.

For the backbone of your garden, it is best to buy seeds or plants raised in the Midwest. Once you find a mail-order nursery that you like, tell your friends.

Edible Flowers and Ferns

We are visual creatures, feasting with our eyes before we ever touch our food. An easy way to make food more appealing is to add flowers. Try a fresh summer salad decorated with the delicate blue star-shaped flowers of borage, or an entree sprinkled with a confetti of chopped parsley and rose petals.

Not all flowers can be eaten safely. Unless you are absolutely certain that a flower or plant is edible, leave it alone. People with serious allergies should avoid eating flowers, and everyone should avoid flowers sprayed with chemicals. All florists, nurseries, and grocery stores use chemicals on their flowers.

With these precautions under consideration, surprise your family with the bright addition of colorful edible flowers. One or two plants of any of these will be more than enough for most kitchens.

Successful edible flower gardens start here:

S Stay with natural gardening techniques. Choose chemical-free fertilizers and pesticides.

T To use flowers, immerse in cool water to dislodge any hidden bugs, wash, separate the petals, and cut with scissors into flower confetti. Or use whole blossoms as a garnish to brighten summer entrees.

A Always use small amounts of flowers to decorate—too many on a plate can be overwhelming.

R Remember to match botanical names on seed packets.

T Think color when choosing what to grow in your garden.

Edible Flowers and Ferns to Try

Borage; *Borago officinalis*

Borage has a sharp cucumber flavor and blue stars for flowers. It is one of easiest flowers to grow. Leave one plant to self-seed each fall and borage will come up every year on its own.

Calendula; *Calendula officinalis*

Calendula have a tangy peppery flavor and loose petals in hot colors. These flowers like full sun. Save the seed from your biggest plant and use them to replant every year.

Johnny-Jump-Up; *Viola tricolor*

Johnny-jump-up has a sharp wintergreen taste with a yellow and violet face. These are cool-weather flowers whose seed should be sown around St. Patrick's Day.

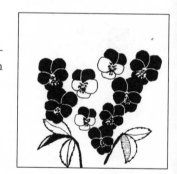

Marigold 'Lemon Gem'; *Tagetes signata pumila*

Lemon gem marigolds have a bitter flavor, a lemon scent, and yellow ruffles. Plant seeds in full sun when you add peppers and tomatoes to your garden. Save seed from the best plant for next year's crop.

Nasturtium; *Tropaeolum majus*

Nasturtiums have a peppery taste and hot colors. Sow seeds in the garden when you plant your first crop of lettuce. Nasturtiums are a wonderful companion plant for tomatoes. Purchase fresh seed every year.

Fiddlehead Fern; *Matteuccia struthiopteris,* also known as *Matteuccia pensylvanica*

Fiddlehead fern is found wild in river bottoms and cultivated in woodland gardens. In early spring, coiled leaf buds push through the ground and begin to unroll. To harvest, cut the fiddleheads when they are two to three inches tall and still tightly coiled. Store them in the refrigerator as you would lettuce. To use, rinse in running water to remove the papery coating, boil three minutes, drain, and use in salad, stir-fry, or however else you can imagine.

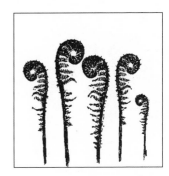

What Edible Flowers and Ferns Need

Edible flowers and ferns can be grown in your herb and vegetable garden or in pots. During the summer, those added to the garden will need average soil, mulch, and one inch of water per week. Perennial flowers and ferns should be planted around the outside or at one end of your garden. Annuals can be interplanted with other plants to confuse pests. After the ground freezes, perennials should be mulched with shredded leaves to protect them from frost heaves. In the spring, pull the mulch aside and lay between rows to keep the mud off your shoes.

Purchasing Edible Flowers and Ferns from Local Garden Centers

Reread your planting list and bring your botanical names. Experienced staff love plants and are wonderful. Inexperienced nursery staff members can often mislead you with good intentions and misinformation.

Purchasing Edible Flowers and Ferns from Mail-Order Sources

Local selection of plants and seeds is often limited. Shopping for plants by mail is an easy way to increase variety in your garden. For the backbone of your garden, it is best to buy seeds or plants raised in the Midwest. Once you find a mail-order nursery that you like, tell your friends and other Midwest gardeners about it.

Popular Vegetables

Tomatoes, beans, and salad greens are the three most popular vegetables grown in Midwest kitchen gardens. People have been growing these vegetables for the entire written history of mankind, and you can too.

Successful vegetable gardens start here:

S Select healthy, nutrient-rich soil. Have a soil sample tested by your county extension office to find out if your soil needs additives.

T Turn under and break up your soil each fall to a depth of six inches to make it easy for plant roots.

A Add a diluted liquid fertilizer when transplanting seedlings and sowing seeds.

R Rake or hoe to control early spring weeds. Mulch with untreated grass clippings, first between rows and then after mid-June between plants.

T Thin plants while they are small to allow remaining plants to grow larger.

Tomato

Tomatoes have been cultivated since pre-Columbian times in South America, and wild tomatoes still grow in the foothills of the Andes. Spanish explorers distributed tomatoes throughout the Old World as an ornamental curiosity. Possibly because of their origin, tomatoes were wrapped in folklore and superstition. Tomato stems and leaves are poisonous. Up until the 1700s, it was considered foolhardy to eat a tomato. Thomas Jefferson was one of the first Americans to grow tomatoes as a food.

Scientifically considered a fruit, the tomato was officially ruled a vegetable by the U.S. Supreme Court when an importer refused to pay taxes, claiming the tomato as a fruit and not subject to duty. The Supreme Court declared that the use of tomatoes in main courses and soups earned it the designation of vegetable. Today tomatoes are the mainstay of summer gardens, and many consider them preventive medicine for cancer.

Originally tomato plants required a mild climate, but by careful breeding cultivars have been developed for colder climates. At last count there were over three hundred tomato types, shapes, and colors available to home gardeners. Tomatoes are the most popular home-grown vegetable in the Midwest. They can be grown in hanging baskets, tubs, or in the ground. No other vegetable conveys the joys of gardening better than a hand-picked tomato. Whether you pluck one fresh from the garden and let the warm, sweet flavor explode in your mouth or spend hours preparing gourmet ketchup, there is nothing in the world quite like a home-grown tomato.

Getting Ready For Early Summer Tomatoes

- Cherry tomato seeds can be planted as soon as the soil is turned in the fall. Next spring these will pop up on their own as the soil warms.
- Start seeds indoors in a warm window in early spring. Cover seeds lightly with a nonsoil planting mix and water from the bottom.
- Gently brush seedlings daily with a piece of notebook paper to simulate a gentle breeze and encourage strong stems.
- In the garden, bury seedlings in the ground up to their first set of leaves when nighttime soil temperatures reach sixty degrees.
- Soil temperature can be increased by covering plants with black plastic, water-filled minigreenhouses, or the tops of plastic milk jugs.
- Transplant seedlings to the garden on a cloudy day, or protect from direct sun for two days. Feed with a diluted natural fertilizer.
- Plant tomatoes in a different garden spot each year to avoid soil-borne diseases and pests.
- Plan for a longer tomato season by planting a few early-ripening hybrids like 'Early Girl' or 'Spring Giant' plus main season varieties like 'Jetstar', 'Better Boy', 'Celebrity', or 'Burpee VF'.
- Try 'Sweet 100' for a cherry tomato.
- Top heirloom tomatoes include: 'Brandywine', 'Big Rainbow', 'Cherokee Purple', 'Hugh's', and 'Green Zebra'.
- Consider interplanting tomatoes with companion plants: chives, marigolds, onions, carrots, garlic, or nasturtiums.
- Make tomato selections based on pest and disease resistance. Tomatoes that have the initials F.V.N.T. after them provide the best protection. F means fusarium resistant; V means verticillium resistant; N means nematode resistant, and T means tobacco mosaic virus resistant.
- Hybrid varieties are usually "determinate" tomatoes, forming flower clusters at the end of stems and growing only to a certain height.
- Older varieties are usually "indeterminate" tomatoes, forming flower clusters on lateral branches as they keep growing and growing. These produce lots of fruit but are late to mature.

In Your Garden

- To encourage early ripening, dig a natural fertilizer high in phosphorus and low in nitrogen in a ring just outside the plant roots. The roots will grow into the fertilized ring.

- For richer color, try adding a light sprinkling of potassium around plants in late June.

- Begin adding organic mulches about the first of July.

- Harvest ripe tomatoes by gently twisting the stem.

- For a higher yield, pick continuously.

- Pinch off all new blossoms at the end of August.

- Trim off yellow and wilting foliage. Destroy infected leaves.

- Water regularly and deeply, at least one inch of water at a time.

- Mulch four inches deep around plants to prevent rot and cracking.

- Keep tomato leaves dry. Leaf blight can travel two hundred miles to mature on wet leaves.

- As nighttime air temperatures drop below fifty degrees, ripen green tomatoes by uprooting plants and hanging them upside down out of the sun in a cool place with good air circulation.

- Remove all plant debris in fall and till the remaining mulch into the soil.

- Save seeds from nonhybrid plants. Dry seeds can be stored up to three years by sealing them in a dark, airtight container with, but not touching, powdered milk or silica gel.

In Your Kitchen

- Ripen green tomatoes stem-end down out of the sun. A ripening bowl or brown paper bag speeds up the ripening process.

- Large numbers of green tomatoes can be held for four to six weeks if stored covered with newspapers at sixty-five degrees in a dark room.

- Dry sliced, seeded tomatoes in a food dehydrator for winter salads and soups.

- Freeze chopped tomatoes for winter sauces.

- Can sauces and salsa for quick-fix meals.

- Grill, broil, stew, fry, bake, stuff, saute, and steam fresh tomatoes.

- For recipe ideas, check the cookbooks at your public library.

- Herbs that go well with tomatoes include rosemary, thyme, oregano, garlic, dill, and basil.

- Tomato paste can be made by allowing the juice of blended plum tomatoes to drip through cheesecloth.

- Peel single tomatoes by heating in the microwave, then stripping off the skin.

- Remove seeds before processing or drying tomatoes, as they turn bitter when heated.

- One pound of tomatoes will yield one cup of pulp. One pound equals three to four 'Early Girl', eight 'Roma', or one 'Beefsteak'.

Beans

Beans are so ancient that they are mentioned in the Bible and have been found at Bronze Age sites and in Egyptian tombs. Extremely high in protein, carbohydrates, and phosphates, beans have been and still are a staple food in many countries and cultures throughout the world.

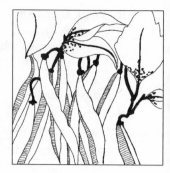

There are hundreds of bean varieties for home gardens, including filet beans, green beans, kidney beans, lima beans, shelling beans, snap beans, and wax beans. Snap, shell, and dried beans are different phases in a bean's development. Snap beans are immature pods. Shell beans are the mature fresh seed. Dried beans are seeds that have dried in the pod. Any bean will give you all three stages but not necessarily good flavor at each stage. Inside each group there are beans that grow on bushes and bean vines that climb poles. Green bush beans were once called string beans, because of a fiber that ran along the seam of the pods. Plant breeders have reduced these fibers and these beans are now called snap beans.

Getting Ready For Early Summer Beans

- In early spring, plant seeds in peat pots filled with a nonsoil seed mixture.
- Fava or broad beans can be planted anytime after St. Patrick's Day. Other beans need a soil temperature in the garden of sixty degrees to germinate.
- Once seedlings are up, place them in a warm window and water from the bottom.
- Gently brush seedlings daily with a piece of notebook paper to simulate a gentle breeze and encourage strong stems.
- Transplant to the garden when the nighttime soil temperature reaches sixty degrees.
- When burying peat pots, cover the rim with soil. If left above ground, the peat will act as a wick, drying faster than the soil around it and dehydrating the young seedling.
- Soil temperature can be increased by covering plants with black plastic, water-filled minigreenhouses, or the tops of plastic milk jugs.
- Transplant seedlings to the garden on a cloudy day, or protect from direct sun for two days. Feed with a diluted natural fertilizer.
- Try growing purple bush snap beans. They taste just like green snap beans, turn dark green when cooked, and rabbits seem to pass them by.

In Your Garden

- Try bean and pea inoculant, a collection of friendly bacteria, when planting to increase your harvest.
- Plant beans every two weeks for a continual supply.
- Beans grow well in ordinary garden soil.
- Bush beans mature quicker than pole beans.
- Bush beans spread two feet wide and tall.
- Pole beans will have more beans over a longer period of time and only need to be planted once.
- Pole beans spread two feet wide and can climb twenty feet.
- Pick beans after the dew on their leaves has dried to prevent spread of disease.
- Pick beans while young and tender. The more you pick, the more beans you get.
- Trim off yellow and wilting foliage. Destroy infected leaves.
- Water regularly and deeply, at least one inch of water at a time.
- Mulch four inches deep around plants.
- Water every two weeks with a diluted natural fertilizer.
- Remove all plant debris in fall and till remaining mulch into soil.
- Matured snap beans can be dried and used as dry beans. Dried matured lima beans become butter beans.
- Save seeds from nonhybrid plants. Dry seeds can be stored up to three years by sealing them in a dark, airtight container with, but not touching, powdered milk or silica gel.

In Your Kitchen

- Harvest by snapping off the stem end.
- Tradition has taught us to snap the bean tip off too, but newer stringless varieties are so tender, there is no longer a need to do this.
- For recipe ideas, check the cookbooks at your public library.
- Herbs that go well with beans include summer savory, lemon verbena, chives, and tarragon.
- One pound of fresh snap beans equals four cups.
- One pound of fresh shell beans equals one and one-half cups.
- To freeze fresh snap beans: drop into boiling water for three minutes, chill in ice water for three minutes, drain, and store in freezer bags.

Salad Greens

Salad greens are an increasingly popular vegetable in the United States. Because they are a basic ingredient in salads, greens are eaten more often than any other vegetable. Greens can be eaten fresh with dressing, used as a garnish, stuffed with cheese, braised in a light broth, wilted with warm vegetable oil and vinegar, or mixed with other fresh vegetables.

Greens germinate and grow at low temperature. They are one of the first vegetables to be planted in the spring and one of the last to be planted in the fall. Most greens tolerate a moderate freeze and do best in cool, fifty- to sixty-degree weather. Hot weather causes greens to become bitter and seed stalks to form. If you grow summer greens in the shade and water frequently, you can harvest from early spring through fall.

Amaranth, arugula, celtuce, dandelion, endive, escarole, French sorrel, garden cress, lettuce, mesclun, parsley, New Zealand spinach, radicchio, salad burnet, spinach, smoky fennel, and sweet cicely are all considered salad greens. They can be grown together and harvested as a mixed salad.

Getting Ready For Early Spring Greens

- Start seeds inside and set seedlings into the garden around when the soil reaches thirty-five degrees. Remove the bottoms of gallon-size milk jugs or clear two-liter soft-drink bottles and place over the seedlings to protect them from spring frosts and wildlife.
- At the same time you set out seedlings, sow additional seed and cover lightly with fine soil. Plantings ten to fifteen days apart will supply fresh greens for the growing season.
- When buying seed, try some mesclun (mes-cloon). This is a mixture of classic French and Italian-style greens, delightful when harvested young and tossed into salads.
- Greens also adapt well to hydroponic culture in greenhouse or window box production. Gardening with greens in almost any type of container can be successful.

In Your Garden

- Greens need frequent applications of natural nitrogen.
- Greens can be grown in neat rows of single varieties or in a wide band of mixed varieties. To grow a wide band of greens, broadcast seeds lightly and cover with soil in an area one or two feet wide and as long as is practical.
- For gardeners with limited space, greens can serve double duty as a border plant in flower gardens that are feed with natural fertilizers.
- Greens are a useful crop in settings where shaded sites must be used for gardens because most will grow quite well under low light conditions.

- There are five different types of lettuce: crisp head, leaf, butterhead, cos or Romaine, and stem.
- Allow six inches between butterhead lettuce varieties and twelve inches between crisp-head lettuce varieties.
- The crisp-head varieties, with dense, firm heads and crisp leaves, are by far the most important commercial types. Strains of 'Great Lakes', an All-American winner, and 'Imperial' mature about seventy-five days from planting and withstand warm weather better than most.
- 'Black-seeded Simpson', 'Early Prizehead', 'Oak Leaf', 'Grand Rapids', and 'Ruby Red' are leaf lettuce varieties that mature about forty-five days from seed planting.
- Butterhead lettuce produces a loose, soft head with an oily feel. Butterhead varieties mature slightly earlier than crisp-head varieties and prefer cooler weather. 'Big Boston', 'Bibb', and 'Buttercrunch', an All-American winner, are popular varieties that do best when started early indoors or in cold frames and are transplanted into the garden.
- Romaine types of lettuce develop an elongated head of stiff, upright leaves about eighty days from planting. This lettuce is hard to grow in Midwest gardens.
- Stem lettuce often is listed in catalogs under the name of celtuce. Its name is adapted from a combination of the words "celery" and "lettuce." Celtuce is grown for its fleshy, elongated stem, which is peeled and eaten raw like celery.
- Bolting and bitter flavor caused by high temperatures can be delayed by shading the crop. Row covers, cheesecloth, or other shading material can be effective. Selecting a planting site that will be shaded in the afternoon is another alternative.

In Your Kitchen

- Crisp head lettuce is ready for harvest when the heads are solid and the tops become yellowish green.
- Butterhead varieties may be harvested when a loose head is formed.
- Head lettuce should be cut at or slightly below the soil surface.
- Leaf lettuce may be harvested at any time after the plants are large enough to use. You can either cut the top off, leaving one inch of plant to grow back, or thin the row by pulling out the entire plant.
- To store greens, wrap in a damp towel, place in a perforated bag, and refrigerate.
- To use, soak greens in a sink of cool water for ten minutes. Then rinse, checking the undersides of leaves for insects. Remove excess water by blotting or with a salad spinner.
- Summer greens can be sweetened by drizzling with honey or sprinkling with sugar before adding salad dressing.

- Tear rather than cut greens.
- Apples, pears, and cantaloupes give off an ethylene gas that causes rust spots on greens.
- Try wilted greens in quiches. Try fresh greens in stir-fries.

Table Vegetables
A to Z

Eating vegetables every day is one of the most important things you can do to maintain your good health and bright smile. According to the American Cancer Society, cabbage family vegetables—broccoli, cauliflower, brussels sprouts, cabbage, kale—appear to protect you against stomach and respiratory diseases. Potatoes, spinach, and tomatoes are thought to protect you against colon cancers. Yellow vegetables like carrots and squash may fight off cancers of the esophagus, larynx, and lung. And the vitamin C in tomatoes, red and green peppers, and broccoli may help protect you against cancers of the esophagus and stomach.

The garden vegetables in the table below are good for you and easy to grow. They are grouped and alphabetized according to planting dates to help you with your spring planting. Check with your county extension office for varieties recommended for your area. Check soil temperature with a soil test thermometer. These can be purchased at garden centers or through many mail-order catalogs. The thermometer should have a range up to 90 degrees and cost under twenty dollars.

VERY HARDY VEGETABLES
(Planted in early spring, depending on soil temperature and variety.)

	Start inside	Start in garden	Plants or seeds	Mini-mum soil temp.	Plant and row spacing (in inches)	What works
Asparagus	■	■	P / S	45°	12 / 24	• Plant in 14-in.-deep trenches with lots of composted manure; • harvest after the third year by snapping spears; • fertilize in June after last harvest.
Broccoli	■	■	P / S	45°	12 / 24	• Pick heat-resistant variety for spring-planted summer crop; • heavy feeder, side-dress with nitrogen; • plan for spring and fall crops by planting in each season; • needs consistent moisture.
Brussels Sprouts	■		P	45°	24 / 36	• Might overwinter if mulched; • cover plants with floating row cover to protect from white cabbage butterfly caterpillars; • harvest from the bottom up when sprouts are 1 in. in diameter, remove leaves at the same time.
Cabbage	■		P	45°	18 / 36	• Needs consistent moisture; • harvest before heads split; • plant spring and fall crops; • cover plants with floating row cover to protect from white cabbage butterfly caterpillars.
Garlic		■	P	45°	4 / 12	• Plant only the biggest cloves; • pinch off flower buds; • stop watering when leaf tips turn brown; • dig up plants and leave in sun; • skin is papery; braid to store.
Jerusalem Artichoke		■	P	45°	20 / 36	• New tubers need to be planted each year in new location; • look for newer named varieties that have been hybridized from the native plant; • can be grown from tubers purchased in produce section; • often called sunchokes.

	Start inside	Start in garden	Plants or seeds	Mini- mum soil temp.	Plant and row spacing (in inches)	What works
Kohlrabi		■	S	45°	12 / 24	• Cover plants with floating row cover to provide extra warmth and protect from pests.
Leek	■	■	S	35°	6 / 18	• Very slow grower, can be started inside in February; • plant in a trench and bank soil around base of plants when they are the diameter of a pencil to whiten stem; • will winter over and form cloves on the underground portion— these are often sold as elephant garlic.
Onion	■	■	P / S	35°	4 / 12	• Hates weeds, loves water; • no extra nitrogen fertilizer; • allow to dry in the sun for an afternoon after harvesting; • bulbs are easier than seeds if you can find the variety you want to grow.
Parsnip		■	S	35°	4 / 18	• Considered a winter vegetable because its flavor is not fully developed until the roots have been exposed to at least 2 weeks of freezing temperatures.
Peas		■	S	40°	6 / 36	• Snow peas have edible pods; • garden peas are dried and used to make pea soup.
Radish		■	S	45°	2 / 12	• Pick radish variety by season; hot temperatures cause hollow. centers in cool-season varieties.
Salad Greens	■	■	P/S	35°	18	• See previous section, Salad Greens.

HARDY, FROST-TOLERANT VEGETABLES
(Planted in spring depending upon soil temperature and variety.)

	Start inside	Start in garden	Plants or seeds	Mini- mum soil temp.	Plant and row spacing (in inches)	What works
Beets		■	S	50°	3 / 12	• Also known as blood turnip; • tops can be cooked or served as salad greens; • needs cool, moist soils; • make spring and fall plantings.

	Start inside	Start in garden	Plants or seeds	Mini-mum soil temp.	Plant and row spacing (in inches)	What works
Carrots		■	S	50°	3 / 12	• Prefers sandy soil for root development; • cover seeded planting area with clear plastic until seeds germinate; • plump carrots need lots of water; • prepare soil to a depth of 9 in. and remove clumps.
Cauliflower	■		P	50°	24 / 36	• Cover plants with floating row cover to protect from white cabbage butterfly caterpillars; • must have a consistent supply of water; • needs extra nitrogen; • when white head begins to form, tie outer leaves together over top to blanch head and to keep it from turning green and bitter.
Horseradish		■	S	50°	24 / 24	• Hardy perennial started from crown divisions or roots; • roots grow most during cool fall weather; • harvest after first hard frost; • replant smaller roots for next year's harvest.
Kale		■	S	60°	12 / 24	• Susceptible to cabbage-family pests; • plant spring and fall harvests.
Mustard		■	S	60°	12 / 24	• Harvest young leaves; • summer heat causes bitter flavor; • plant spring and fall harvests.
Potatoes		■	S	60°	12 / 36	• Needs fertile, well-drained soil; • mound soil and mulch around plant as it grows to reduce potato sunburn and form potatoes on top of soil; • needs consistent water and lots of mulch.
Shallot		■	S	50°	4 / 18	• Plant 4 in. deep; • clip tops as green onions;

	Start inside	Start in garden	Plants or seeds	Mini-mum soil temp.	Plant and row spacing (in inches)	What works
						• allow plants to die down in summer, dig and allow to dry outside for an afternoon;
						• if tops are green when harvested, they can be braided;
						• hardy, will overwinter;
						• shallots from grocery store can be used as starter seed.
Sunflower		■	S	60°	varies	• Bag heads after pollination to protect from birds.
Swiss Chard		■	S	50°	10 seeds/ft.	• Thin and harvest young plants;
						• mature plants, harvest outside leaves;
						• late plantings escape leaf-miner infestation.
Turnip		■	S	60°	3 / 12	• Plant in spring, late summer, and fall;
						• often confused with its cousin, rutabaga, which has a longer growing season and is harder to grow in our area.

TENDER VEGETABLES, EASILY INJURED BY FROST
(Planted in early summer, depending on soil temperature and variety.)

	Start inside	Start in garden	Plants or seeds	Mini-mum soil temp.	Plant and row spacing (in inches)	What works
Artichoke	■		P	65°	12 / 24	• Easy to grow in cool summer areas;
						• pick quick-maturing varieties and plant in shade.
Beans	■	■	P/S	65°	2 / 30	• See previous section, Beans.
Corn, Sweet	■	■	P/S	60°	9 / 36	• Pollinated by the wind, plant at least 3 rows across;
						• expect 1 ear per plant;
						• pruning will not increase yields;
						• fertilize, fertilize, fertilize.
Cucumber	■	■	P/S	60°	12 / 48	• Plant dwarf varieties in small gardens;
						• shallow roots need mulch and lots of water;
						• floating row covers protect from cucumber beetle, remove when first female blossom (flower with tiny cucumber) forms for pollination.

	Start inside	Start in garden	Plants or seeds	Mini-mum soil temp.	Plant and row spacing (in inches)	What works
Eggplant	■		P	75°	12 / 24	• Exotic varieties can be grown in containers; • fertilize when plants are half-grown and after first harvest.
Husk Tomato	■	■	P/S	65°	18 / 24	• Berrylike fruits used in pies and jelly; • needs same care as tomato.
Okra	■		S	65°	24 in hills	• Poor seed germination; • start seeds in warm place in wet paper towel and plastic bag; • remove mature pods daily.
Peppers, Hot	■		P	65°	12 / 24	• Use low-nitrogen fertilizer; • plants have shallow roots, so mulch heavily; • plant inside open-ended juice cans if you've seen cutworms in your garden; • leave a small piece of stem on pepper when harvesting.
Peppers, Sweet	■		P	65°	12 / 24	• Use low-nitrogen fertilizer; • plants have shallow roots, so mulch heavily; • plant inside open-ended juice cans if you've seen cutworms in your garden; • leave a small piece of stem on pepper when harvesting.
Pumpkin	■	■	P/S	70°	varies	• Match variety to your needs; • try naked-seed types for roasted seeds, another for pies, another for jack o' lanterns.
Squash, Summer	■	■	P/S	70°	48 / 48	• Bush plants, harvest while young; • if attacked by squash borer, cover stems with soil and plant will reroot; • use floating row covers until you find first female blossom (flower with tiny squash attached); companion-plant dill to attract wasps that feed on squash beetles.

	Start inside	Start in garden	Plants or seeds	Mini- mum soil temp.	Plant and row spacing (in inches)	What works
Squash, Winter	■	■	P/S	70°	60 / 60	• Harvest in fall when rind is hard; • leave 2 in. of stem attached to squash when harvesting; • store in a cool place, single layer, with newspaper between squashes.
Sweet Potatoes	■		P	70°	18 / 36	• Plant in a raised ridge; • harvest before first frost; • allow to dry on ground all after- noon; • cure for 10 days in warm room, then store in cool location; • mice have been known to harvest sweet potatoes before people do.
Tomatillo	■		P	65°	24 / 36	• Used in green salsa; • needs same care as tomatoes.
Tomato	■		P	65°		• See previous section, Tomato.

What Vegetables Need

Vegetables need a different spot in your garden plot each year, full sun, one inch of water per week, mulch, natural soil fertilizer in the spring, and a midsummer application of liquid fertilizer. Each fall the entire vegetable garden should be tilled under to prepare for your spring garden.

In the spring, avoid working the soil too early. Heavy clay soils compact into hard clumps if cultivated when the soil is too wet. If spring fever gets you while the soil is still cold, choose the kinds of vegetable seeds that can live with cool soil or start seeds inside. Use a soil thermometer to check soil temperatures and be patient with Mother Nature. Seeds that love warm soil will rot in cold, wet soil. In the Midwest, very hardy vegetables not injured by winter freezing can often be planted in early spring. These include asparagus, broccoli, brussels sprouts, cabbage, Jerusalem artichoke, kohlrabi, leek, onion, parsnip, pea, radish, and salad greens. Hardy frost-tolerant vegetables are planted in spring. These include beet, carrot, cauliflower, garlic, horseradish, kale, mustard, potato, rutabaga, shallot, Swiss chard, and turnip. Tender vegetables easily injured by frost may be planted in early summer. These include artichoke, bean, cucumber, eggplant, husk tomato, okra, peppers, pumpkin, sweet corn, squash, sweet potato, tomato, and tomatillo.

Which Seed to Buy

Besides eating fresh from the garden, this is the most fun part of gardening—selecting seeds. There are several seed varieties (cultivars) in each of the vegetable categories that have been available since the turn of the century and will be probably be available well past the twenty-first century. As seed companies compete for your gardening dollars, new seed cultivars are introduced each year. Just because something is new does not make it better. But the other side of the coin is valid too—an old seed cultivar is not necessarily better. Best and better is what works in your garden.

Old, established seed cultivars are called "heirlooms." Most heirlooms are open-pollinated and allowed to set seed without the hand of man. Seed from heirloom vegetables will grow true, which means that any new plants grown from heirloom seeds will be very similar to the parent. Heirloom stock is improved by selecting and planting the seed from the best offspring.

Newer varieties are called hybrids. Hybrid seeds are made by cross-pollinating two varieties to get the best qualities of both. New hybrids can only be maintained by crossing the same parent types every year. Seeds from hybrid plants will not grow true and cannot reproduce the traits of both parents.

Both your county's agricultural extension service and your state's university horticultural department have public trial gardens with heirloom and hybrid plants. Each year the results of these tests are available at a minimal cost or free of charge to home gardeners. Just ask your extension agent or university for the most recent listing of heirloom and hybrid vegetables recommended for your area.

Once you have your list of what will give you the best result in your area, it's time to buy seeds. A successful garden begins with the selection and use of high-quality seed of adapted superior varieties. Start by purchasing seed from a reputable seed company. You can purchase seeds locally or through mail-order catalogs. Save records of your seed orders, so if you have a complaint you can contact the sales company. Saving records of your seed orders is also useful for keeping track of the varieties you planted.

On many seed packets you will see an emblem identifying it as an All-America Selection. The All-America Selection (AAS) was established in 1933 to evaluate new cultivars grown from seed in trials all over North America. Over the years home gardeners have benefited from the AAS trials through the identification of cultivars with improved disease resistance, earlier bloom, increased uniformity, and new and improved flower colors.

All seed packets are required to show the year they were packaged for, number of days to harvest, planting directions, and the germination percentages expected. When buying seeds, you get what you pay for.

Asparagus for a Lifetime

Every so often, articles are published explaining that asparagus can be planted at a shallower level than tradition advises. No matter how tempting this is, don't do it. These recommendations usually involve commercial plots and commercial growers who remake their beds every few years. In the home garden, traditional planting fourteen inches deep will produce excellent results for a lifetime. Dig deep once and be done with it.

Beware of Green Potatoes

Throw away any green potato you find. Potato skins turn green because of a chlorophyll buildup that can be toxic if too much is eaten. There are edible blue, yellow, red, and white potatoes, but all green potatoes are toxic.

Cheap, bargain, off-brand seeds tend to produce inferior vegetables. What you save in money, you will lose in vegetable production.

Many of the older seed cultivars can also be taken directly from garden plants, dried, stored, and planted next year. It is possible to store vegetable seeds for up to three years without refrigeration if the seeds are stored in a dark area in airtight jars with a moisture-absorbing ingredient such as dried rice, powdered milk, or commercial desiccant. The dark jars that vitamin pills are packaged in are wonderful for this purpose.

Each spring, check leftover seed for germination. If germination is poor, discard it and buy fresh seed. To test for germination, place seeds between paper towels. Moisten the seeds and place the paper towels in a plastic bag to prevent the seeds from drying out. Place on top of the refrigerator or in another warm place. If most of them sprout, the seed is good. If only a percentage sprout, use more seeds when planting or buy fresh seed.

Where to Put Your Garden

Location is the key factor to good vegetable gardens. Garden size depends on how many vegetables you would like and the time you have to tend them. Rural gardeners often have more choice than suburban or city gardeners. If your space is large, lay out your garden in mounded rows east to west with walking paths between. The idea of planting in raised mounds is thought to come from early Midwest Indian tribes who used mounds for both practical and ritual purposes. Wherever the idea came from, mounding between footpaths keeps soil from being compacted and is a very effective way to garden.

Place the garden away from other landscaping as trees and shrubs will compete with vegetables for water and nutrients. Walnut trees should be avoided entirely as they produce a root toxin that injures other plants. If your space is small, be creative. Vegetables will grow in pots, in raised beds, in flower beds, even in window boxes as long as there is well-drained fertile soil, water, and full sun.

No matter what size your garden, it is important to rotate the location of your plants every year to allow the soil a chance to recharge, curb any pest infestations, and discourage disease. It is possible to grow more than one vegetable in the same place by planting quick-growing vegetables with slow-growing vegetables. By the time the quick-growing vegetable is ready to be pulled out of the ground, the slow-growing one is just getting started.

Heavy mulching with untreated grass clippings saves a tremendous amount of time weeding and watering. Another timesaver is to layer compost (tuck pulled or trimmed plant material under the grass mulch as you go along).

Pests in the Vegetable Garden

When solving a problem, start with the simplest solution and move up the ladder of complication. If you have garden pests or diseases, use a spray of soapy water to wash plants. If the problem continues, add garlic, salad oil, and cayenne pepper to the soapy spray. Tilling your soil over each fall and rotating the position of vegetables each year prevents problems before they begin. Marigolds, garlic, and chives interplanted in vegetable rows is a wonderful way to offset most problems.

To find out more about healthy soil, see Great Gardens Start Here in Section One. Be sure to check Section Six for public gardens with vegetable patches that you can visit.

Plant Groups and Associations

National Hot Pepper Association
400 NW 20th Street
Ft. Lauderdale, FL   33311

Annual $20 membership dues include a quarterly newsletter, contact with both local chapters and the national organization, and other growers and cooks interested in spicy foods.

Seed Savers Exchange
3076 North Winn Road
Decorah, IA 52101

Annual membership of $25 gives members access to over twelve thousand unique varieties of vegetables.

Purchasing Vegetable Seeds and Plants from Local Garden Centers

This is a reliable but usually rather expensive way to buy seeds and plants. Local nurseries stand behind their products but tend to be somewhat conservative and limited in their selection.

Purchasing Vegetable Plants and Seeds from Mail-Order Sources

Local selection of plants and seeds is often limited, and sometimes plants are mislabeled. Shopping for plants by mail is a way to increase variety in your garden. Once you find a mail-order nursery that you like, tell your friends and other Midwest gardeners about it.

Small Fruits

Sweet strawberries, plump blueberries, tart rhubarb, and unforgettable grapes are the stuff that makes our mouths water as we leaf through mail-order catalogs. Yet fresh fruit is the most expensive and the most disappointing item we buy in Midwest grocery stores. The only reliable way to get these delectable treats is fresh from a garden. The small fruits listed in this chapter are easy to grow even in gardens of limited space. Use the information listed here to avoid the common mistakes of choosing the wrong variety, planting in the wrong place, or pruning at the wrong time.

Successful fruit gardens start here:

S Select healthy, nutrient-rich soil. Have a soil sample tested by your county extension office to find out if your soil needs any amendments to grow fruit.

T Time your plant order so that plants arrive in time for early spring planting.

A Add a diluted liquid fertilizer when transplanting seedlings and sowing seeds.

R Rake or lightly hoe to control early spring weeds. Mulch with untreated grass clippings and bark.

T Trim and prune plants as needed to keep in shape and encourage new growth.

Small Fruits for Midwest Gardens

Blueberry

BOTANICAL NAME: *Vaccinium*

PLANT TYPE: hardy perennial shrub; highbush blueberries are 4 to 6 feet tall with an open habit of growth. Try 'Blue Crop', 'Blue Gold', 'Blue Jay', 'Duke', 'Earliblue', 'Elliot', 'Jersey', 'Nelson', 'Northland', 'Patriot', 'Sierra', 'Toro'. Half-high blueberries are 3- to 4-foot hybrids of highbush and wild lowbush. Try 'Friendship', 'North Country', 'Northblue', 'Northsky', 'St. Cloud'

STARTING: bareroots, soak overnight before planting; use a soil mix of 50% peat or compost, 25% topsoil, 25% sand and nitrogen; mix spent coffee grounds into mulch; remove fruit buds the first year; plant more than one variety to increase production

CULTIVATION: full sun; needs acid soil, pH of 4.0 to 5.6; lots of water; mulch; fertilize in early spring with acidic liquid fertilizer; prune a portion of old canes in early spring to encourage new growth

PROBLEMS: relatively disease and insect free; wash with soapy water in midsummer; protect from birds in summer, rabbits in winter; yellow leaves are a sign of iron deficiency caused by alkaline soil

HARVESTING: two days after berries turn blue

IN YOUR KITCHEN: fresh or wonderful for pies, preserves, freezing

Cranberry, American

BOTANICAL NAME: *Vaccinium macrocarpon*

PLANT TYPE: native perennial low-growing shrub

STARTING: soak roots overnight; plant in any type of acid soil 2 feet apart; mulch and water frequently

CULTIVATION: easy, easy, easy; full sun; pink flowers in spring; fruit in autumn; roots easily from cuttings; commercial growers use boggy areas to grow cranberries because of their traditional high pH—they harvest berries by flooding fields and letting the fruit float; in home gardens, cranberries can easily be picked by hand

HARVESTING: pick berries before temperatures go below freezing

IN YOUR KITCHEN: sauce, jelly, baking, and pie fillings; wash and freeze in bag

Currants, Gooseberries, and Jostaberries

BOTANICAL NAME: *Ribes*

PLANT TYPE: hardy perennial canes and bushes. Gooseberries have thorns and taste like grapes. Fruit ranges from green to white, yellow, red, and purple and from pea to plum size. Try: 'Achilles', 'Catherina', 'Hinnonmaki Yellow', 'Welcome', 'Whitesmith'. Currants are tiny, grow in clusters, and can be red, black, or white. They are used in jams and jellies. 'Pixwell' and 'White Imperial' are good choices. Jostaberry is a gooseberry-and-black-currant hybrid from Europe, free of thorns, rust resistant, and no pruning needed.

STARTING: soak roots overnight

CULTIVATION: plants can live 20 years; full sun to partial shade; well-drained fertile soil; mulch; prune any canes older than 3 years

PROBLEMS: generally pest free; susceptible to mildew in humid weather; some varieties are susceptible to white pine blister rust disease

HARVESTING: pick when fully ripe

IN YOUR KITCHEN: fresh or use in pies, sauces, jellies; will keep in refrigerator for 2 weeks

Grapes

BOTANICAL NAME: *Vitis*

PLANT TYPE: hardy perennial vine; try 'Beta', 'Canadice', 'Concord', 'Edelweiss', 'Swenson Red', 'Fredonia', 'Reliance', 'Valiant', 'Worden'

STARTING: bareroots, soak overnight; plant 8 feet apart; prune to largest cane; plant in a sheltered, sunny location on south side; well-drained soil

CULTIVATION: full sun; good air circulation; prune and spray with dormant oil in late winter before buds begin to swell; grapes are produced on second-year vines; feed in fall or early spring with a complete fertilizer; fruit forms on new spring growth

PROBLEMS: takes 3 years to produce from roots; susceptible to mildew and fungus diseases; not consistently hardy; save planting instructions as correct pruning is very important; winter mulch with 4 inches of loose bulky material when the temperature drops to 20° and stays there

HARVESTING: grapes stop ripening when picked; use scissors to clip clusters

IN YOUR KITCHEN: great in juices, jellies, jams, wine; can be stored in shallow layers in wood or wicker (not plastic or metal) at 32° for several months

Kiwi, Hardy

BOTANICAL NAME: *Actinidia kolomikta*

PLANT TYPE: compact perennial vine

STARTING: soak roots overnight; mix a slow-release complete fertilizer in planting hole; mulch; needs trellis or fence to climb

CULTIVATION: sun; rich, well-drained soil; protect from wind; 1 male plant per 8 female plants needed; hand pollinate if bees don't visit; prune to shape in summer; in early spring prune back to 18 inches

PROBLEMS: relatively free of pests and diseases

HARVESTING: ripens in late summer; ripe when soft to touch

IN YOUR KITCHEN: eaten raw like grapes, skin and all; can be stored in refrigerator for several weeks; ripens at room temperature

Raspberries

BOTANICAL NAME: *Rubus*

PLANT TYPE: hardy perennial canes. Summer-bearing raspberries set fruit buds in summer and bear fruit that same fall. After frost, prune dead-looking canes to the ground, top healthy ones to 3 feet. Varieties to try: 'Algonquin', 'Boyne', 'Canby', 'Estate', 'Latham', 'Killarney', 'Nordic', 'Nova'. Everbearing (fall-bearing) raspberries bear fruit on the top half of first-year-canes from late summer to frost. They overwinter and produce a second crop on the lower half of the canes the following summer. The easiest way to keep track of all this is to prune these to the ground each fall. You lose part of your summer harvest, but you have hardier canes and a larger fall harvest. Varieties to try: 'Autumn Bliss', 'Fall Gold', 'Fallred', 'Heritage', 'Redwing'

STARTING: soak roots overnight; use a rooting stimulant; plant 2 feet apart; shallow planting; prune canes to 6 inches; mulch; mix both summer-bearing and everbearing berries for a full-season harvest

CULTIVATION: full sun; plant in hills or rows; fertilize in early spring with a balanced natural fertilizer; add wood ashes; proper pruning is important when growing raspberries—keep instructions that come with planting packet so you will know when and how to prune; limiting the number of canes improves crop; winter mulch with 4 inches of loose bulky material when the temperature drops to 20° and stays there; burn or destroy all old canes

PROBLEMS: birds in summer, rabbits in winter; susceptible to tomato and potato virus; can catch viruses from wild raspberries; red spider mites tend to attack during droughts, wash leaves with soapy water to discourage

HARVESTING: berries separate from stem when ripe; pick early in morning; rinse just before serving

IN YOUR KITCHEN: fresh; freeze whole on cookie sheet and bag

Rhubarb

BOTANICAL NAME: *Rheum*

PLANT TYPE: perennial vegetable roots. Try 'Canada Red', 'Crimson Red', 'Linnaeus', 'McDonald', 'Ruby', 'Valentine', 'Victoria'

STARTING: soak for an hour before planting; add compost and a complete fertilizer in 12-inch-deep planting hole; space 2 feet apart

CULTIVATION: sun to partial shade; heavy feeders; use natural complete fertilizers spring and summer; need water and mulch; remove all flower stalks

PROBLEMS: needs room to grow

HARVESTING: pull stalks from ground; cut leaves off and toss them into compost or use for mulch; begin harvesting in early spring and stop on July 4

IN YOUR KITCHEN: stalks are used for pies and sauces; to freeze, wash, slice, and bag; 3 cups per 9-inch pie

Rose Hips

BOTANICAL NAME: *Rosa rugosa, R. acicularis, R. cinnamomea, R. laxa, R. moyesii*

PLANT TYPE: perennial shrub

STARTING: soak roots for an hour; mulch and water frequently; plant in 50% compost, 25% sand, and 25% topsoil in a pesticide- and herbicide-free area

CULTIVATION: full sun; good air circulation; cover in winter with soil and extra mulch over crown of plant; uncover in spring, then prune brown canes; use only natural fertilizers

HARVESTING: pick rose hips when they turn from orange to light red; trim off blossom ends, cut lengthwise, remove tiny hairs and seeds, rinse and pat dry

IN YOUR KITCHEN: tea, soup, jelly, jam, sauce, syrup, wine; wash and freeze in bag; dry

Strawberries

BOTANICAL NAME: *Fragaria*

PLANT TYPE: perennial plants. "Day-neutral" strawberries produce a summer crop and keep going through frost. Try 'September Sweet', 'Tribute'. Everbearing strawberries produce in midsummer with a second crop in late summer, continuing until frost. Remove blossoms through July 4. Try 'Ft. Laramie', 'Gem', 'Northland', 'Ogalalla', 'Ozark Beauty', 'Tristar'. June-bearing strawberries produce in early summer. Remove all blossoms the first year. Try: 'Dunlap', 'Earliglow', 'Glooscap', 'Honeoye', 'Jewel', 'Redcoat', 'Sparkle', 'Surecrop', 'Stoplight', 'Trumpeter'

STARTING: order for spring planting; return any moldy plants to shipper or nursery center; new plants can be stored wrapped in damp paper towels and a plastic bag in refrigerator until ground can be worked; soak plants in water while planting; needs full sun, rich well-drained soil—the better the soil, the bigger the berries

CULTIVATION: use a pyramidal terraced planter, a strawberry pot, or the "matted row" system—set plants 2 feet apart in rows that are 3 feet apart; dig a 5-inch-deep hole and set the plants so that just the tip of the crown is exposed and the roots are down in the hole; water twice a week; apply a light summer mulch to conserve water; winter mulch with 4 inches of loose bulky material when the temperature drops to 20° and stays there; plants only produce for two years—renovate a section of your bed by replacing old plants with young plant offshoots every spring; fertilize with a natural low-nitrogen formula—high nitrogen will give you more leaves than berries

PROBLEMS: plants grown too close together result in small berries and problems; birds love berries

HARVESTING: pick early in the morning or later in the day when the fruit is cool; use within 2 or 3 days of picking; cover and store them unwashed in the refrigerator

IN YOUR KITCHEN: fresh or frozen; in pies, sauces, smoothies, cakes; 1 quart equals 4 or 5 servings, 8 quarts equals 13 pints frozen, 1 1/2 quarts makes 1 9-inch pie

For a small strawberry garden in a pot, try the project described earlier in this section under Potted Herb Garden, using various kinds of strawberry plants instead of herbs. This makes a great gift.

What Small Fruits Need

During the summer, fruit needs rich soil, mulch, and one inch of water per week. Fruit should be planted around the outside or at one end of your garden. After the ground freezes, fruit should be mulched heavily with shredded leaves to protect from winter winds. In the spring, pull the mulch aside and lay between rows to keep the mud off your shoes.

Plant Groups and Associations

The International *Ribes* Association
PO Box 428
Booneville, CA 95415

Annual membership dues are $20 and include a quarterly newsletter, the *Ribes Reporter,* and membership networking. They also offer a cultural guide for $10 and a cookbook for $6.50.

North American Fruit Explorers
Route 1, Box 94
Chapin, IL 62668

Annual dues of $10 include quarterly newsletter, *Pomona,* and lending library.

Purchasing Roots and Canes from Local Garden Centers

This is a reliable but rather expensive way to buy new plants and seeds. Local nurseries stand behind their products but tend to be somewhat conservative and limited in their selection.

Purchasing Roots and Canes from Mail-Order Sources

Local selection of plants is often limited, and sometimes plants are mislabeled. Shopping for plants by mail is a way to increase variety in your garden. Most plants you receive will be in dormant condition. It will take at least two years for these plants to flourish. Check each catalog's warranty policy and allow each new plant time to acclimatize. If plants do not show growth in three weeks, contact the catalog company and ask for new plants.

For the backbone of your garden, it is best to buy plants raised in the Midwest. Once you find a mail-order nursery that you like, tell your friends and other Midwest gardeners about it.

Sustainable Landscaping

Deciduous Trees and Shrubs

Evergreen Conifers

Green Lawns

Ground Covers and Vines

Native Prairies

Romantic Meadows

Trees, shrubs, lawns, and ground covers raise property values, decrease the cost of home utilities, provide wildlife habitats, and enrich our lives. Sustainable landscaping uses low-maintenance plants and places them where they will thrive and flourish with a minimal amount of care. Once you know what you need, it's easy to select a plant to meet that need. When selecting landscaping materials ask yourself these questions:

- Why is this plant needed?
- How long-lived should this plant be?
- How much space does this plant need when it is full grown? Are there overhead wires or underground pipes that will be in the way of its growth? Are there sidewalks that will hamper roots or collect seeds?
- What are the soil conditions that this plant will live in?
- How much care will this plant receive?

Answering these questions as you read about the plants in this section will help you determine which hardy plant to select for your Midwest garden. All can be found by botanical or common name in traditional garden centers, in mail-order catalogs, or in state-run forest nurseries that sell groups of seedling plants for wildlife habitats and natural landscaping projects. Some commercial nurseries consider many of these plants "weeds" because they need very little attention, fertilizer, and pesticides. Other nurseries are more progressive and understand that risking our health applying pesticides or expending our resources on plants that will never be happy in our gardens is a waste of time.

Deciduous Trees and Shrubs

Deciduous trees and shrubs are plants that drop their leaves each fall. They shade our yards and color our streets with spring flowers and autumn color. Tree and shrub selection is one of the more important investment decisions a gardener can make when planning a new garden. Since most trees and shrubs can outlive the gardeners who plant them, selection can influence lifetimes.

To optimize the growth and health of trees and shrubs, proper planting is as important as choosing the correct tree or bush. Autumn is a good time to plant trees and shrubs if new plantings can be protected from drying winter winds and watered until the ground freezes. During spring plantings, daily watering and shade cloths might be needed until the new plants are established.

The trees, shrubs, and plants in this section are tolerant of the Midwest's stressful weather and have few insect or disease problems.

Successful low-maintenance landscaping with deciduous trees and shrubs starts here:

S Space. Do you have enough for the tree or shrub you are planting? To find out, use a garden hose to mark off the area the mature plant would occupy.

T Too many trees can cause problems too. While shade can be wonderful, too much shade can be depressing.

A Always ask for a written warranty when buying a tree or shrub.

R Real estate values increase as landscaping matures. Trees and shrubs are a smart investment.

T Take your time choosing your landscape plants. Use these recommendations to judge the wonderful trees and shrubs that are available for your home landscape.

Trees and Shrubs in the Midwest

Deciduous means leaf-dropping. Most deciduous trees are hardwood. Coniferous or conifer means cone-bearing. Most conifers are softwood.

DECIDUOUS TREES AND SHRUBS FOR THE MIDWEST AT A GLANCE

USDA Zone	Height in feet	Width in feet	Moist Soil	On Street	In Yard	Name	Garden Interest				
							spring	summer	late summer	fall	winter
4	1	1		✔	✔	Spirea	✔	✔	✔		
4	1	1		✔	✔	Japanese Barberry	✔	✔	✔	✔	✔
3	2	2		✔	✔	Shrub Roses		✔	✔	✔	
2	2	2	✔	✔	✔	Potentilla		✔	✔	✔	
4	3	3	✔		✔	Arctic Blue Leaf Willow	✔	✔	✔	✔	
2	6	6		✔	✔	Weigela	✔	✔	✔		
4	3	3		✔	✔	Japanese Barberry	✔	✔	✔	✔	✔
2	4	4	✔	✔	✔	Potentilla		✔	✔	✔	
2	4	4		✔	✔	Lilac	✔	✔	✔	✔	
4	4	4	✔	✔	✔	PJM Rhododendron	✔				
3	4	4	✔		✔	Azalea	✔				
2	4	4		✔	✔	Viburnum		✔		✔	✔
4	4	5	✔	✔	✔	Hydrangea			✔	✔	✔
4	6	8		✔	✔	Beautybush	✔		✔		
4	6	6	✔	✔	✔	Inkberry	✔	✔	✔	✔	✔
2	6	6		✔	✔	Weigela	✔	✔	✔		
3	6	6	✔	✔	✔	Winterberry		✔	✔	✔	✔
3	8	5		✔	✔	Shrub Roses		✔	✔		
4	8	8	✔		✔	Fothergilla	✔		✔		
2	8	10		✔	✔	Sand Cherry	✔	✔	✔	✔	
4	10	10		✔	✔	Spirea	✔	✔	✔		
3	10	10		✔	✔	Bayberry					✔
3	10	10		✔	✔	Dogwood	✔	✔	✔	✔	✔
4	12	12		✔	✔	Crabapple	✔		✔	✔	✔
2	12	12		✔	✔	Lilac	✔	✔	✔	✔	
3	12	15		✔	✔	Bottlebrush Buckeye		✔		✔	
4	15	10	✔	✔	✔	Hydrangea Tree			✔	✔	✔
3	15	15		✔	✔	Amur Maple				✔	
4	15	15			✔	Burning Bush				✔	
3	15	15	✔		✔	Witch Hazel				✔	✔
5	15	20		✔	✔	Smokebush		✔	✔	✔	
4	20	15		✔	✔	Star Magnolia	✔			✔	
4	20	25		✔	✔	Thornless Hawthorn	✔			✔	✔
3	25	15		✔	✔	Japanese Lilac Tree		✔		✔	
5	25	15			✔	Paperbark Maple				✔	✔
3	25	15	✔	✔	✔	Serviceberry	✔		✔	✔	✔
2	25	20		✔	✔	Canadian Cherry	✔	✔		✔	
2	25	25	✔	✔	✔	Pagoda Dogwood	✔	✔	✔	✔	
2	30	30		✔	✔	Viburnum		✔		✔	✔

USDA Zone	Height in feet	Width in feet	Moist Soil	On Street	In Yard	Name	Garden Interest				
							spring	sum-mer	late summer	fall	winter
3	35	35		✔	✔	American Hornbeam		✔	✔		
3	40	40			✔	Corktree			✔	✔	
4	40	40		✔	✔	Magnolia	✔		✔		
4	45	35	✔		✔	River Birch			✔	✔	
3	50	40		✔	✔	Red Maple			✔		
3	50	55	✔	✔	✔	Yellowwood		✔	✔	✔	
3	55	40	✔	✔	✔	Ginkgo			✔		
3	60	50	✔	✔	✔	Swamp White Oak			✔		
2	60	30			✔	Quaking Aspen			✔	✔	
4	65	40	✔	✔	✔	Kentucky Coffee Tree	✔	✔	✔	✔	
4	70	40		✔	✔	Pin Oak			✔	✔	
3	75	50		✔	✔	Sugar Maple			✔		
3	80	50		✔	✔	Red Oak			✔		
3	80	80		✔	✔	Bur Oak			✔		

Aspen, Quaking

Quaking aspen is the most widely distributed tree in America. It can be found in forty-eight states. Aspen are hardy trees with round, pointed-tip leaves that hang from long stems and flutter in every breeze. Aspen pollen is carried by the wind. Mature seed capsules split open and release small seeds with mats of long silky hair that also drift on the wind. Planted in wooded, naturalized areas it becomes a preferred food source for wildlife.

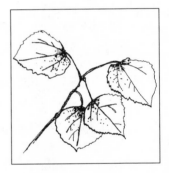

BOTANICAL NAME: *Populus tremula*

WINTER HARDINESS: −50°

MATURE HEIGHT: 60 feet

MATURE WIDTH: 30 feet

CROWN: triangular

BARK: gray-white

FLOWERS: warm brown catkins

FRUIT: small capsules

SUMMER COLOR: green and silver

FALL COLOR: gold

WILDLIFE: attracts butterflies: mourning cloak, red-spotted purple, viceroy, swallowtail

PROBLEMS: needs to be planted in groups; some suckering; weak wood

Landscaping Adds Value

❦ Landscaping can increase a home's value by fifteen percent.

❦ A mature tree can have an appraised value of ten thousand dollars.

❦ Trees can reduce summer temperatures around your house as much as ten percent.

❦ A tree removes twenty-six pounds of carbon dioxide and releases thirteen pounds of oxygen a year—enough oxygen for a family of four.

Azalea

Hardy azalea are introductions from the University of Minnesota Landscape Arboretum. Spring-blooming hybrid strains include 'Golden Lights', gold; 'Mandarin Lights', peach; 'Northern Lights', pink; 'Orchid Lights', lilac; 'Rosy Lights', dark pink; 'Spicy Lights', salmon; and 'White Lights', light pink fading to white. Azaleas need full sun, a moist site, and acid soil.

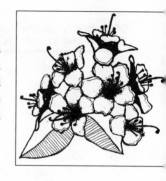

BOTANICAL NAME: *Rhododendron*

WINTER HARDINESS: −40°

MATURE HEIGHT: 4 feet

MATURE WIDTH: 4 feet

INTEREST: spring flowers

SHAPE: rounded, fan-shaped

PROBLEMS: needs well-drained soil; no serious diseases or pests unless stressed; slow-growing

Barberry, Japanese

Japanese barberry are very hardy shrubs. Most have sharp thorns. Some are red all year, and others are green or gold. These are excellent as barrier plants, hedges, and colorful focal points.

BOTANICAL NAME: *Berberis thunbergii*

WINTER HARDINESS: −30°

MATURE HEIGHT: 1 to 3 feet

MATURE WIDTH: 1 to 3 feet

INTEREST: year-round

SHAPE: mounded or vase-shaped

PROBLEMS: subject to winter burn from reflected sun; shear to maintain shape

How Close to Your House Should You Plant Shade Trees?

To stay in proportion and leave room for tree roots, the tallest trees surrounding your home should be twice as tall as your home. A tree that will be one hundred feet tall should be planted seventy-five feet away from your house. A tree that will be twenty feet tall should be planted fifteen feet away.

Bayberry

A salt-tolerant shrub with shiny dark leaves and white fruit for winter interest. Prefers sandy, well-drained, poor soil but will tolerate clay.

BOTANICAL NAME: *Myrica pensylvanica*

WINTER HARDINESS: −40°

MATURE HEIGHT: 10 feet

MATURE WIDTH: 10 feet

INTEREST: winter fruit

SHAPE: upright, rounded

PROBLEMS: will need iron supplements in alkaline soil

Beautybush

Beautybush is an old-fashioned shrub that is native to China and was introduced to America in the early 1900s. Beautybush accepts a wide range of soil types. It will tolerate partial shade but blooms best in full sun. Arching branches need to be pruned annually after flowering in spring.

BOTANICAL NAME: *Kolkwitzia amabilis* 'Pink Cloud', 'Rosea'

WINTER HARDINESS: −30°

MATURE HEIGHT: 6 feet

MATURE WIDTH: 8 feet

INTEREST: pink flowers in spring; yellow fall leaves

SHAPE: fan-shaped

PROBLEMS: becomes leggy with age; needs pruning

Birch, River

River birch is a tree native to Midwest riverbanks and flood plains. The 'Heritage' hybrid is very attractive, with wonderful cinnamon-colored, textured bark that is resistant to birch bark borers. It has a short life planted as a street tree, but will live longer planted in moist lawns away from sidewalks. Falling male flowers, catkins, are messy and will stain concrete.

BOTANICAL NAME: *Betula nigra* 'Heritage'

WINTER HARDINESS: −30°

MATURE HEIGHT: 45 feet

MATURE WIDTH: 35 feet

CROWN: triangular

BARK: brown peeling

FLOWERS: long catkins

FRUIT: small nutlets

SUMMER COLOR: green

FALL COLOR: yellow

WILDLIFE: attracts mourning cloak and swallowtail butterflies

PROBLEMS: susceptible to leaf miners and moisture stress; place mothballs around tree as preventive medicine

Bottlebrush Buckeye

Bottlebrush buckeye is a summer-flowering dwarf shrub of the horse chestnut family. A fast-growing native, each bush will spread into a broad, rounded clump.

BOTANICAL NAME: *Aesculus parviflora*

WINTER HARDINESS: −30°

MATURE HEIGHT: 12 feet

MATURE WIDTH: 15 feet

INTEREST: large sprays of white flowers in summer, fall color

SHAPE: round

PROBLEMS: because of the way it spreads, use in shrub borders where it has room

Burning Bush

Burning bush is a beautiful, mounded shrub from Asia that is attractive all year. Slow to grow. Useful in borders, hedges, or as a specimen plant.

BOTANICAL NAME: *Euonymus*

WINTER HARDINESS: −30°

MATURE HEIGHT: 15 feet

MATURE WIDTH: 15 feet

INTEREST: red leaves in fall, bark all year

SHAPE: rounded

PROBLEMS: too much water or drought or any type of stress can cause winterkill; needs full sun to turn red, and protection from drying winter winds

Cherry, Canadian

Canadian cherry is a hardy native tree whose leaves unfurl green and turn deep purple in the sun. White flowers bloom in May and are followed by edible red fruit in July.

BOTANICAL NAME: *Prunus virginiana* 'Canada Red'

WINTER HARDINESS: −50°

MATURE HEIGHT: 25 feet

MATURE WIDTH: 20 feet

CROWN: round

BARK: shiny

FLOWERS: white

FRUIT: red, edible

SUMMER COLOR: purple

FALL COLOR: purple

WILDLIFE: attracts 49 species of birds

PROBLEMS: suckering tendency; requires well-drained soil

Coffee Tree, Kentucky

Kentucky coffee tree is a native tree of the Midwest needing full sun and moist soil. It is free of disease, pest resistant, and great as a specimen tree in lawns. Because of its bare branches six months of the year, grass will grow under its canopy. Kentucky coffee tree prefers moist, fertile soils.

BOTANICAL NAME: *Gymnocladus dioicus*

WINTER HARDINESS: −30°

MATURE HEIGHT: 65 feet

MATURE WIDTH: 40 feet

CROWN: oval

BARK: curled scales

FLOWERS: yellow clusters

FRUIT: pods on female trees

SUMMER COLOR: blue-green

FALL COLOR: yellow

PROBLEMS: pods can cause cleanup problems; slow recovery after transplanting

Corktree

Corktree is a tall, wide, pest-free tree, tolerant of drought and pollution. Wonderful for large areas. 'Shademaster' is a fruitless male hybrid.

BOTANICAL NAME: *Phellodendron amurense* 'Shademaster'

WINTER HARDINESS: −40°

MATURE HEIGHT: 40 feet

MATURE WIDTH: 40 feet

CROWN: oval

BARK: rough cork

FLOWERS: none

FRUIT: none

SUMMER COLOR: dark green

FALL COLOR: yellow

PROBLEMS: availability limited; shallow root system needs space in lawn, not street

Crabapple

More than six hundred varieties of flowering crabapple trees are grown in the United States. Unfortunately all but a few are susceptible to every Midwest apple disease there is, including scab, cedar apple rust, mildew, and fireblight. Several varieties have been developed by regional universities and plantsmen for disease resistance: 'Adams', pink; 'Centurion', pink; 'Prairifire', pink; 'Professor Sprenger', white; 'Red Baron', red; 'Sentinel', white; 'Snowdrift', white; 'Sugartyme', white; and 'Donald Wyman', white.

BOTANICAL NAME: *Malus* hybrids

WINTER HARDINESS: −30°

MATURE HEIGHT: 12 to 20 feet

MATURE WIDTH: 12 to 20 feet

CROWN: oval or round

BARK: attractive

FLOWERS: pink, white, or red

FRUIT: various with hybrid

SUMMER COLOR: none

FALL COLOR: minimal

WILDLIFE: attracts 29 species of birds

PROBLEMS: order tree by name to prevent problems; lower branches of street trees need to be pruned for clearance; some suckering

Dogwood

Dogwoods are multistemmed shrubs that spread by underground stems to form hardy clumps of colorful twigs. Easy to clone by burying part of a branch, allowing it to root, then cutting it away from parent plant.

BOTANICAL NAME: *Cornus*

WINTER HARDINESS: −40°

MATURE HEIGHT: 10 feet

MATURE WIDTH: 10 feet

INTEREST: variegated variety for summer color; red, gold, or gray branches for winter color

SHAPE: fan-shaped

WILDLIFE: Attracts 47 species of birds; spring azure butterfly

PROBLEMS: hard-prune to the ground in early spring; winter color comes from first-year twigs only

Dogwood, Pagoda

Pagoda dogwood is a hardy large shrub or small tree. If pruned into a single trunk, the branches will arrange themselves in flat, spreading tiers that really do look like oriental rooftops. This is wonderful in courtyards and at entrances. Pagoda dogwood is also recommended as a street tree under the shade of taller trees.

BOTANICAL NAME: *Cornus alternifolia*

WINTER HARDINESS: –40°

MATURE HEIGHT: 25 feet

MATURE WIDTH: 25 feet

CROWN: rounded horizontal

BARK: average

FLOWERS: creamy white

FRUIT: blue-black

SUMMER COLOR: green

FALL COLOR: deep red

PROBLEMS: must be pruned while young into a single trunk; needs moist soil and partial shade

Fothergilla, Large

This native shrub is a two-season stunner with white bottlebrush flowers in spring and mixed yellow, orange, and red fall leaves in sun or partial shade. It prefers a moist, acid soil with plenty of mulch and is unique and excellent in mixed shrub borders.

BOTANICAL NAME: *Fothergilla major*

WINTER HARDINESS: –30°

MATURE HEIGHT: 8 feet

MATURE WIDTH: 8 feet

INTEREST: spring, white flowers; fall, yellow, orange, red leaves

SHAPE: upright

PROBLEMS: drought will cause stress

Ginkgo; Maidenhair Tree

Ginkgo is a tree that bears its seeds in cones and is listed as a conifer, but it is a conifer unlike any other, the sole survivor of a group of trees that once ranged worldwide and left fossilized imprints of their leaves in the rocks of many lands. Ginkgo turns gold each fall and drops its leaves the same way that its ancestors have done for over two hundred million years. This is a tough tree that has outlived all its enemies and is tolerant of urban stresses. Young trees are slender, spreading with age.

BOTANICAL NAME: *Ginkgo biloba* 'Autumn Gold'; 'Lakeview'; 'Sentry'

WINTER HARDINESS: −30°

MATURE HEIGHT: 55 feet

MATURE WIDTH: 40 feet

CROWN: fan-shaped

BARK: furrowed bark

FLOWERS: insignificant

SUMMER COLOR: green

FALL COLOR: gold

PROBLEMS: female cones have a strong smell and are messy; plant male clones

Hawthorn, Thornless

Thornless hawthorn is a small tree that bears white flowers, small fruit, and thrives in adverse conditions including sidewalk salt. Fruit attracts wildlife. 'Hybrid Crusader' is claimed to be more resistant to cedar apple rust than other varieties.

BOTANICAL NAME: *Crataegus crus-galli*

WINTER HARDINESS: −30°

MATURE HEIGHT: 20 feet

MATURE WIDTH: 25 feet

CROWN: flattened globe

BARK: average

FLOWERS: clustered white

FRUIT: red balls

SUMMER COLOR: dark green

FALL COLOR: red

WILDLIFE: Attracts 19 species of birds; red-spotted purple butterfly

PROBLEMS: limited availability of preferred hybrid; susceptible to cedar apple rust and leaf miners; some suckering

Hornbeam, American

American hornbeam is a neat, manageable, attractive tree with smooth gray bark, tolerant of rough conditions and moist soil.

BOTANICAL NAME: *Carpinus caroliniana*

WINTER HARDINESS: −40°

MATURE HEIGHT: 35 feet

MATURE WIDTH: 35 feet

CROWN: rounded column

BARK: blue-gray

FLOWERS: green catkins

FRUIT: nutlets

SUMMER COLOR: blue-green

FALL COLOR: orange

WILDLIFE: Attracts red-spotted purple butterfly

PROBLEMS: sensitive to drought; susceptible to chestnut borer

Hydrangea

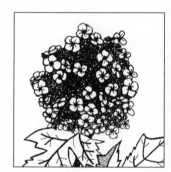

A native of Japan, hydrangea is an old-fashioned large bush with profuse mophead flowers on slender stems, blooming late summer through fall. There are over 350 varieties available, all wonderful in a mixed border or as an accent plant in perennial beds. Hydrangea needs moist, well-drained soil in either sun or partial shade and will tolerate some sidewalk salt. Leave the flower heads for winter interest and prune to the ground in spring. In very cold regions, plant in a sheltered area.

BOTANICAL NAME: *Hydrangea macrophylla*

WINTER HARDINESS: −30°

MATURE HEIGHT: 4 feet

MATURE WIDTH: 5 feet

INTEREST: blue mophead flowers in acid soil, pink flowers in alkaline soil

SHAPE: rounded

PROBLEMS: only flowers on new wood; prune hard in spring

Hydrangea Tree, Panicle

This small flowering tree is an old-fashioned favorite that originated in Japan and has been in America since the 1860s. It is wonderful used as a specimen tree or an understory tree. It needs moist, well-drained soil in either sun or partial shade.

BOTANICAL NAME: *Hydrangea paniculata* 'Grandiflora', 'Tardiva'

WINTER HARDINESS: −30°

MATURE HEIGHT: 15 feet

MATURE WIDTH: 10 feet

INTEREST: late summer flower mopheads persist through winter

SHAPE: upright, arching stems

PROBLEMS: only flowers on new wood

Inkberry

Inkberry is a native shrub holly with dark shiny leaves that is wonderful for naturalizing wet, shaded areas.

BOTANICAL NAME: *Ilex glabra*

WINTER HARDINESS: −30°

MATURE HEIGHT: 6 feet

MATURE WIDTH: 6 feet

INTEREST: green all year; small black fruit

SHAPE: rounded

PROBLEMS: needs heavy pruning to keep leaves on lower branches

Lilac

Lilacs are one of the oldest, hardiest, best-loved, and best-performing flowering shrubs in the Midwest. There are so many colors, flower styles, sizes, fragrances, and blooming sequences available that just reading about them is exciting. Lilacs are happiest planted away from the house and other trees in well-drained soil. They need four hours of full sun per day and bloom on last year's woody stems.

BOTANICAL NAME: *Syringa*

WINTER HARDINESS: −50°

MATURE HEIGHT: 4 to 12 feet

MATURE WIDTH: 4 to 12 feet

INTEREST: spring flowers, *Syringa* x *hyacinthiflora;* summer and late-summer flowers, *Syringa vulgaris, S.* x *prestoniae, S. villosa.* Also see the description of Japanese lilac tree that follows

SHAPE: upright, rounded

WILDLIFE: Attracts tiger swallowtail caterpillars and monarch, swallowtail, painted lady, and red-spotted purple butterflies

PROBLEMS: some types are more susceptible to powdery mildew, borers, and scale than others; pinch back unruly branches each spring; prune after blooming

ORGANIZATION: International Lilac Society
David Gressley
The Holden Arboretum
9500 Sperry Road
Kirtland, OH 44094-5172
A $20 annual membership in this society entitles you to a quarterly journal, technical information about lilacs, a handbook on lilac culture, plant sources, and networking.

Japanese Lilac Tree

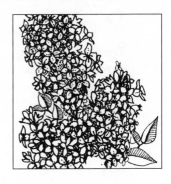

Japanese lilac is a hardy small tree for streets and yards, clean and disease-free with interesting bark. The hybrid 'Ivory Silk' is very drought-resistant, with large creamy flower clusters in summer. It needs four hours of sun per day.

BOTANICAL NAME: *Syringa reticulata* 'Ivory Silk'

WINTER HARDINESS: −40°

MATURE HEIGHT: 25 feet

MATURE WIDTH: 15 feet

CROWN: oval

BARK: shiny

FLOWERS: creamy white lilacs in late summer

FRUIT: clusters of brown seed capsules

SUMMER COLOR: white flowers

FALL COLOR: none

PROBLEMS: susceptible to lilac borer, scale, and powdery mildew; needs well-drained soil

Magnolia

Magnolia is an exotic-looking native that is easily grown as a specimen tree or street tree. The hybrid 'Merrill' blooms with showy, fragrant flowers on bare branches in early spring; leaves follow. Star Magnolia, *Magnolia stellata,* is a wonderful small version that can be used as a specimen tree or landscaping shrub.

BOTANICAL NAME: *Magnolia* x *loebneri* 'Merrill'

WINTER HARDINESS: −30°

MATURE HEIGHT: 40 feet

MATURE WIDTH: 40 feet

CROWN: rounded pyramid

BARK: attractive

FLOWERS: in spring; large, white, fragrant

FRUIT: insignificant

SUMMER COLOR: green

FALL COLOR: gold

PROBLEMS: flower buds are sometimes killed by frosts; susceptible to scale insects and wilts

Maple

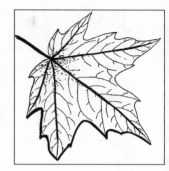

There are over ninety species of maple ranging from one-hundred-foot giants to low shrubs, all pollinated by insects and all casting dense shade. The mature winged seeds can be an irritating feature if trees are placed too near rain gutters and gardens. Recommended varieties for street trees are amur maple: *Acer ginnala* 'Embers', fifteen feet tall and fifteen feet wide; red maple: *Acer rubrum,* fifty feet tall and forty feet wide; sugar maple: *Acer saccharum* 'Green Mountain' and 'Legacy', seventy-five feet tall and fifty feet wide; paperbark maple: *Acer griseum,* twenty-five feet tall and fifteen feet wide.

BOTANICAL NAME: *Acer*

WINTER HARDINESS: −40°

MATURE HEIGHT: 15 to 75 feet

MATURE WIDTH: 15 to 50 feet

CROWN: oval

BARK: rough

FLOWERS: very small

FRUIT: winged

SUMMER COLOR: green

FALL COLOR: reds

PROBLEMS: hard to grow grass under tree; seeds and flowers are messy

Oak

Oaks are the most useful and important native trees in the Midwest. Grown primarily for shade, these trees are very long-lived and slow growing. Most have leaves that drop each fall, although many will retain their dead leaves for some time. Pollen is wind carried. The oak's biggest downfall as a landscape tree is its acorns, which feed wildlife and make sidewalks messy. It is very tolerant of drought, salt, and soil compaction. Recommended types are bur oak: *Quercus macrocarpa*, eighty feet tall and eighty feet wide; pin oak: *Quercus palustris*, seventy feet tall and forty feet wide; red oak: *Quercus rubra*, eighty feet tall and fifty feet wide; and swamp white oak: *Quercus bicolor*, sixty feet tall and fifty feet wide.

BOTANICAL NAME: *Quercus*

WINTER HARDINESS: −40°

MATURE HEIGHT: 70 to 80 feet

MATURE WIDTH: 40 to 80 feet

CROWN: wide oval

BARK: furrowed

FLOWERS: inconspicuous

FRUIT: acorns

SUMMER COLOR: green

FALL COLOR: reds and golds

WILDLIFE: attracts a wide variety

PROBLEMS: requires ample space; iron supplements may be needed to treat alkalinity created by old, crumbling driveways and sidewalks

Potentilla

Potentilla is an incredibly versatile, carefree shrub that can be used almost anywhere. It will tolerate dry soil but really shines in situations close to its native meadows and bogs.

BOTANICAL NAME: *Potentilla fruticosa*

WINTER HARDINESS: −50°

MATURE HEIGHT: 2 to 4 feet

MATURE WIDTH: 2 to 4 feet

INTEREST: yellow, white, or orange flowers from summer to frost

SHAPE: rounded

PROBLEMS: suffers in drought and from the mites that dry spells can bring; prune a few of the older canes to the ground each spring to encourage growth

Rhododendron

The PJM hybrids were introduced by a nursery in Massachusetts and are very hardy. Because the spring flowers are really bright, plant this shrub only in front of or next to colors that go with purple. Prefers moist, well-drained acid soil, mulch, and partial shade.

BOTANICAL NAME: *Rhododendron* 'PJM'

WINTER HARDINESS: −30°

MATURE HEIGHT: 4 feet

MATURE WIDTH: 4 feet

INTEREST: lavender flowers in spring

SHAPE: rounded

PROBLEMS: will wind-burn in winter

Rose, Shrub

Shrub roses are wonderfully hardy, repeat bloomers that are salt tolerant. They have clusters of flowers, single flowers, or double flowers in pinks, reds, yellows, whites, and oranges. Hardiness varies with type. The 'Explorer' series and 'Parklands' hybrids were developed in Canada. Antique roses, hybrid roses grown on their own roots, and the Griffith Buck rose series developed at Iowa State University are also good low-maintenance shrubs.

BOTANICAL NAME: *Rosa*

WINTER HARDINESS: −40°

MATURE HEIGHT: 1 to 8 feet

MATURE WIDTH: 1 to 5 feet

INTEREST: summer to fall flowers

SHAPE: spreading and upright

PROBLEMS: not many; prune each spring

Sand Cherry, Purple-leaf

Purple-leaf sand cherry is a shrub with wonderful intensely colored leaves that hold their color from spring to frost. White flowers in spring are followed by small black fruits.

BOTANICAL NAME: *Prunus* x *cistena*

WINTER HARDINESS: −50°

MATURE HEIGHT: 8 feet

MATURE WIDTH: 10 feet

INTEREST: leaves, spring through fall; flowers, spring

SHAPE: irregular, spreading

PROBLEMS: strong, beautiful color but plagued by many garden pests

Serviceberry

Serviceberry is a native all-season tree with drooping clusters of white spring flowers and strong autumn color. Native to the moist soils of the North and Midwest. A wildlife food source, serviceberry can be used as a street tree, lawn tree, or woodland tree. It is also known as Juneberry and shadbush.

BOTANICAL NAME: *Amelanchier*

WINTER HARDINESS: −40°

MATURE HEIGHT: 25 feet

MATURE WIDTH: 15 feet

CROWN: upright, rounded

BARK: average

FLOWERS: white in spring

FRUIT: small, dark purple

SUMMER COLOR: green

FALL COLOR: red

PROBLEMS: lower branches of street trees need to be pruned; sensitive to drought; can be attacked by insects

Smokebush

Sometimes called smoke tree, smokebush is beautiful shrub either as part of a grouping or as a specimen. Introduced to American nurseries as early as 1656, it was the height of fashion by the 1790s. Leaves are blue-green changing to yellow, red, or purple each fall, and when crushed, they smell like oranges. Smokebush prefers full sun and well-drained soil.

BOTANICAL NAME: *Cotinus coggygria*

WINTER HARDINESS: −20°

MATURE HEIGHT: 15 feet

MATURE WIDTH: 20 feet

INTEREST: smoke-like flower plumes in late summer; fall colors

SHAPE: oval

PROBLEMS: in colder areas plant will die back to ground; in warmer areas careful spring pruning is needed to remove dead wood but preserve flower buds; keep mulch away from crown to prevent crown rot

Spirea

Spirea is shrub that is available in every store and nursery center. There are short spirea, tall spirea, mounded spirea, and arching spirea with white, pink, and purple flowers. If this bush is planted in full sun with good air circulation, it is an easy-care choice for borders and ground covers. 'Bridal Wreath' is a wonderful, old-fashioned variety.

BOTANICAL NAME: *Spirea*

WINTER HARDINESS: −30°

MATURE HEIGHT: 1 to 10 feet

MATURE WIDTH: 1 to 12 feet

INTEREST: spring, summer, late summer flowers

SHAPE: various

WILDLIFE: attracts red-spotted purple butterfly

PROBLEMS: prune each type after it blooms to keep in shape

Viburnum

The viburnum family includes over 225 shrubs and trees that are easy to grow and generally problem-free if mulched and fed regularly. Highbush cranberry, *V. trilobum,* has edible fruit and attracts over twenty-eight species of birds.

BOTANICAL NAME: *Viburnum*

WINTER HARDINESS: −50°

MATURE HEIGHT: 4 to 30 feet

MATURE WIDTH: 4 to 30 feet

INTEREST: all-season

SHAPE: various

WILDLIFE: attracts birds

PROBLEMS: sulphur sprays will cause leaves to drop; prune and shape immediately after blooming before plant sets blossoms for next year

Weigela

Weigela is an old-fashioned, very hardy shrub that blooms in pink, white, purple, or red once each spring or summer and then once again—a great choice for borders.

BOTANICAL NAME: *Weigela*

WINTER HARDINESS: –50°

MATURE HEIGHT: 3 to 6 feet

MATURE WIDTH: 3 to 6 feet

INTEREST: spring, summer, late-summer flowers

SHAPE: upright, rounded

PROBLEMS: branches frequently die back to the ground; prune after blooming

Willow, Arctic Blue Leaf

Arctic blue leaf willow has hazy blue slender leaves that make a wonderful background or hedge. Prefers moist soil.

BOTANICAL NAME: *Salix purpurea* 'Nana'

WINTER HARDINESS: –30°

MATURE HEIGHT: 3 to 6 feet

MATURE WIDTH: 3 to 6 feet

INTEREST: leaves

SHAPE: upright, rounded

PROBLEMS: messy near sidewalks

Winterberry

Also known as inkberry and Michigan holly, winterberry is a native, twiggy shrub that drops its leaves in winter but keeps its bright red berries. Wonderful in borders, this shrub has no serious insect or disease problems. It prefers wet soil.

BOTANICAL NAME: *Ilex verticillata*

WINTER HARDINESS: –40°

MATURE HEIGHT: 6 feet

MATURE WIDTH: 6 feet

INTEREST: white summer flowers; glossy red berries in late summer through winter; yellow fall leaves

SHAPE: rounded

WILDLIFE: 20 species of birds

PROBLEMS: requires acid soil; needs male plant in grouping for berry production

Witch Hazel

Witch hazel is a native shrub with leaves that turn yellow in the fall. Small, sweet-smelling flowers cover bare branches late each fall when nothing else is blooming. Branches of witch hazel are used as divining rods to locate water and minerals. It prefers moist, acid soil.

BOTANICAL NAME: *Hamamelis*

WINTER HARDINESS: −40°

MATURE HEIGHT: 15 feet

MATURE WIDTH: 15 feet

INTEREST: yellow autumn flowers

SHAPE: rounded

PROBLEMS: weak branches if grown in shade; prune after flowering

Yellowwood

Yellowwood is a tree native to the Midwest with an upright spreading crown of yellow fall leaves and a wonderful summer show of white fragrant flowers. Brown pods are of winter interest. An attractive street tree, yellowwood withstands prolonged drought, extreme cold and heat, and wet soils.

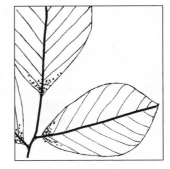

BOTANICAL NAME: *Cladrastis kentukea*

WINTER HARDINESS: −30°

MATURE HEIGHT: 50 feet

MATURE WIDTH: 55 feet

CROWN: flat oval

BARK: gray

FLOWERS: white clusters

FRUIT: brown pods

SUMMER COLOR: green

FALL COLOR: gold

PROBLEMS: susceptible to wilt and bark damage from lawn mowers

Buying Trees and Shrubs

Trees and shrubs come packaged in four ways: bare-rooted with no soil on the roots; with a burlapped soil ball around the roots; rooted in plastic or metal containers; or field grown and transferred into paper or fiber pots before sale.

Bare-rooted stock is most reasonably priced. Most mail-order catalogs sell bare-rooted stock, which is available only in the early spring. When your new plants arrive, you will need to soak them overnight

Celebrating with Trees

To mark the end of construction and the joy of moving into new surroundings, our Scandinavian ancestors placed a decorated tree or wreath at the highest point of a newly finished building. This topping-out ceremony was often followed by a celebration honoring the workers who made the project come to life.

in a diluted fertilizer solution before planting. If you cannot plant immediately, store the stock in a cool place out of sunlight and wind.

Balled and burlapped stock is encased in soil. You can plant any time the ground is not frozen as long as you water deeply and faithfully. When planting, remove the burlap to prevent wicking, or wind-drying of the roots.

Container-grown and potted trees and shrubs can be planted any time the ground is not frozen. If you cannot plant container-grown plants immediately, water them daily and fertilize with diluted liquid fertilizer weekly. To plant, gently untangle the outer edges of the root system with your fingers. Water with a plant-starter fertilizer. This will encourage the root system to expand into its new home.

Field-grown stock in paper or fiber pots can also be planted at any time. Cut vertical slots into the outside edges to help the roots emerge. Score the bottom. Then plunge the entire paper pot into the ground. Any rim left above the ground should be trimmed off so that it doesn't wick and dry out the roots.

Eight Steps to Planting Your Trees and Shrubs

1. Make a hole as deep as the root ball and three times as wide.

2. Amend the soil dug from the hole with sand, compost, slow-release fertilizer, or peat as needed. Fertilizing with fast-acting fertilizer too soon after planting is like giving a person who is just recovering from surgery a full meal—it can be too much for a weakened system. Add only specially formulated slow-release fertilizers directly in the planting hole. Water-soluble starter fertilizers that will help your plant recover can be applied to the rootball when planting, to the leaves, or to the ground any time after planting.

3. Plant your new tree or shrub as close to the original nursery depth as possible. Setting the plant too deep could kill it.

4. Replace the amended soil around the plant roots. Rather than stepping on the soil, water liberally to settle the soil and eliminate air pockets.

5. Use the techniques listed below for all newly planted stock.

6. Water deeply every week but do not fertilize with regular fertilizer for the first season.

7. Add four inches of mulch to help with soil moisture and temperature.

8. Use herbicides sparingly. Herbicides applied around tree roots are often fatal—this includes heavy applications of degradable preparations such as Roundup.

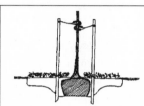

Dig wide hole. Place root ball on undisturbed soil. Remove burlap or fold down wire basket. Stake with slack wire through rubber hose. Fill with good soil. Add three to five inches of mulch up to, but not touching trunk. Water to settle soil.

When to Prune Deciduous Ornamentals

Timing is everything. It is best to prune in early spring, before new growth begins and when pruning wounds heal quickly. Particularly in early spring, trees and shrubs produce a hormone that stimulates cell division to develop a special protective layer of bark similar to scar tissue. For spring-flowering ornamentals, prune immediately after the flowers have faded. Pruning before this will cut off flower buds.

It is good gardening practice to regularly remove two to three of the oldest canes or stems from all mature woody shrubs. Shrubs maintained in this manner will always be attractive, vigorous, and healthy.

Deciduous trees need to be pruned to eliminate double leaders (two top stems splitting from the main trunk); weak crotches (two top stems that have matured, leaving a Y); branches that cross and rub against each other; diseased or broken branches; or lower branches that bump people's heads.

Some trees "bleed" or exude sap from pruning wounds when pruned in early spring. For this reason, maples, birches, elms, and black walnuts are usually pruned after they leaf out in the spring and their sap has slowed down.

Overgrown woody shrubs may be given a new lease on life though proper pruning. Pruning and clipping are different. Clipping is used to shape. Pruning is used to renew.

Pruning involves selective removal of the oldest, heaviest branches closest to the ground. Pruning stimulates the new shoots just below the pruning cuts, and new growth takes place at the base of the shrub. If top pruning is practiced, the natural form of the shrub is destroyed by the new butch haircut you have just given it.

Tools needed for pruning are a long-handled lopping shear and a pruning saw.

Deciduous Tree Pruning Fundamentals

1. Always make pruning cuts at a bud or at an adjoining side branch so that no branch stubs remain to rot and cause disease.

2. When removing large branches, make an initial undercut to prevent the bark from tearing with the weight of the branch as it falls from the tree.

3. Sterilize your tools with a ten-percent bleach solution between pruning jobs and trees to prevent the spread of disease.

4. Save your money and leave pruning paints and dressing on the shelf—research has shown that they don't help or hinder tree recovery.

5. Consult a competent arborist for large jobs. (See When Trees Need Help, at the end of this section.) Ladders and chainsaws can be the most life-threatening things in your neighborhood.

Mulching Trees

A mixture of compost, shredded leaves, woodchips, pine needles, and a slow-release nitrogen fertilizer will keep weeds and grass from stealing the water and nutrients tree roots need. Spread mulches two to four inches deep from the tree trunk to the dripline—the area under the tree's outer branches. Once the mulch is in place, remove or rake back any mulch that actually touches the bark of the trunk.

National and State Registry of Big Trees

There is a national registry of big trees through American Forests (see under Plant Groups and Associations) and several Midwest states including Indiana, Iowa, Kansas, Michigan, Missouri, Ohio, Nebraska, Pennsylvania, and Wisconsin also have Big Tree or Champion Tree programs where mature, full-size trees are identified, named, and hopefully protected.

Plant Groups and Associations

American Forests
910 17th Street, NW, Suite 600
Washington, DC 20006

Founded in 1875, this group focuses on conserving America's forests. An annual membership of $30 brings a lot of good information including a quarterly magazine. Ask for *Famous and Historic Trees,* a brochure that entertains and lets you participate by purchasing a 6-month membership plus a famous and historic tree for your yard.

Elm Research Institute
Elm Street
Westmoreland, NH 03467

Remember when elms graced our streets? This group is encouraging homeowners and towns to replant Main Street with new disease-resistant American elms. This elm is the product of more than twenty years of research and is a purebred American elm with the classic vase shape and a high resistance to Dutch elm disease. For a period of time, they are offering a first-time annual membership of $30 that includes a two-foot-tall American elm sapling.

International Oak Society
PO Box 310
Pen Argyl, PA 18072-0310

Annual dues of $15 include seed exchange, membership list, and the yearly publication *Journal of the International Oak Society.*

When Trees Need Help

Trees are so big that their problems, when they have any, can be overwhelming. Arborists are specialists in handling tree problems, but it may not be easy to choose one who is qualified. An unqualified arborist may damage the tree, and more importantly may not be insured, leaving you with a liability that can run into the tens of thousands of dollars if a worker should be injured on the job. Here are some recommendations for finding a qualified arborist:

- Check your telephone directory's yellow pages under Tree Services. While anyone can list themselves in the phone book, a listing at least indicates some degree of permanence. Be cautious of any arborist that advertises topping as a service. Topping always damages trees and should not be done.

- Ask if the arborist is certified by either your state arborists' association or the International Society of Arboriculture. Certification is not required by every state but it does indicate that the arborist has a certain degree of credibility.

- Ask for certificates of insurance, including proof of liability for personal and property damage and workman's compensation. Then contact the insurance company to make sure the policy is current. Under some circumstances, you can be held financially responsible if an uninsured worker is hurt on your property or if the worker damages a neighbor's property.

- Ask for local references. Take a look at some of the work, and if possible, talk with former clients. Experience, education, and a good reputation are signs of a good arborist.

- Don't rush into a decision just because you are promised a discount if you sign an agreement now. Be sure you understand what work is to be done for what amount of money. It is not generally a good idea to pay in full until the work is completed.

- Most reputable tree care companies have all the work they can handle without going door to door. People who aren't competent arborists may solicit tree work after storms, seeing an opportunity to earn quick money. Storm damage creates high-risk situations for both workers and property.

- If possible, get more than one estimate.

- A conscientious arborist will not use climbing spikes except when removing a tree. Climbing spikes open unnecessary wounds that could lead to decay.

- Good tree work is expensive. An arborist must carry several kinds of insurance as well as pay for specialized equipment. Beware of estimates that fall well below the average.

Purchasing Trees and Shrubs from Local Garden Centers

This is a reliable but usually rather expensive way to buy new trees and shrubs. Local nurseries stand behind their products but are more conservative and limited in their selection than mail-order sources. Locally purchased plants tend to be large and healthy. Always ask if the nursery grew the plant or imported it. Ask if the plant is guaranteed to winter over—if so, keep your receipt and packaging materials.

Reread your planting list and plan before you go. Experienced staff love plants and are wonderful. Inexperienced nursery staff members can often mislead you with good intentions and misinformation. If they can't talk you into substitutions, many nurseries will often order the plants you want from their suppliers at no extra cost.

Purchasing Trees and Shrubs from Mail-Order Sources

Local selection of plants is often limited, and sometimes plants are mis-labeled. Shopping for plants by mail is a way to increase variety in your garden. Most plants you receive will be in dormant condition. It will take at least two years for these plants to flourish.

Check each catalog's warranty policy and allow each new plant time to acclimatize. If plants do not show growth in three weeks, con-tact the catalog company and ask for new plants.

For the backbone of your garden, it is best to buy plants raised in the Midwest. Once you find a mail-order nursery that you like, tell your friends and other Midwest gardeners about it.

Be sure to check Midwest Mail-Order Plant and Seed Sources in Section Six for suggestions about where to buy trees and shrubs in the Midwest.

Evergreen Conifers

Conifers bear cones. Even though not all cones look like cones, cones make the conifer. Conifers are one of the oldest plant families. There are over 650 species, and they all grow only in the northern hemisphere. Nearly all conifers are evergreens with needle leaves all year-round and strong trunks. From the tall giants to specimen dwarfs, conifers are the backbone of the Midwest garden.

Most evergreen conifers need full sun and water year-round. Conifers are available in a wide choice of shapes, colors, textures, and sizes. They are used for backgrounds, foundations, windbreaks, hedges, gardens, and in formal landscapes because of their classic shape.

Successful low-maintenance landscaping with evergreen conifers starts here:

S Start any new landscape plan with evergreen placement. Since conifers stay green all year, they are a permanent part of any landscape design. Use a garden hose to mark off the area the mature tree would occupy.

T Too many trees can cause problems too. While shade can be wonderful, too much shade can be depressing.

A All birds, most butterflies, and small mammals use evergreen foliage for cover.

R Real estate values increase as landscaping matures. Trees and shrubs are a smart investment.

T Take your time choosing your landscape plants. Use these recommendations to judge the wonderful trees and shrubs that are available for your home landscape.

CONIFER TREES AND SHRUBS FOR THE MIDWEST AT A GLANCE

NAME	Arbor Vitae *Thuja*	False Cypress *Chamaecyparis*	Fir *Abies*	Hemlock *Tsuga*	Juniper *Juniperus*	Larch *Larix*	Pine *Pinus*	Spruce *Picea*	Yew *Taxus*
FORM									
Globe	✔	✔	✔				✔	✔	✔
Ground Cover					✔			✔	
Specimen	✔	✔		✔	✔		✔	✔	
Spreading		✔			✔		✔	✔	✔
Tree			✔	✔		✔	✔	✔	
Upright	✔			✔	✔		✔	✔	✔
COLOR									
Blue-green	✔	✔			✔		✔	✔	
Gold	✔	✔			✔		✔		
Gray-green					✔				
Plum		✔							

Arbor Vitae

Also known as northern white cedar, arbor vitae are a group of large, slow-growing, upright trees that are often used as landscaping plants. Their needles are overlapping small scales. Body shapes tend to be globes, cones, and tubes. Cones are small and mature during the first year. Arbor vitae need well-drained, moist soil in full sun to partial shade. This was the first tree exported from America to Europe after a tea made from its needles was used to cure an expedition of scurvy.

BOTANICAL NAME: *Thuja occidentalis*

PROBLEMS: even slow-growing trees get big, usually outgrowing other mature plantings; susceptible to storm damage and winter burn on the south side of buildings; rabbits and other wildlife will eat twigs and foliage

Cypress, False

False cypress, a form of Atlantic white cedar, is an unusual and interesting addition to Midwest gardens. Its leaves are narrow, scalelike, and rounded. Some have beautiful gold foliage. Some have deep plum foliage. All produce half-inch cones. Most commercial varieties are descended from three North-American natives and two imports. Their resonant wood is used for organ pipes and ship building, and they tend to be insect resistant.

BOTANICAL NAME: *Chamaecyparis*

PROBLEMS: needs protection from drying winds; heavy soil can cause root rot; each spring a jet of water and pruning should be used to remove spent foliage; a favorite food of deer

Fir

Firs have short, flat needles that leave circular scars on their branches when they shed. Erect cones mature the first year and shatter after ripening. There are nine firs that are native to North America, seven to the West, and two to the East. One of our best native Christmas-tree choices, fir seeds attract wildlife.

BOTANICAL NAME: *Abies*

PROBLEMS: slow-growing; dislike hot, dry winds; twigs are nibbled by deer and rabbits; porcupines like to gnaw the bark

Hemlock

Hemlock is a graceful native evergreen with flattened needles and horizontal, drooping branches. Cones mature in one season and often remain over the winter. The hemlock is the state tree of Pennsylvania and one of our most beautiful forest trees. Thickets of hemlock make excellent winter cover for wildlife. Hemlock prefer locations sheltered from the wind with well-drained, moist acid soil. Once established in the right location, hemlock is trouble-free and long-lived.

BOTANICAL NAME: *Tsuga canadensis*

PROBLEMS: hot sun and wind can scorch needles in summer and winter; buy locally raised trees to offset this problem. This is a poor Christmas tree because its needles shed when dry; deer and rabbits eat twigs

Juniper

Junipers are favorite evergreens for foundation plantings, ground covers, and accent plants. They have scalelike prickly needles and cones that resemble berries. There is a form for almost every garden and landscape use. Their hardiness varies according to type and where they are planted. Junipers prefer sandy, well-drained soil and a sunny, open area. Oil from the needles is used in perfumes, incense, and flavorings. The wood itself is used to make pencils, chests, and fenceposts. Juniper seed cones are eaten by over fifty types of birds.

BOTANICAL NAME: *Juniperus*

PROBLEMS: tend to outgrow their space; water and automatic sprinkler stress can encourage disease and root rot; subject to winter burn; can be infected with cedar apple rust and should not be planted near apple orchards

Larch

Larch is a group of deciduous conifers with fluffy clusters of needles that turn gold and orange each fall before falling to the ground. They are our only native conifer that drop their needles in autumn. The bright reddish purple cones stay on the tree, creating winter interest.

BOTANICAL NAME: *Larix*

PROBLEMS: needs moist soil; plant in front of background, but away from sidewalks, as it loses all its needles in winter; seeds and twigs are eaten by rabbits and deer

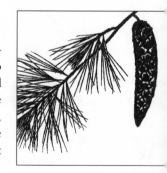

Pine

Pines have needle-shaped leaves arranged in clusters of two to five needles. Fertilization is by wind, and pine cones need at least two years to mature. Pines are used for foundation plantings, as ground covers, and as borders. Pine branches grow in a circle around the trunk, with one circle of growth added per year. Of the hundred known pine species, thirty-six are natives of North America. Only a few species of pine are native to our area. As a rule, Midwest pines will be happiest in Midwest gardens. Seeds from cones attract wildlife.

BOTANICAL NAME: *Pinus*

PROBLEMS: susceptible to air pollution and drought; five-needle pines are susceptible to the fatal white pine blister rust disease; deer will eat pine needles during hard, lean winters

Spruce

Spruce are triangular trees with sharp four-sided needles arranged singularly on branches. Cones hang from the trees like Christmas ornaments and mature during the first season. Red spruce, white spruce, and black spruce are native to our area. Colorado blue spruce are imported from the Rockies as popular lawn trees. Spruce are valuable for making paper pulp, piano sounding keys, guitars, and boats.

BOTANICAL NAME: *Picea*

PROBLEMS: watch for aphids that can attack trees in very early spring; watch for pine-needle scale in spring; needles dry and fall too quickly, so spruce are poor Christmas trees

Yew

Yew are slow-growing and excellent for shearing and pruning into hedges and screens. They all have dark green, smooth needles. Female plants have single-berry cones that birds love. Mature plants are drought tolerant but do better if sprayed down with water in summer heat. Yews prefer the north and east sides of buildings in partial shade, and mid-pH soil. The yew's botanical name, *Taxus,* is from the ancient Greek word for bow.

BOTANICAL NAME: *Taxus*

PROBLEMS: subject to winter-burn from reflected light on west and south walls; deer and moose will eat needles in hard winters

Pruning Evergreens

Arbor vitae and junipers can be pruned at any time during the summer and late-summer months. You can trim anything as long as you do not cut behind the living foliage of the branches into the dead zone. Once evergreens have established a dead zone, they will never grow leaves in that section again. Use hedge shears on compact, definitely formed trees. Hand shears can be used on other forms such as globe or spreading types.

Pines are pruned only in spring when the buds (called candles) are beginning to lengthen. Pinch back the candles halfway. Pruning can be done by cutting with shears or by breaking off the bud end with your fingers.

To keep spruce in bounds, prune every spring by cutting back last year's branches along one of the lateral (side) buds. If older wood is to be removed, cut back to another branch. Yews can be clipped in spring.

Water

Evergreen roots spread out rather than down. Mulch is important. Water is vital at all times.

Mulching Evergreens

A mixture of compost, shredded leaves, woodchips, pine needles, and a slow-release nitrogen fertilizer will keep weeds and grass from stealing the water and nutrients tree roots need. Spread mulches two to four inches deep from the tree trunk to the dripline—the area under the tree's outer branches. Once the mulch is in place, remove any mulch that actually touches the bark of the trunk.

Plant Groups and Associations

American Conifer Society
PO Box 360
Keswick, VA 22947-0360

Founded in 1983, this group has a Central Region chapter with spring and fall meetings. They sponsor garden tours, a seed exchange, and plant sales and auctions. Annual membership of $25 also includes the quarterly *Bulletin*. Here are a few tips from their brochure: yews and hemlocks are the easiest to control by pruning new spring growth; firs, cedars, and spruce all have easily identifiable buds that can be pruned to maintain size; pines, junipers, arbor vitae, and false cypress are all difficult to prune.

Rule of Six

Six inches of anything—mulch, stones, dirt, or water—will smother roots and suffocate any established tree or bush.

Green Lawns

The word "lawn" originally referred to a natural area of grass without trees. Lawns became popular in late-eighteenth-century Europe, when architects designed several lawn areas for the palace of Versailles. Lawns were rapidly adopted by the court aristocrats. And because grass grew easily in these mild climates, lawns became a gardening mainstay. In the new world, colonists adopted these same sophisticated lawn designs in an attempt to tame the wilderness that surrounded them.

Today green lawns are a billion-dollar industry in America. Grass grows in schoolyards, in public parks, on golf courses, in front of buildings, along sidewalks, and around our homes. Experts estimate that the replacement value of America's lawns would exceed twelve billion dollars, and annual maintenance costs just to keep grass green have been estimated at over four billion dollars.

There are four reasons for cultivating a lawn:

1. to control mud and dust,
2. to play on,
3. to please the eye,
4. from habit.

If any of the first three are important to you, read on. If number four has raised questions in your mind, skip forward to Native Prairies and Romantic Meadows for other possibilities for your grassy area.

Lawn grasses are divided into two groups. Cool-season grasses thrive in the cool climates of the northern United States and warm-season grasses are adapted to the southern part of the country. In the Midwest, we can grow both warm- and cool-season grasses, but neither very well.

In Midwest lawns, warm-season grasses will turn green late in spring, glow through the summer, and fade with the first fall day. Cool-season grasses will green up during winter's end, go dormant and sometimes die during our hot summers, and bounce back until Thanksgiving. Turf experts recommend a mixture of three grasses for Midwest lawns: Kentucky bluegrass (*Poa pratensis*), red fescue (*Festuca rubra*), and perennial ryegrass (*Lolium perenne*).

Kentucky bluegrass and perennial ryegrass will dominate the open, sunny areas. Red fescue will take over in the shade. A good seed mixture should contain at least fifty percent Kentucky bluegrass and percentages of fescue and ryegrass.

Beautiful green lawns start here:

S Select the right seed mix: fifty percent Kentucky bluegrass and percentages of fescue and ryegrass.

T Time your seed planting or sodding with spring or autumn rains for fast and consistent seed germination.

A Always feed in early spring and late fall.

R Reel mowers, power mowers, or scissors, whichever you use, make sure they are sharp when you cut your grass.

T Thin and bare spots should be scraped to remove the top layer of soil, new topsoil added, and grass seed mixed in.

When to Seed

Lawns may be seeded any time during the summer if water is available during the two weeks needed to establish seedlings. The best times to start a new lawn are in spring, mid-May through the end of May, and in late summer and fall, mid-August through mid-September, when the temperatures are cooler and there is rainfall. Late summer and fall are the best times, as there is less competition from weed seeds and the soil is warm for faster seed germination.

How to Seed

Grass roots need good topsoil, at least four and ideally six inches of a level base that is firm and free of large lumps. Before seeding, use a commercial fertilizer that is high in phosphorus and potassium, 0-20-20, at the rate of twenty pounds per thousand square feet. Use a rototiller to mix the fertilizer into the bottom layer of topsoil. Use a seed spreader to distribute two pounds of seed per thousand square feet of lawn. Seeding in two directions will bring the most even coverage. Next broadcast slow-release nitrogen pellets over the seeds. Rake the surface lightly to put the seed in contact with the soil. Mist the area with water after seeding and fertilizing. A light mulch of burlap, or one inch of clean straw or even grass clippings, can be used to keep the seeds moist. During warm weather, water twice a day to keep the germinating seedlings damp. After the grass seed has sprouted, watering may be reduced to twice per week, depending on the weather.

Sodding a Lawn

Sodding will give you an instant green lawn. It is important to buy freshly cut sod from a local dealer to make sure that the base soil types are compatible. Sodding can be done any time if adequate water is available. Sod must be kept out of the sun and laid within a few hours of delivery. Preparation should be as thorough for sodding as it is for seeding. The lawn area needs four to six inches of good topsoil and fertilizer raked to a smooth, firm surface. Topsoil should be moist when sod is laid. Sod should be staggered with the ends in contact but not covering each other. The finished lawn should be rolled lightly to ensure contact with the topsoil and then watered deeply. Water frequently for the next month until sod roots reach into the topsoil.

When to Water an Established Lawn

In the summer, you can allow your lawn to turn brown and go dormant or you can water. If you want to water your lawn, start in June before the grass turns brown. All cool-season lawns will turn some color of brown from too much heat in July and August. Lawns can be kept almost green by deep watering once a week for clay or silty soils and twice a week for sandy soils. Early-morning watering cuts down on surface evaporation. Deep, long watering encourages deep, hardy roots. Shallow watering encourages the roots to grow near the top of the soil where they are more exposed to evaporation. The average water loss from a grass-covered area through evaporation is one inch per week. It takes about three hours of sprinkling to replace the inch of water lost through evaporation.

One way to check the output of your sprinkler is to place small straight-sided containers at different intervals in the sprinkling area to catch the water for an hour. Measuring the depth of water in each container will give you an idea of how long you need to water to give your lawn the inch it needs. Watering longer or more frequently invites serious lawn diseases.

When to Mow Your Lawn

Mowing height is the key to keeping lawns healthy and attractive. In the spring and fall, you will need to mow your lawn weekly to keep it two inches tall. Cutting off more than thirty percent at any time will stress your lawn and damage grass plants.

During the summer months, lawn growth will slow as cool-season grasses become dormant. To help your lawn stay cool, raise your mower to three and one-half inches and mow only as needed. Grass leaves cut to this height shade the root systems and keep summer weed seeds from establishing themselves. Mowing the grass shorter during hot weather weakens it, making it susceptible to disease. Short grass has a shallow root system and really suffers during summer's heat.

To adjust your mower to the right height, place it on a hard surface and measure from the blade to the hard surface. Always mow at the same height each season. Letting the grass grow long in the fall makes the lawn difficult to mow again and invites mice and other pests to overwinter in your lawn.

It is important to have sharp mower blades. Dull blades tear the leaf tips rather than cutting them and turns them brown. Dull mowers also take more power or fuel to operate.

You can use grass clippings to mulch flower and tree areas or allow grass clippings to lie on the lawn. This recycles nutrients and moisture, saves on fertilization costs, and cuts down the time you spend mowing.

In the fall, use your mower to chop up and mulch fallen leaves. Large clumps will smother the grass, but small pieces will recycle into the lawn area.

When and What to Feed Your Lawn

Feed your lawns while they are growing. Dormant summer lawns are not growing and do not need fertilizer. Fertilizing at this time will cause thatch buildup and stress your lawn's root system. If broadleaf weeds are a problem during midsummer, wait until early fall to control them or catch them with a special fertilizer mix next spring. If crabgrass is a problem, apply crabgrass preventive with your spring feeding. Crabgrass is an annual grass that reseeds itself every year. Crabgrass preventive forms a gaseous barrier that stops crabgrass from germinating during its growth window each spring. There isn't one "wonder chemical" that will deal with all lawn pests, predators, and diseases. Lawn chemicals can be hazardous to your health. It is saner and safer to use as few as possible. A healthy, properly maintained lawn will repel most problems.

To have a healthy lawn you will need to fertilize it each spring and fall. "Slow-release" nitrogen is pelleted with a coating that dissolves slowly, feeding your lawn little bits over a longer period. Slow-release nitrogen along with potassium and phosphorus applied in the fall will guarantee a green spring lawn. A spring lawn fed with a good nitrogen lawn food will bounce back quickly each fall as the weather cools.

Lawn fertilizers range from chemical mixes to all-natural types. When you apply them at the proper rate, you can expect good results from any type. Chemical fertilizers containing water-soluble nitrogen may burn grass if you apply them too heavily. Slow-release and natural fertilizers will not usually burn when you use them as directed. No matter which you choose, lawns are high-maintenance landscaping features that need a steady supply of fertilizers, water, and care.

What to Do about Bare Spots

Lawns often have areas of thin or bare spots. Scattering seed over these spots is a waste of time and money. To reestablish good grass growth, mow the area and get rid of as much existing vegetation as possible. Remove the top layer of soil so that bare earth is exposed. Replace this top layer with fresh topsoil, filling any low spots, and add a grass seed mix. Mulch lightly and keep the area moist until the grass is up. Sod is an instant repair, but remember that it needs to be fresh cut.

Growing Green Lawns in Shade

It is hard to grow a dense stand of grass in the shade. When you plant grass in a shady location, purchase a shady lawn seed mixture. This will have a higher percentage of red fescue than Kentucky bluegrass.

It will help if you can prune large trees to let in more sunlight. Shade-grown grass needs half the fertilizer and less mowing than grass grown in full sun. In heavy shade you may find that even the shady lawn mixtures do not do well and you will need to plant one of the ground covers or vines listed in the next section.

Ground Covers and Vines

Sometimes you need something more than shrubs, trees, and flowers. Ground covers and vines are plants that spread by crawling either vertically or horizontally. Because of their ability to wander, these plants can be used to carpet an area, to cover walls and fences, and to screen for privacy or shade. Treat these plants as you would other garden flowers, choosing colors that complement your garden design and leaf shapes that contrast with walls, walks, and fences.

Successful ground-cover carpets and winding vines start here:

S Select healthy, nutrient-rich soil. Have a soil sample tested by your county extension office to find out if your soil needs any additives. Bed preparation is the most important step to beautiful ground covers and vines. See Great Gardens Start Here in Section One for more information on mulches and soil.

T Think about how your young plants will look when they reach full size and place accordingly.

A Add a diluted liquid starter fertilizer when transplanting young plants, and water frequently.

R Rake or hoe to control early spring weeds. Mulch with untreated grass clippings to improve soil or add wood chips to give your beds a tidy, unified look.

T Thin and share plants with neighbors as they mature and fill up their allocated garden space.

GROUND COVERS FOR THE MIDWEST AT A GLANCE

Common Name	Botanical Name	Hardiness	Interest	Leaves and Flowers
	A ▼			
Maidenhair Fern	*Adiantum pedatum*	–40°	—	height: 12–18 in. leaves: green
Goutweed	*Aegopodium podagraria*	–40°	—	height: 12 in. leaves: variegated, green and white
Carpet Bugle	*Ajuga reptans*	–40°	spring	height: 6 in. leaves: variegated, green, bronze flowers: blue, white, purple
Rock Cress	*Arabis*	–30°	spring	height: 6 in. leaves: evergreen— soft green flowers: white or rose
Bearberry	*Arctostaphylos uva-ursi*	–40°	summer	height: 6 in. leaves: evergreen— deep green flowers: white, pink with red berries
Sandwort	*Arenaria montana*	–40°	spring	height: 6 in. leaves: gray flowers: white
Silver Mound	*Artemisia schmidtiana*	–30°	summer	height: 12 in. leaves: silver-green flowers: white
Wild Ginger	*Asarum*	–40°	spring	height: 6 in. leaves: deep green flowers: deep red, not significant
Sweet Woodruff	*Asperula* also known as *Galium*	–40°	summer	height: 12 –18 in. leaves: deep green flowers: white, yellow
Japanese Painted Fern	*Athyrium goeringianum*	–40°	—	height: 6 in. leaves: variegated purple, gray, green
Purple Rock Cress	*Aubrieta*	–30°	spring	height: 6 in. leaves: gray-green flowers: rose to purple
Basket of Gold	*Aurinia saxatilis* also known as *Alyssum saxatile*	–40°	spring	height: 12 in. leaves: gray-green flowers: gold

Common Name	Botanical Name	Hardiness	Interest	Leaves and Flowers
	B ▼			
Heartleaf	*Bergenia*	−40°	spring	height: 12 –18 in. leaves: light green flowers: pink
	C ▼			
Bellflower	*Campanula carpatica*	−40°	summer	height: 12 in. leaves: medium green flowers: pink, blue, white
Snow in Summer	*Cerastium tomentosum*	−40°	—	height: 6 in. leaves: variegated
Plumbago	*Ceratostigma*	−20°	late summer	height: 12 in. leaves: green flowers: blue
Ground Clematis	*Clematis recta*	−40°	summer	height: 12 in. leaves: medium green flowers: white
Lily of the Valley	*Convallaria majalis*	−40°	spring	height: 6 in. leaves: deep green flowers: white bells
Bunchberry	*Cornus canadensis*	−40°	summer	height: 6 in. leaves: deep green flowers: yellow with red berries
Crown Vetch	*Coronilla varia*	−40°	summer	height: 18 in. leaves: medium green flowers: light pink
	D ▼			
Mock Strawberry	*Duchesnea indica*	−40°	summer	height: 6 in. leaves: medium green flowers: yellow with red berries
	E ▼			
Barrenwort	*Epimedium alpina*	−40°	spring	height: 12 in. leaves: medium green flowers: white, pink, yellow
Wintercreeper	*Euonymus fortunei*	−30°	—	height: 12 in. leaves: evergreen— variegated

Common Name	Botanical Name	Hardiness	Interest	Leaves and Flowers
	F ▼			
Blue Fescue	*Festuca*	–40°	—	height: 12 in. leaves: blue-green-silver
Wild Strawberry	*Fragaria*	–30°	summer	height: 6 in. leaves: dark green flowers: pink, white with red berries
	G ▼			
Wintergreen	*Gaultheria procumbens*	–40°	spring	height: 6 in. leaves: evergreen— deep green flowers: white with red berries
	H ▼			

Ivy	*Hedera helix*	–40°	—	height: 6 in.
				leaves: evergreen—
				    light green, dark green,
				    variegated

Rose of Sharon	*Hypericum calycinum*	–30°	spring through late summer	height: 12 in. leaves: medium green flowers: yellow
	I ▼			
Candytuft	*Iberis sempervirens*	–30°	spring	height: 12 in. leaves: dark green flowers: white
	L ▼			
Yellow Archangel	*Lamiastrum galeobdolon*	–30°	spring	height: 10 in. leaves: variegated flowers: yellow
Spotted Dead Nettle	*Lamium maculatum*	–40°	spring	height: 12 in. leaves: gold, yellow-green, variegated flowers: white, pink
	M ▼			
Mint	*Mentha*	–40°	—	height: 12–18 in. leaves: medium green

Common Name	Botanical Name	Hardiness	Interest	Leaves and Flowers
	P ▼			
Japanese Spurge	*Pachysandra terminalis*	–40°	early spring	height: 8 in. leaves: medium green, variegated flowers: white
Virginia Creeper	*Parthenocissus*	–40°	—	height: 10 in. leaves: medium green, red in fall
Creeping Phlox	*Phlox*	–40°	spring	height: 6 in. leaves: evergreen— dark green flowers: pink, blue, red, white
Fleeceflower	*Polygonum*	–40°	summer	height: 6 in. leaves: medium green flowers: pink
Cinquefoil	*Potentilla*	–40°	summer	height: 3–18 in. leaves: medium green flowers: red, orange, yellow
Self-Heal	*Prunella grandiflora*	–30°	summer	height: 8–16 in. leaves: medium green flowers: violet, rose, white
	S ▼			
Pearlwort	*Sagina subulata*	–30°	summer	height: 2–4 in. leaves: evergreen— mossy green flowers: white
Rock Soapwort	*Saponaria ocymoides*	–40°	spring	height: 10 in. leaves: medium green flowers: pink to rose
Low Stonecrop	*Sedum*	–40°	summer through late summer	height: 2–12 in. leaves: evergreen— blue, burgundy, green, green-yellow, bronze flowers: yellow, red
Hen and Chickens	*Sempervivum*	–20°	summer	height: 4–8 in. leaves: light green-gray plus variations flowers: yellow, red
Lamb's Ear	*Stachys byzantina*	–40°	summer	height: 12 in. leaves: soft gray flowers: white, purple

Common Name	Botanical Name	Hardiness	Interest	Leaves and Flowers
T ▼				

Creeping Thyme	*Thymus serpyllum*	–40°	summer	height: 6 in.
				leaves: evergreen—
				    green, gold, gray,
				    variegated
				flowers: pink, white, red

Foamflower	*Tiarella cordifolia*	–40°	spring	height: 8 in. leaves: medium green flowers: white, pink
V ▼				
Cowberry	*Vaccinium vitis-idaea*	–40°	summer	height: 8 in. leaves: evergreen—green flowers: pink with red berries
Speedwell	*Veronica incana*	–30°	summer	height: 12 in. leaves: gray-green flowers: blue
Periwinkle	*Vinca minor*	–40°	spring through late summer	height: 6 in. leaves: evergreen— dark green flowers: purple, white, red
Violet	*Viola*	–40°	early spring through spring	height: 8 in. leaves: dark green flowers: yellow, pink, purple, blue, white
W ▼				
Barren Strawberry	*Waldsteinia ternata*	–40°	summer	height: 6 in. leaves: dark green flowers: yellow

VINES FOR MIDWEST GARDENS AT A GLANCE

Common Name	Botanical Name	Hardiness	Interest	Profile
A ▼				
Hardy Kiwi	*Actinidia kolomikta*	–40°	spring, summer fall	woody climber with 6-in. heart-shaped leaves; white flowers and fall berries; 5 feet wide to 20 feet long
Pepper Vine	*Ampelopsis brevipedunculata* 'Elegans'	–30°	late summer	aggressive climber with turquoise berries that turn purple; fast growth to 25 feet
Dutchman's Pipe	*Aristolochia durior*	–30°	summer	twining, fast growth to 30 feet, sun to shade, huge leaves, brown pipe-shaped flowers
C ▼				
Trumpet Vine	*Campsis* sp.	–30°	summer	clinging, slow grower; takes 5 years to flower, sun to partial shade, orange or red flowers that resemble trumpets
Bittersweet	*Celastrus* sp.	–40°	fall, winter	twining, fast growth, sun to partial shade, orange or yellow berries in fall, male and female plant needed
Clematis	*Clematis* x hybrids	–40°	all	twining, medium growth, sun to partial shade, flowers, likes heavy mulch
Mountain Glory	*Cobaea*	all	summer	climbing annual with huge balloon buds and bellflower-like blooms, sun to partial shade
D ▼				
Hyacinth Bean	*Dolicho*	all	summer	climbing ornamental annual bean with white and purple flowers, sun to partial shade
E ▼				
Wintercreeper	*Euonymus fortunei*	–20°	all	perennial, clinging, aggressive, partial shade or shade, likes north side of buildings

Common Name	Botanical Name	Hardiness	Interest	Profile
	H ▼			
Ivy	*Hedera helix*	–40°	all	perennial, clinging, fast growth, partial shade, grow on trellis
Climbing Hydrangea	*Hydrangea anomala*	–30°	summer	clinging, slow growth, partial to full shade, white flowers
	I ▼			
Moonflower	*Ipomoea*	all	summer	climbing annual with huge white trumpets that bloom at night, sun
Morning Glory	*Ipomoea*	all	summer	climbing annual with blue or red trumpets, sun
Cardinal Climber	*Ipomoea multifida*	all	summer	climbing annual with red trumpets, sun
	L ▼			
Everlasting Pea	*Lathyrus*	–40°	late summer	perennial pea; deadhead to prolong flowering; full sun; well-drained soil a must; growth to 8 feet
Sweet Pea	*Leguminosae*	all	summer	climbing annual, scented, old-fashioned favorite, sun
Honeysuckle	*Lonicera* sp.	–40°	summer	perennial, twining, fast growth to 30 feet, sun to partial shade, fragrant flowers
Luffa	*Luffa acutangula*	all	fall	climbing annual with vegetable sponges; sun
	P ▼			
Virginia Creeper	*Parthenocissus quinquefolia* also known as Woodbine	–40°	summer	perennial, twining, fast; fall growth to 60 feet, sun to shade, fall color
Boston Ivy	*Parthenocissus tricuspidata*	–30°	summer and fall	perennial, clinging, fast growth to 60 feet, sun to partial shade, fall color
Silver Lace Vine	*Polygonum aubertii* also known as Silver Fleece Vine	–30°	summer	perennial, twining, fast growth to 30 feet, sun, flowers

Common Name	Botanical Name	Hardiness	Interest	Profile
	R ▼			
Climbing Rose	*Rosa*	–30°	summer to late summer	perennial, tie canes, medium growth, sun, fragrant flowers, check with extension office for hardy varieties
	T ▼			
Black-Eyed Susan	*Thunbergia*	all	summer	climbing annual with dark-eyed trumpet flowers in white, yellow, and orange, sun
Nasturtium	*Tropaeolum majus*	all	summer	climbing annual with warm-colored trumpets, sun
Canary-Bird	*Tropaeolum peregrinum*	all	summer	sprawling fast-growing annual with pale yellow flowers; to 8 feet
	V ▼			
Grape	*Vitis* sp.	–40°	summer	perennial, tendrils, fast growth, fruit, check with extension office for hardy varieties; prune hard in February
	W ▼			
Japanese Wisteria	*Wisteria floribunda*	–30°	summer	perennial, twining growth to 10 feet, partial shade, fragrant purple and white flowers

What Ground Covers and Vines Need

A low-maintenance garden is a healthy garden. Ground covers and vines are disease resistant, long lasting, and easy to care for if they have their basic needs of good soil and mulch met, if old flower heads and yellow leaves are removed and destroyed, and if they have enough water.

HOW MANY VINES DO YOU NEED?

Use your plant's size and garden square footage (width × length) to figure how many plants per square foot you will need for your garden project.

Plant Size	Number of Plants Needed
On 9-in. centers or 18 in. across	1.75
On 10-in. centers or 20 in. across	1.50
On 12-in. centers or 24 in. across	1
On 18-in. centers or 36 in. across	.50
On 24-in. centers or 48 in. across	.25

GROUND COVER PLANNING CHART

Based on a 100-sq.-ft. garden space

Plant Size	Number of Plants Needed
On 6-in. centers or 12 in. across	400
On 8-in. centers or 16 in. across	200
On 9-in. centers or 18 in. across	175
On 12-in. centers or 24 in. across	100
On 24-in. centers or 48 in. across	25

Plant Groups and Associations

American Ivy Society
PO Box 2123
Naples, FL 34106–2123

Annual membership is $20 and includes the yearly *Ivy Journal,* an ivy source list, an ivy identification service, and three newsletters per year.

Purchasing Vines and Ground Covers from Local Garden Centers

This is a reliable but usually rather expensive way to buy new plants and seeds. Local nurseries stand behind their products but are more conservative and limited in their selection than mail-order sources. Plants purchased locally tend to be large and healthy. Always ask if the nursery grew the plant or imported it. Ask if the plant is guaranteed to winter over—if so, keep your receipt and packaging materials.

Perennials and Annuals

Perennials usually take two to three seasons to come into their own. Perennials and annuals are the main categories of vines. A perennial is a vine that will survive for longer than two years. An annual will last for only one growing season. Annual vine seeds need to be started inside and moved to their home after frost.

Cool Off with Vines

Perennial vines can be used to reduce sun glare on the walls of your home. If you have a home with painted siding, hinge the vertical support for the vines so that the entire plant can be laid on the ground while painting or cleaning.

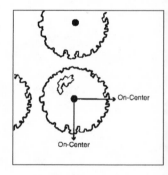

Purchasing Vines and Ground Covers from Mail-Order Sources

Local selection of plants is often limited, and sometimes plants are mis-labeled. Shopping for plants by mail is a way to increase variety in your garden. When shopping by mail, gardeners must be on their toes. Some nurseries grow their own plants and sell them through catalogs. Many mail-order companies buy plants from all over and sell them through catalogs. Many catalogs show pictures of mature plants in all their glory, and then fill your order with seedlings or two-inch pieces of roots. Most plants you receive will be in dormant condition. It will take at least two years for these plants to flourish.

Check each catalog's warranty policy and allow each new plant time to acclimatize. If plants do not show growth in three weeks, contact the catalog company and ask for new plants.

Kudzu

The vine "that ate the South," kudzu, was imported from Asia and introduced into American gardens in the 1920s. Growing a foot a day and blanketing our southern states, kudzu is a reminder of what can happen when a plant leaves its native environment. The kudzu story might have a happy ending—scientists are working on ways to use the vine as a replacement for tree pulp in papermaking.

Native Prairies

The word "prairie" came from a French word that meant "a meadow grazed by cattle." It was originally used by explorers to describe their discovery of the vast triangular heartland of North America. When pioneers first encountered our prairies, they found an inland sea of tall grasses. Shorter bluestems, buffalo grass, and sagebrush blanketed the high plains west to the Rocky Mountains. To the south, a vast desert stretched to Mexico. To the east were lush woodlands of oak, black walnut, buckeye, and maple. The northern forests were mixes of pine, spruce, red cedar, hemlock, beech, sugar maple, and basswood.

In summer, intense heat waves shimmered across the grasses, hot winds parched the soil, and dust was everywhere. In the fall, endless rusty golds and incredible rich smells of prairie recycling itself filled the air. In the winter, howling gales and wind-chill factors of seventy degrees below zero were normal. The word "blizzard" was a term coined just to describe a prairie snowstorm. Spring was unforgettable as flowers once again burst into bloom, insects buzzed, birds sang, and a brisk wind blew.

These first settlers, mostly from forest regions, found the vast prairie overwhelming. They were not used to the biting insects, humid summer heat, windy winters, lightning storms, and raging prairie fires. Their need for firewood and timber prompted most to settle at the edges of the prairie along riverbanks. The prairie was not farmed during early settlement because of the tough grassy root systems that defied plows. It was not until 1837, when John Deere invented the steel-bladed, self-scouring plow in Grand Detour, Illinois, that it became possible to farm the prairie. In a remarkable fifty years, most of the prairies were plowed under. Today corn, soybean, wheat, and livestock fill the heartland. Approximately seventy percent of America's food comes from these converted prairie grasslands.

Prairies are an important part of the Midwest heritage. In the past few years there have been numerous conferences, radio programs, popular articles, books, television shows, and scientific papers on prairies. This growing awareness of prairies and the ecological movement has led many people to experiment with the native plants that were here before the settlers came and with wild prairie plots in their home landscapes.

Creating a little piece of true prairie is not easy. After all, it took years and millions of dollars in machines, chemicals, and hard work to eliminate prairies. Restoration is unpredictable and takes time. But when planting is done right, the payoff is wonderful.

Successful prairie restoration starts here:

S Start small. If your neighbors have groomed yards, rather than converting your whole lawn, pick an area that can be edged by lawn or sidewalk. Keep your plant materials in scale with your plot size. Place larger plants in large areas, smaller plants in small areas.

T Tilling and preparation of a weed-free planting area and a seed or plant mix of at least two to three dozen species exactly suited to your area is vital.

A Addition of attractive features like stepping stones and benches will make your prairie visually appealing.

R Realize that not everyone will appreciate tall grass, but that most people will appreciate and understand prairie flowers. Choose a mixture of sixty percent grass to forty percent flowers.

T Tell everyone what you are doing. This is your chance to shine and share your views about gardening and your environment.

Native Prairie Grasses

Many native prairie grasses grow in clumps, need full sun, and are adaptable to a wide range of soils. When selecting grasses for prairies, avoid those that spread by underground rhizome, have "creeping" in their names, or are labeled "exotic" (introduced).

Short Grasses

Shorter grasses are good backdrops to set off perennials and smaller plantings.

Buffalo Grass; *Buchloe dactyloides*

Buffalo grass is a hot-summer grass that is currently enjoying a revival as a lawn and garden pathway grass. Researchers are developing new varieties of this sod-forming grass to fit a wider range of conditions. Buffalo grass requires less maintenance than traditional cool-season Kentucky bluegrass lawns and paths.

Sideoats Grama; *Bouteloua curtipendula*

Sideoats grama has seed stalks with oatlike seeds that tangle to one side.

Blue Grama; *Bouteloua gracilis*

Blue grama has seed stalks of curved spikes.

Medium Grasses

Medium grasses are good backdrops to set off perennials in lawn-replacement prairies.

Little Bluestem; *Andropogon scoparius*
Little bluestem is the most widely used prairie grass for wildflower beds and meadows. The blue leaves and stems turn a deep rust each fall and contrast with silver seed heads.

Splitbeard Bluestem; *Andropogon ternarius*
Splitbeard bluestem is used as an ornamental grass. The leaves and stems turn rust red each fall and fluffy white seed heads are scattered over the length of each stem.

Switchgrass; *Panicum virgatum*
In fall, switchgrass turns golden yellow with large, loose seeds heads. Of the native grasses, it is the most resistant to ice and snow. When puchasing switchgrass, choose the species rather than the more aggressive cultivated varieties.

Prairie Dropseed; *Sporobolus heterolepis*
Prairie dropseed has the thin, arching leaves of fountain grass. It is the most handsome of the prairie grasses.

Tall Grasses
Plant taller grasses for a dramatic accent or in large prairie plantings.

Big Bluestem; *Andropogon gerardi*
Big bluestem is a dramatic eight-foot-tall grass for a wide range of soils. In late summer, big bluestem produces a distinctive three-part seed head that resembles a turkey's foot—hence one of its common names. The bluish stems turn a deep rust red after frost and occasionally topple over in heavy winter snows.

Indian Grass; *Sorghastrum nutans*
Indian grass grows five to seven feet tall, with a large silky plume following yellow flowers in late summer. Stems are gold after frost.

Eastern Gama; *Tripascum dactyloides*
Eastern gama grows in a large circle and has broad leaves that make an impressive hedge or screen. Its seed heads sit on top of four- to eight-foot stalks and look like a primitive sort of corn. This grass turns orange in the fall and forms small mounds over winter.

Native Prairie Wildflowers

Native plants are adapted to the rainfall and soil types of their region. Once prairies are established, they usually do not need extra water or fertilizer of any kind. "Xeriscape" is a term coined by the Denver, Colorado water department to describe their program promoting the use of drought-tolerant plants in home landscapes. Going native takes this sensible program one step further. Native landscapes provide habitats for wildlife and save money the gardener would normally spend on the water and chemicals necessary to support nonadapted plants.

See Section Two: Domesticated Wildflowers for more detailed profiles of many of these plants. Still others are profiled in *The Best Flowers for Midwest Gardens.*

NATIVE PRAIRIE WILDFLOWERS

Early Spring

These are short, quick-start plants.

Pasque Flower; *Anemone patens*

Dog-Tooth Violet; *Erythronium mesochoreum*

Prairie Smoke; *Geum triflorum*

Blue-Eyed Grass; *Sisyrinchium campestre*

Spring

These are medium-sized plants, seldom exceeding two feet.

Indigo; *Baptisia* spp.

Camass; *Camassia scilloides*

Coreopsis; *Coreopsis* spp.

Shooting Star; *Dodekatheon meadia*

Flowering Spurge; *Euphorbia corollata*

Wild Strawberry; *Fragaria virginiana*

Yellow-Star Grass; *Hypoxis hirsuta*

Sheep Sorrel; *Oxalis violacea*

Wood Betony; *Pedicularis canadensis*

Western Phlox; *Phlox pilosa*

Bird's-Foot Violet; *Viola pedata*

Summer

Prairie plants increase in height as the summer progresses. These are over one foot tall.

Leadplant; *Amorpha canescens*

Milkweed; *Asclepias* spp.

Indian Paintbrush; *Castilleja coccinea*

New Jersey Tea; *Ceanothus americanus*

Coneflower; *Echinacea* spp.

Rattlesnake Master; *Eryngium yuccifolium*

Bee Balm; *Monarda* spp.

Prairie Clovers; *Petalostemum* spp.

Black-Eyed Susan; *Rudbeckia*

Rosinweed; *Silphium integrifolium*

Compass Plant; *Silphium laciniatum*

Prairie Dock; *Silphium terebinthinaceum*

Culver's Root; *Veronicastrum virginicum*

Do You Know Your State's Floral Emblem?

Goldenrod was adopted as the state flower of Nebraska in 1895. Late goldenrod (*Solidago gigantea*) is over four feet tall and blooms August through October. A two-foot-tall blue-green grass, little bluestem (*Andropogon scoparius*) is Nebraska's state grass.

Illinois	Violet
Indiana	Peony
Iowa	Wild Prairie Rose
Kansas	Sunflower
Michigan	Apple Blossom
Minnesota	Lady's Slipper
Missouri	Red Hawthorn Blossom
Nebraska	Goldenrod
North Dakota	Wild Prairie Rose
Ohio	Scarlet Carnation
Pennsylvania	Mountain Laurel
South Dakota	Pasque Flower
Wisconsin	Wood Violet

Prairie Talk

dry	very dry
dry mesic	well drained
mesic	average garden soil
prairie	full sun
savanna	partially shaded
wet	soggy most of the year
wet mesic	dry in summer, wet all other times
woodland	full shade

Autumn

Autumn is dominated by plants with daisy-shaped blooms, some reaching six feet tall or more.

Aster *Aster* spp.

Downy Gentian; *Gentiana puberulenta*

Sunflower; *Helianthus* spp.

Blazing Star; *Liatris* spp.

Goldenrod; *Solidago* spp.

Planting and Caring for Your Prairie

Prairie enthusiasts tend to scorn "meadow-in-a-can" mixes. If these attract your attention, consider planting a meadow instead of a prairie (see the following section on Romantic Meadows). Native prairie plants and seeds are probably best purchased from mail-order sources. Seeds can range from thirty-five to two hundred dollars a pound depending on variety. Plant prices are the same as for other perennials. Generally seeds are better for large prairies and plants are better for smaller prairies.

1. Prepare the site by spraying grass and weeds with the chemical herbicide glyphosate, commercially available as Roundup, and shallow tilling.
2. Sow the seed or plant the transplants in early fall or early spring, when we normally have heavy rains.
3. The first year, set your mower at six inches and mow in late fall.
4. The next spring, reseed bare spots.
5. Mow every other fall.
6. All seeds, wildflower or garden flower, need water to germinate. If drought is forecast or if rain doesn't fall, consider watering to protect your investment of time and money.

Be sure to check the listing of Midwest gardens in Section Six for prairies you can visit.

Free Stuff from Your Department of Transportation

The Department of Transportation (DOT) in many Midwest states prints wonderful four-color foldout brochures of the wildflowers that they have planted along our highways. These are free just for the asking. You can find some of these at rest stops or call and request that they be sent to you. Two favorites: *Discover Iowa's Roadside Flowering Plants and Grasses* and *Wildflowers and Grasses along Nebraska Roadsides.*

Plant Groups and Associations

Missouri Prairie Foundation
PO Box 200
Columbia, MO 65205

Founded in 1966 to focus on prairie development and education. Dues are $25 for one year and include their quarterly, *Missouri Prarie Journal.*

Purchasing Prairie Plants and Seeds from Local Garden Centers

This is getting easier to do, as you can now find many common prairie plants at local nurseries, but it can be very difficult to find a great selection of prairie seed. Most suppliers of prairie seed are small family businesses and their products are not carried by the chains.

Purchasing Prairie Plants and Seeds from Mail-Order Sources

You can purchase some prairie plants by mail (see Midwest Mail-Order Plant and Seed Sources in Section Six) though most suppliers prefer to supply seeds. Seeds for prairies vary in price. Order several catalogs and compare.

Romantic Meadows

A romantic meadow is tall green grasses swaying in the wind, dotted with bright flowers and surrounded by woodland. Wildflowers and uncut grasses are beautiful, hardy, and, once established in a meadow, require less maintenance than a conventional lawn or landscape. Meadows also provide food and shelter for a host of birds, butterflies, and beneficial insects. Meadow landscaping has been incorporated into both private and public spaces, creating a sense of place and increasing our connection to nature.

Meadows differ from prairies in that prairies use only native plants that were present before European immigration and were not introduced as part of that process of settlement. Meadows incorporate colorful wildflowers from all over the world. Teachers of biodiversity tell us that the more plant types we use, the greater will be the number of birds, butterflies, and small mammals that can live around us. And the more life forms we can keep alive around us, the better chance we, our children, and our grandchildren have of inheriting a beautiful and balanced world.

It took three billion years of evolution just to create the creatures that live in the seas. Today there are more kinds of life than ever, all descendants of ancestral organisms that lived billions of years ago. Modern wildflowers are part of this group, composed of survivors that managed to dodge and weave through billions of good and bad years of evolution.

Creating romantic meadows with a wide range of plant materials supports the environment. Meadows do not require pesticides, fertilizers, weekly mowing, or watering. Not only are meadows good for the environment, but once they are established, they save time and money.

Successful meadows start here:

S Starting from scratch, you can seed with wildflower mixes and remove weeds that will appear the first year, like burdock, ragweed, and crabgrass. The first year, annual wildflowers will color the bare ground. The second year, perennial wildflowers will join the show. Every fall mow the meadow, leaving grass and plant stalks six to eight inches high to protect seeds and tender roots from winter winds.

T To begin from an established lawn, you will need to use an herbicide such as glyphosate, commerically available as Roundup, to kill sod-forming grasses that will choke out young wildflowers.

A Advertise—explain to your neighbors what you are doing. Many meadows look like unmowed lawns the first few years. Signs and explanations help smooth ruffled feathers.

R Relax from mowing chores and enjoy the wildlife that will visit your meadow.

T Timing is everything when planting wildflower seeds. The rains of autumn and very early spring give seeds the moisture they need. Freezing and thawing cycles help with germination.

WILDFLOWERS FOR ROMANTIC MEADOWS

Here's a list of wildflowers you'll find in meadow seed mixes, nurseries, and backyard gardens. Some are profiled in Section Two: Domesticated Wildflowers. Others are described in *The Bes Flowers for Midwest Gardens.*

Name	Botanical Name	Flower Color	Plant Size
Yarrow	*Achillea*	yellow, white	medium
Butterfly Weed	*Asclepias tuberosa*	orange	medium
New England Aster	*Aster novae-angliae*	purple	tall
Indigo	*Baptisia*	purple, white	medium
Bluebell	*Campanula*	blue	medium
Bachelor's Button	*Centaurea cyanus*	blue	medium
Chicory	*Chichorium intybus*	blue	medium
May Daisy	*Chrysanthemum maximum*	white	medium
Tickseed	*Coreopsis*	yellow, red	medium
Rocket Larkspur	*Delphinium*	blue	medium
Coneflower	*Echinacea*	purple	medium
Blanketflower	*Gaillardia*	red, yellow	medium
Baby's Breath	*Gypsophila*	white	medium
Sunflower	*Helianthus*	gold	medium, tall
Dame's Rocket	*Hesperis matronalis*	purple	tall

Name	Botanical Name	Flower Color	Plant Size
Gayfeather	*Liatris*	purple	medium
Wild Snapdragon	*Linaria*	mixed	short
Blue Flax	*Linum lewisii*	blue	short
Scarlet Flax	*Linum rubrum*	red	short
Lupine	*Lupinus*	purple	medium
Bee Balm	*Monarda*	purple	medium
Evening Primrose	*Oenothera*	yellow	medium
Corn Poppy	*Papaver rhoeas*	red	short
Prairie Clover	*Petalostemum*	purple	short
Phlox	*Phlox*	purple	short
Obedient Plant	*Physostegia*	pink	medium
Mexican Hat	*Ratibida*	yellow, rust	medium
Black-Eyed Susan	*Rudbeckia*	yellow	medium
Catchfly	*Silene armeria*	pink	short
Goldenrod	*Solidago*	gold	medium, tall
Creeping Thyme	*Thymus*	white	short
Ironweed	*Vernonia*	purple	tall
Johnny-Jump-Up	*Viola*	purple and yellow	short

Grasses for Romantic Meadows

Nonaggressive grasses, such as Chewings fescue or hard fescue, and clovers can be added to meadow mixes to stablilize soils. Ornamental grasses work well too. See previous section on Prairies for more suggestions about grasses. Avoid aggressive sod-forming grasses such as bluegrass or rye grass; these will choke out plants. Native grasses are hardy but more difficult to establish in home gardens. Whatever grasses you choose, they should make up at least half your meadow.

What Romantic Meadows Need

Meadow plants and seeds can be purchased from the mail-order sources listed in Section Six or as "Meadow-in-a-Can" mixes. Usually wild-flower mixes are a combination of "nurse" seeds and perennial flower seeds. The nurse seeds are annuals that grow quickly and bloom the same year, protecting the perennial seeds while they grow. Perennial seeds establish their root systems in the first year and bloom the second year. Wildflower seeds can range in price from thirty-five to fifty dollars a pound depending on the variety. Plant prices are the same as that of other perennials. Generally, seeds are better for large meadows and plants for smaller meadows.

Planting and Caring for Your Meadow

1. Prepare the site by spraying grass and weeds with the chemical herbicide glyphosate, commerically available as Roundup, and till shallowly.
2. Sow the seed or plant the transplants in early fall or early spring, when we usually have heavy rains.
3. The first year, set your mower at six inches and mow in late fall.
4. The next spring, reseed bare spots.
5. Mow every other fall.
6. All seeds need water to germinate. If drought is forecast or if your meadow seems dry, consider watering to protect your investment of time and money.

Be sure to check the listings of Midwest gardens in Section Six for meadows you can visit.

Free Stuff from Your Department of Transportation

The Department of Transportation (DOT) in many Midwest states prints wonderful four-color fold-out brochures of the wildflowers they have planted alongside our highways. These are free for the asking. You can find them at rest stops or phone and request that they be sent to you. Two favorites: *Discover Iowa's Roadside Flowering Plants and Grasses* and *Wildflowers and Grasses along Nebraska Roadsides.*

Purchasing Meadow Seeds and Plants

Both grass and wildflower seeds and many wildflower plants are readily available at local garden centers and by mail order. Commerical wildflower mixes are wonderful for meadows. For individual wildflower varieties or for grasses, always purchase by botanical name.

Wildlife Gardens

Captivating Butterflies

Enchanting Birds

At a time when many of us worry that the wilderness areas around us are disappearing, wild creatures have become a symbol of what we want to preserve, and our gardens echo the wild places that inspire us. Birds entertain us with their songs, hummingbirds and butterflies add colorful splashes, and plants soothe us with their beauty.

Wildlife gardens can be organized or untamed. Both will attract different creatures as the seasons change. In spring and fall, exotic songbirds and butterflies stop by on their migratory routes. In summer, our permanent birds will raise their young and familiar caterpillars will chew our plants. In winter, small mammals will leave their footprints around our feeders and birds will fill cold, frozen landscapes with life.

When planning your wildlife garden, think long term and short term. For short-term, immediate success, plant more shrubs and flowers than trees. Trees can take years to mature and should be considered long-term additions. Flowers and shrubs grow faster and can be used immediately by wildlife.

Water is the most important feature in the wildlife garden, attracting a greater variety of wildlife than anything else. When temperatures are above freezing, a pond with running water is wonderful, but even a pan of fresh water set outdoors will help. Finding water during dry, cold winters is more of a problem for most wildlife—consider adding a heated water source for the wildlife in your garden.

Establishing and maintaining your wildlife garden is a delicate balancing act. Refrain from using chemical pesticides, herbicides, and fungicides. Trust that most problems in your garden will work out without intervention. Too many rabbits will invite owls or falcons, but be aware that birds of prey can't tell the difference between small pets and wild rabbits. An overabundance of one type of flower might be just what migrating monarchs have been looking for. Nature is unpredictable and surprising. Design your wildlife garden and then allow yourself the pleasure of watching nature at work.

Captivating Butterflies

Butterflies are the jewels of summer memories for old and young alike. Yet as their habitats are destroyed, they are disappearing from our gardens and meadows. There are not as many butterflies today as there were in the summers of our childhoods. The butterflies' fading presence touches each of us in ways that we often cannot even find words for. That the world is constantly changing, we can accept. That our children and grandchildren might never catch a glimpse of a butterfly on a warm summer breeze is heartbreaking.

Butterflies make up a large group of insects with the family name of Lepidoptera, derived from a combination of the Greek words for scale and wing. Over twenty thousand types of butterflies have been identified. In the United States today, even though much of their habitat has been destroyed, there are seven hundred species of butterflies grouped into nine families. In the Midwest, there are butterflies from five of these family groups that can still be easily found: brush-footed, gossamer-winged, skippers, swallowtails, and whites and sulfurs. Rather than sit by and watch the wildness of nature slowly slip away, many gardeners are taking personal steps to provide habitats for these small flashing summer jewels.

All butterflies need nectar flowers and a safe place to lay eggs. Caterpillars need food plants to eat and places to hibernate and turn into butterflies. Butterfly populations vary widely from year to year depending upon the conditions. But rain or shine, making a place for butterflies in your garden will give them a chance to thrive and spread throughout the Midwest.

As you succeed in attracting butterflies to your garden, you'll find that you want them to come more often and remain longer. To keep them coming back, you'll need to provide food, water, and nursery plants in a sunny site that is protected from the wind.

Successful butterfly gardens start here:

S Start by looking through the following section to find out which variety you would like to invite into your garden.

T Take an inventory of what you have in your garden and match it with the profiles that follow to find out what you need to add for each variety.

A Add the missing elements.

R Record which butterflies visit, when they visit, and what attracted them.

T Try a few new plantings to attract more butterflies next year.

Midwest Garden Butterflies

Just like flowers, trees, and birds, butterflies are grouped into families related to each by some aspect of anatomy or reproduction. If you would like to learn more about the butterflies that love Midwest gardens, use a full-color butterfly identification field guide for the eastern region, looking up each butterfly by its scientific name (in italics).

Where to Look for Butterflies

Butterflies are cold-blooded creatures. They need the sun's heat to warm their blood and muscles. Because of this, they are drawn to warm daylight hours and wind-free locations. Look for butterflies basking on hot rocks and warm wood surfaces. When observing butterflies, move slowly. Rapid movements will frighten them into flight. If you wear bright colors, they might even move closer to observe you.

Brush-Footed Family (Nymphalidae)

This is the largest and most diverse butterfly family. Close to two hundred of the three thousand species currently recognized worldwide are living in North America. Some of our most easily recognized butterflies are part of this group: admirals, angle-wings, checkerspots, crescent spots, fritillaries, leafwings, longwings, painted ladies, and tortoiseshells. Brush-footed butterflies are large, with unifying characteristics of knobby antennae, a short set of front legs that is useless for walking, and a combination of orange and black wings. Most eggs laid by brush-footed butterflies are ribbed. Two to three broods of eggs hatch each year. Emerging caterpillars have matching ridges. Chrysalises are usually spiked at the top and hang upside down by a silken thread. Most overwinter as caterpillars or chrysalises, although some of the more famous of the group are strong fliers and migrate and overwinter as adults. Brush-footed butterflies are territorial and return to the same locations year after year.

MIDWEST SPECIES:

American Painted Lady; *Vanessa virginiensis*
Buckeye; *Junonia coenia*
Comma Anglewing; *Polygonia comma*
Monarch; *Danaus plexippus*
Mourning Cloak; *Nymphalis antiopa*
Painted Lady; *Vanessa cardui*
Question Mark; *Polygonia interrogationis*

Red Admiral; *Vanessa atalanta*
Red-spotted Purple; *Basilarchia astyanax* or
   Limenitis arthemis astyanax
Tawny Emperor; *Asterocampa clyton*
Viceroy; *Basilarchia archippus* or
   Limenitis archippus

NECTAR PLANTS AND FEEDERS: aster, black-eyed Susan, cone-flowers, cosmos, fleabane, gayfeather, globe thistle, goldenrod, ironweed, Joe-Pye weed, lilac, marigold, may daisy, milkweed, mint, pinks, stonecrop, fruit, and grape jelly or sugar water from feeders

DRINKING: will land on sun-warmed rock placed in birdbath or other backyard water; dew from flowers

PLACES TO HIDE: evergreens, woodpiles

PLACES TO LAY EGGS: aster, grasses, milkweed, elm, willow, poplar, birch, hackberry, hollyhock, cherry, apple, oak, plum

Migrating Brush-Footed Monarchs

When monarch butterflies are migrating, you see them on the highway. You find them smashed on your windshield. You see them floating above your flowers. Some lucky people find them massed together on pine trees waiting for a change in weather.

Each fall great hordes of flame-colored butterflies gather together, sweeping south from the Great Lakes region through the Midwest. With a cruising speed of only twelve miles per hour, monarchs have developed inborn strategies to take advantage of winds and weather. As the days cool and the jet stream changes, monarchs will hitch a ride on any weather system headed south. Reaching Texas and the Gulf of Mexico, they will continue to meet up with other monarchs and fly to central Mexico. Their final destination is a baseball-diamond-sized forest colony where their parents spent the previous winter. Nine different colonies will form in this small mountainous area to wait for the warming days of spring.

As the days grow longer in February and March, these same monarchs mate and begin their journey back the way they came. Unlike their journey south, their return trip is a race against time. The female monarch has just a short time to live. She rarely stops, not even to eat. On her return journey north, she lays over six hundred eggs, one small jeweled egg per milkweed leaf.

You can raise your own monarch by searching the underside of milkweed leaves in the spring. When you find an egg, gather the stems and leaves from the entire plant. Keep the extra stems in water for caterpillar food. Wrap the end of the egg-bearing leaf and stem in a wet paper towel and a plastic sandwich bag. Place this in a large clean jar with air holes, or make a rearing cage from a shoebox with plastic wrap on the side for a viewing window. Then watch and wait for the caterpillar to hatch and begin to eat. It will eat so much and grow so fast that it will shed its skin four times as it grows to three thousand times its birth weight.

In two weeks, the caterpillar will be two inches long and will begin spinning its chrysalis at the top of the rearing cage. In about ten days, a new monarch butterfly will emerge, ready to grace your garden until it is time to fly south once more.

Other Traveling Butterflies

In addition to our native monarchs, a cousin of our common sulfur, the cloudless sulfur *Phoebis sennae,* is also a great traveler. This small butterfly spends the summers in the Midwest and winters in Mexico. *Vanessa cardui,* the painted lady, is a worldwide traveler who can easily fly 620 miles in one lifetime. This globetrotting beauty is found throughout Asia, Africa, Europe, and North America. And, each autumn, hordes of buckeye butterflies—*Junonia coenia*—gather together and drift southward in great groups.

Anyone Can Be a Butterfly Gardener

Butterflies are insects and have needs that flowers and trees cannot always meet. If your garden isn't attracting as many butterflies as you'd like, try putting out wine, beer, salt, and overripe fruit. Whether you start with one bowl of overripe apples or acres of land, anyone can be a butterfly gardener.

Gossamer Wings Family (Lycaenidae)

The gossamer wings' common name refers to the iridescent light-refracting scales on their upper wings. Gossamer wings are the first butterflies of spring. The most notorious member of this family, the harvester, or *Feniseca tarquinius,* is the only carnivorous butterfly in North America, feeding on sweet plump aphids. Gossamer eggs are flattened discs with ribbing. The caterpillars eat buds, flowers, and fruit, and then exude a sweet fluid that ants love. In return for this treat, the ants protect the caterpillars from parasites. Overwintering chrysalises are compact and may be attached to plants or just lie on the ground amid leaf litter, emitting a crackling sound that helps discourage predators.

MIDWEST SPECIES: Banded Hairstreak; *Satyrium calanus*
Eastern Tailed Blue Hairstreak; *Everes comyntas*
Bronze Copper Hairstreak; *Lycaena thoe*
Spring Azure; *Celastrina argiolus*

NECTAR PLANTS AND FEEDERS: goldenrod, milkweed, mint, queen Anne's lace, violet, and grape jelly or sugar water from feeders

DRINKING: will land on sun-warmed rock placed in birdbath or other backyard water; drinks dew from flowers; fond of puddles

PLACES TO HIDE: evergreens, tall grasses and plants

PLACES TO LAY EGGS: cherry, clover, corn, dogwood, hibiscus, hollyhock, mint, oak, viburnum

Skipper Family (Hesperiidae)

The skippers' common name refers to their unique darting, skipping flight pattern. They have furry mothlike bodies and triangular wings that fold flat against their gold and brown bodies when not in use. When sunning, they look like folded paper airplanes. Midwest skippers are about half an inch long but compete successfully with larger butterflies for food. Because they are small, their eggs are tiny. Their fat green caterpillars have large heads and protect themselves by weaving loose shelters of leaves. Chrysalises are smooth, covered with a waxy powder and a loose-woven covering. Both the caterpillar and chrysalis will overwinter.

MIDWEST SPECIES: Checkered Skipper; *Pyrgus communis*
Hoary Edge Skipper; *Achalarus lyciades*

NECTAR PLANTS AND FEEDERS: aster, clover, fleabane, gayfeather, globe thistle, Joe-Pye weed, zinnia, and grape jelly or sugar water from feeders

DRINKING: will land on sun-warmed rock placed in birdbath or other backyard water; drinks dew from flowers

PLACES TO HIDE: tall grasses

PLACES TO LAY EGGS: bean, hibiscus, honey locust, and hollyhock foliage and stems

Swallowtail Family (Papilionidae)

Swallowtails are the biggest butterflies in North America and are easily recognized by their long tails and bright wings in contrasting patterns of yellows, blacks, and blues. Most have a wingspan of two to five inches. Their eggs, however, are smaller than a round sesame seed, and the caterpillars that hatch from these eggs look like bird droppings. As the caterpillars mature, they begin to take on the colors of what they will become. When the caterpillars are threatened they rear up and thrust out a small forked organ that emits a strong smell. When mature, caterpillars spin a chrysalis that looks like bits of leaves or bark. This chrysalis hangs at a twenty-five-degree angle from a twig, secured by a silken thread. When the days are warm, caterpillars are transformed into flamboyant creatures that flit from flower to flower. Swallowtails will produce two to three broods a year. The last group of caterpillars will hibernate over winter.

MIDWEST SPECIES: Eastern Black Swallowtail; *Papilio polyxenes*
Giant Swallowtail; *Heraclides cresphontes*
Tiger Swallowtail; *Pterourus glaucus*

NECTAR PLANTS AND FEEDERS: bee balm, clover, coneflower, dame's rocket, goldenrod, Joe-Pye weed, lilac, milkweed, phlox, viburnum, zinnias, fresh oranges, and grape jelly or sugar water from feeders

DRINKING: dew from flowers; will land on sun-warmed rock placed in birdbath or other backyard water

PLACES TO HIDE: aspen, ash, birch, cherry, cottonwood, evergreens, willow

PLACES TO LAY EGGS: ash, aspen, birch, carrot foliage, cherry, cottonwood, dill, parsley, poplar, queen Anne's lace, willow

White and Sulphur Family (Pieridae)

The family Pieridae are the most widely distributed in the United States. All the butterflies in this family are the shade of white, yellow, yellow-green, or pale orange with wingspans between one and two inches. Several have black wing borders. Their colors may change from season to season and from male to female as they flit among nectar sources. Adults have six legs that they use to walk, on the ground and across flowers. This group includes the infamous white butterfly whose eggs turn into green caterpillars on cabbages in our gardens and then overwinter as cone-headed chrysalises hanging from silken cords. Eggs are spindle shaped, laid one to a leaf; the caterpillars are smooth and sleek.

MIDWEST SPECIES: Cabbage White; *Artogeia rapae*
Common Sulfur; *Colias philodice*
Orange Sulfur; *Colias eurytheme*

NECTAR PLANTS: aster, bee balm, cabbage family, globe thistle, gold-enrod, milkweed, pea family, phlox

DRINKING: will gather by riverbanks and puddles to sip minerals

PLACES TO HIDE: common in meadows and parks; chrysalis overwinters or adults migrate in groups

PLACES TO LAY EGGS: cabbage-family vegetables, clovers, vetch, wild indigo

What to Plant for Butterflies

Not all plants are suitable for all butterflies all the time. Trees are generally used by butterflies as a caterpillar food source and as resting places. Most flowers are sources of energy-building nectars. Whether for food or shelter, the following plants and trees will attract a variety of adult butterflies and their caterpillars to your yard. Some of the plants listed below are profiled in earler sections of this book. Others are described in *The Best Flowers for Midwest Gardens.*

Flowers

Allium (*Allium*)

Anise Hyssop (*Agastache*)

Aster (*Aster*)

Bee Balm (*Monarda*)

Black-eyed Susan (*Rudbeckia*)

Butterfly Weed (*Asclepias*)

Candytuft (*Iberis*)

Columbine (*Aquilegia*)

Coneflower (*Echinacea*)

Coral Bell (*Heuchera*)

Cosmos (*Cosmos*)

Cranesbill (*Geranium*)

Dame's Rocket (*Hesperis*)

Daylily (*Hemerocallis*)

Fairy Candle (*Cimicifuga*)

Fleabane (*Erigeron*)

Gayfeather (*Liatris*)

Globe Thistle (*Echinops*)

Goldenrod (*Solidago*)

Heal-All (*Prunella vulgaris*)

Helen's Flower (*Helenium*)

Hollyhock (*Alcea*)

Ironweed (*Vernonia*)

Joe-Pye Weed (*Eupatorium*)

Leadplant (*Amorphia*)

Lupine (*Lupinus*)

Marigold (*Tagetes*)

May Daisy (*Chrysanthemum*)

Mum (*Chrysanthemum*)

Petunia (*Solanaceae*)

Phlox (*Phlox*)

Pincushion Flower (*Scabiosa*)

Pink (*Dianthus*)

Queen Anne's Lace (*Daucus*)

Rose Mallow (*Hibiscus*)

Sage (*Salvia*)

Sea Holly (*Eryngium*)

Speedwell (*Veronica*)

Statice (*Limonium*)

Stonecrop (*Sedum*)

Sunflower (*Helianthus*)

Tickseed (*Coreopsis*)

Turtlehead (*Chelone glabra*)

Violet (*Viola*)

Wild Indigo (*Baptisia*)

Yarrow (*Achillea*)

Zinnia (*Zinnia*)

Herbs

Bee Balm (*Monarda*)

Catmint (*Nepeta*)

Chicory (*Cichorium*)

Chive (*Allium*)

Dill (*Anethum*)

Mint (*Mentha*)

Parsley (*Petroselinum*)

Sage (*Salvia*)

Thyme (*Thymus*)

Wormwood (*Artemisia*)

Shrubs

Azalea (*Rhododendron*)

Blueberry (*Vaccinium*)

Conifers, various

Dogwood (*Cornus*)

Gooseberry (*Ribes*)

Holly (*Ilex*)

Kinnikinik (*Arctostaphylos*)

Lilac (*Syringa*)

Mountain Laurel (*Kalmia*)

New Jersey Tea (*Ceanothus*)

Viburnum (*Viburnum*)

Willow (*Salix*)

Vines

Honeysuckle (*Lonicera*)   Trumpet Vine (*Campsis*)
Morning Glory (*Ipomoea*)

Trees

Apple (*Malus*)   Hackberry (*Celtis*)
Ash (*Fraxinus*)   Hawthorn (*Crataegus*)
Aspen (*Populus*)   Holly (*Ilex*)
Birch (*Betula*)   Hornbeam (*Carpinus*)
Cherry (*Prunus*)   Magnolia (*Magnolia*)
Cottonwood (*Populus*)   Poplar (*Populus*)
Dogwood (*Cornus*)   Willow (*Salix*)
Elm (*Ulmus*)

Be sure to check Section Six for a listing of Midwest gardens with butterfly habitats or plantings that attract butterflies.

Enchanting Birds

A recent survey found that bird-watching is second only to gardening as the most popular leisure-time activity in America. Although it might seem that feeding and gardening for birds benefits only the birds, gardeners benefit as well, since birds eat pesty insects, property values increase with attractive landscaping, and utility bills decrease when homeowners plant shade trees and windbreaks.

Birds sing to establish nesting territories and attract mates. Each song is a series of notes produced in recognizable patterns by each species. Hormones control how and when birds sing. Each species chooses a different but consistent singing perch. Birds that perch and sing out in the open have shorter songs than birds that sing hidden where predators cannot easily find them. Birds of grasslands tend to have soaring, high-pitched songs. Birds of the woodlands, like whales who sing underwater, have low-pitched songs that spread further in dense vegetation. Some birds are mimics that imitate other birds' songs and even nonbird sounds.

Of our Midwest bird population, over one hundred species are migrants that nest and raise their young during the summer in our backyards, then leave each winter for tropical climates where they can find the insects, fruit, seeds, and flowers they need to survive. Some of these little birds travel for weeks and thousands of miles to reach their winter destinations. Because long-distance travel is dangerous, only half of the fledglings raised in our gardens survive their first trip. Each spring the surviving fledglings return triumphantly to their Midwest homes to mate and start the cycle all over again.

Attracting a wider variety of these amazing birds to your garden can be as simple as making a place for them. Birds cheer us and respond to us. They seem to welcome our efforts to help them and to keep them near. Specific conditions attract specific birds. Match those conditions in your garden and you will attract the birds of your choice.

Steps to a successful songbird garden include:

S Start by looking through the following section to find out which birds you would like to invite into your garden.

T Take an inventory of your current garden and match it with the bird profiles that follow to find out what you need to add for each variety.

A Add the missing elements.

R Record which birds visit, when they visited, and what attracted them.

T Try a few new plantings to attract a few new birds next year.

Midwest Garden Birds

Just like flowers, trees, and butterflies, the birds in our gardens are grouped into families related by some aspect of anatomy or reproduction. If you would like to learn more about identifying birds, use a full-color bird identification field guide for the eastern region. To find out more about birds that love Midwest gardens, look through the following bird profiles under their family's scientific name.

A Word of Caution

There are state, federal, and international laws specifically protecting over eight hundred varieties of songbirds. Taking or molesting songbirds, their nests, or their eggs is prohibited by these laws and subject to fines and other penalties. It is also illegal to possess feathers, eggshells, nests, or any bird part without a special permit. This includes helping baby bird "orphans." If you find untended baby birds or are interested in the laws that govern your locality, contact a state or federal wildlife agency.

Common Name	Scientific Name	Family Group
American Goldfinch	Fringillidae	Bunting, Finch, Grosbeak, and Sparrow
American Robin	Turdidae	Bluebird and Thrush
Black-capped Chickadee	Paridae	Chickadee and Titmice
Blue Jay	Corvidae	Crow and Jay
Brown Thrasher	Mimidae	Mockingbird and Thrasher
Cedar Waxwing	Bombycillidae	Waxwing
Chipping Sparrow	Fringillidae	Bunting, Finch, Grosbeak, and Sparrow
Common Redpoll	Fringillidae	Bunting, Finch, Grosbeak, and Sparrow
Crow	Corvidae	Crow and Jay
Dark-eyed Junco	Fringillidae	Bunting, Finch, Grosbeak, and Sparrow
Dickcissel	Fringillidae	Bunting, Finch, Grosbeak, and Sparrow
Downy Woodpecker	Picidae	Woodpecker
Eastern Bluebird	Turdidae	Bluebird and Thrush
Evening Grosbeak	Fringillidae	Bunting, Finch, Grosbeak, and Sparrow
Fox Sparrow	Fringillidae	Bunting, Finch, Grosbeak, and Sparrow
Golden-crowned Kinglet	Sylviidae	Gnatcatcher, Kinglet, and Warbler
Gray Catbird	Mimidae	Mockingbird and Thrasher
Hairy Woodpecker	Picidae	Woodpecker
House Finch	Fringillidae	Bunting, Finch, Grosbeak, and Sparrow
House Sparrow	Fringillidae	Bunting, Finch, Grosbeak, and Sparrow

Common Name	Scientific Name	Family Group
Indigo Bunting	Fringillidae	Bunting, Finch, Grosbeak, and Sparrow
Mockingbird	Mimidae	Mockingbird and Thrasher
Mourning Dove	Columbidae	Pigeon
Northern Cardinal	Fringillidae	Bunting, Finch, Grosbeak, and Sparrow
Northern Flicker	Picidae	Woodpecker
Northern Oriole	Icteridae	Blackbird, Meadowlark, and Oriole
Orchard Oriole	Icteridae	Blackbird, Meadowlark, and Oriole
Pine Siskin	Fringillidae	Bunting, Finch, Grosbeak, and Sparrow
Purple Finch	Fringillidae	Bunting, Finch, Grosbeak, and Sparrow
Red-bellied Woodpecker	Picidae	Woodpecker
Red-breasted Nuthatch	Sittidae	Nuthatch
Red-winged Blackbird	Icteridae	Blackbird, Meadowlark, and Oriole
Rose-breasted Grosbeak	Fringillidae	Bunting, Finch, Grosbeak, and Sparrow
Rufous-sided Towhee	Fringillidae	Bunting, Finch, Grosbeak, and Sparrow
Ruby-crowned Kinglet	Sylviidae	Gnatcatcher, Kinglet, and Warbler
Ruby-throated Hummingbird	Trochilidae	Hummingbird
Song Sparrow	Fringillidae	Bunting, Finch, Grosbeak, and Sparrow
Tree Sparrow	Fringillidae	Bunting, Finch, Grosbeak, and Sparrow
Tufted Titmouse	Paridae	Chickadee and Titmice
White-breasted Nuthatch	Sittidae	Nuthatch
White-crowned Sparrow	Fringillidae	Bunting, Finch, Grosbeak, and Sparrow
White-throated Sparrow	Fringillidae	Bunting, Finch, Grosbeak, and Sparrow
Wood Thrush	Turdidae	Bluebird and Thrush
Yellow-headed Blackbird	Icteridae	Blackbird, Meadowlark, and Oriole

Waxwing Family (Bombycillidae)

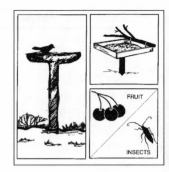

There are three species in this family group—one in Japan, one in the far north, and one in the Midwest. All are migratory.

Cedar Waxwing

Cedar waxwings are group travelers that migrate to the south in winter and come back to the Midwest for spring and summer breeding. Male waxwings communicate in high-pitched reedy trills. Females have a softer version of the same song. These are plump, seven-inch-long birds with creamed-coffee bodies and feathered crests, black wings and tails, and black eye-masks. Waxwings are named for the red markings on their wings and yellow markings on their tails. They lay four to five blue-gray eggs with black dots and will raise a late-summer as well as a spring brood. When they recognize cowbird eggs, they toss them from the nest.

SCIENTIFIC NAME: *Bombycilla cedrorum*

FOOD SOURCES: fruits and berries; fermented berries can make them tipsy; insects

FEEDERS: in spring and fall set out a low tray containing fruit

DRINKING AND BATHING: while migrating in groups will visit birdbaths; prefers rivers and ponds with flying insects

PLACES TO HIDE: open woodlands

PLACES TO RAISE YOUNG: nests of cupped grasses, lichens, and bark strips placed 6 to 20 feet off the ground on horizontal limbs of deciduous trees in open areas

Pigeon Family (Columbidae)

A large family of birds with short legs, round heads, and long tails. There are eight native species and three introduced species in North America.

Mourning Dove

Twelve inches long with a light brown-gray body, darker wings, and a black spot at the lower base of each ear patch, the mourning dove's common name refers to the males' sad cooing at dawn, dusk, and during courtship. There are usually two white eggs in each brood, two to four broods per year; males and females both sit on the nest. In some areas, the mourning dove is considered a game bird. It is a permanent resident of the Midwest.

SCIENTIFIC NAME: *Zenaidura macroura*

FOOD SOURCES: fruit and seeds

FEEDERS: perches or trays—set out corn, millet, safflower, thistle, fruit

DRINKING AND BATHING: birdbath

PLACES TO HIDE: low bushes, brush piles, grassy areas

PLACES TO RAISE YOUNG: stick nests built 10 to 25 feet off the ground in evergreens or shrubs

Crow and Jay Family (Corvidae)

Fifteen species of this family live in North America. All are powerful, large birds that eat meat, fruit, grains, and seeds. Some are more colorful than others, but in all the male and female look alike.

Blue Jay

A noisy, big, twelve-inch-long bird with a raucous call that is at the top of the pecking order in the bird world. Distinct blue feathers, blue crest, black necklace, and gray underbelly make both male and female instantly identifiable. Very territorial and aggressive to squirrels and cats, this bird sings its name. Jays build several trial-run nests before settling down in one, and they raise one brood a year from four or five olive eggs with dark brown spots. The female sits on the nest while the male brings food; both parents feed the young. Jays will migrate in huge flocks if food runs low.

SCIENTIFIC NAME: *Cyanocitta cristata*

FOOD SOURCES: nuts; has been known to rob other nests

FEEDERS: hanging or low tray—set out corn, suet, peanuts

DRINKING AND BATHING: birdbaths

PLACES TO HIDE: dense trees, especially oaks

PLACES TO RAISE YOUNG: nests placed 10 to 25 feet off the ground in crotches of conifers or deciduous trees

Crow

Everyone recognizes these large jet-black birds that croon in soft tones and scold in raucous caws. They are good mimics. Crows are about twenty inches long and can weigh over one pound with a wingspan of three feet. They are cautious parents but basically very social birds that will group together after their nestlings are gone. Crows practice "mobbing"—gathering together to chase away predators. They lay four to six green-spotted eggs in a bowl-shaped, stick- and plant-lined nest.

SCIENTIFIC NAME: *Corvus brachyrhynchos*

FOOD SOURCES: seeds, insects, roadkill, garbage; can be nest robbers

FEEDERS: low-tray or hanging—set out seeds and peanuts

DRINKING AND BATHING: birdbath, puddles, and lawn sprinklers

PLACES TO HIDE: open woodlands

PLACES TO RAISE YOUNG: bowl-shaped nests in dense trees

Bunting, Finch, Grosbeak, and Sparrow Family (Fringillidae)

This is a huge family with seventy-two native species and one species, the house sparrow, introduced. These are small to medium perching birds that eat insects and seeds.

American Goldfinch

An instantly recognizable bird that is five inches long with distinct coloring, the summer male is bright yellow with a white underbelly, black tail, and black wings with white wing bars. Females and winter males are dull yellow with no caps. Breeding males have a black cap. Females lay four pale blue eggs and raise one to two broods a year. Also known as the wild canary, this is the state bird of Iowa. Traveling in large flocks, this bird's song is full of short trills, chirps, and twitters.

SCIENTIFIC NAME: *Carduelis tristis*

FOOD SOURCES: insects and seeds; love thistles

FEEDERS: hanging and window—set out sunflower and thistle seed

DRINKING AND BATHING: birdbaths

PLACES TO HIDE: deciduous trees near lawns; weedy patches, and openings around conifers

PLACES TO RAISE YOUNG: nest-cups of grass in upright forks of deciduous trees or large bushes 4 to 14 feet off the ground

Common Redpoll

This is a five-inch-long lively bird with a gray brown-streaked body, white wing bars, a black chin, and bright red splotchy forehead. Males have pink on their breasts, females have white. Three to six light green speckled eggs are laid for one brood per year. Extremely social, the redpoll's song is a mix of twittering and repeated hissing. They summer in the upper Midwest and winter-migrate in great flocks to the lower Midwest.

SCIENTIFIC NAME: *Carduelis flammea*

FOOD SOURCES: tree seeds

FEEDERS: hanging and window—set out sunflower and thistle seed, suet

DRINKING AND BATHING: birdbaths

PLACES TO HIDE: during winter will sleep in snow tunnels, small trees, and bushes

PLACES TO RAISE YOUNG: grass- and feather-lined nests in alder and spruce trees

Dark-Eyed Junco

Juncos are winter visitors to the Midwest and are often called snowbirds by their many fans. They are five to six inches long with slate gray tops and white underbellies, outer tail feathers, and beaks. Males are darker gray. Females are lighter gray. Colors change from area to area. Juncos spend summers in Canada forests and arrive in the Midwest with winter snows. Traveling in groups, members stay in touch with each other by buzzing trills that carry from yard to yard on still winter days. At feeders, groups use a pecking order to establish who gets to eat what when. When mating, males pick a territory and sing to prospective mates from the highest branch of trees. Juncos lay four to five pale blue, brown-spotted eggs and raise two broods per year.

SCIENTIFIC NAME: *Junco hyemalis*

FOOD SOURCES: seeds and insects

FEEDERS: ground and low trays—set out millet, corn, sunflower seed, peanuts

DRINKING AND BATHING: whole groups in a birdbath

PLACES TO HIDE: conifers

PLACES TO RAISE YOUNG: nests are cups of twigs, grass, pine needles built on the ground under tree roots

Dickcissel

Friendly, social small birds that spend summers in our grasslands and winters in Mexico, males are polygamous, mating with many females. This bird says its name when its sings. Females look like house sparrows with yellow cheeks and eye stripes. Males look like small meadowlarks with black bibs and rusty shoulder patches. When they migrate to Mexico and South America, dickcissels mix with sparrows and visit garden feeders. Females lay three to five pale blue eggs per brood; mowing ditches destroys many nests and nestlings.

SCIENTIFIC NAME: *Spiza americana*

FOOD SOURCES: meadow seeds and insects

FEEDERS: hanging and low trays—set out sunflower seed and cracked corn

DRINKING AND BATHING: birdbaths

PLACES TO HIDE: weeds and grasses

PLACES TO RAISE YOUNG: cups of grass in grass clumps on the ground

Finch

Perched on treetops, finches sing bubbly songs of rapid high whistles in paired sequence. Small, perky five- to six-inch birds that travel in groups except during breeding season, when they are territorial, groups of finches can dominate feeders. Both house finches and purple finches are permanent residents of the Midwest.

Male house finches are bright rose red with brown-streaked underbodies and dark wings. Females are brown streaked. House finches are natives of Mexico introduced to North America on Long Island, New York in the 1940s. They have spread and are now one of our most common feeder birds. They are cheerful, clear singers.

Male purple finches are raspberry colored with brown wings; females are brown streaked and lay four to five pale blue eggs with black spots.

MIDWEST SPECIES: House Finch; *Carpodacus mexicanus*
Purple Finch; *Carpodacus purpureus*

FOOD SOURCES: seeds and fruits

FEEDERS: hanging feeder—set out sunflower, safflower, thistle, millet seed; peanuts; suet

DRINKING AND BATHING: birdbaths

PLACES TO HIDE: mixed woods near lawns

PLACES TO RAISE YOUNG: cups of twigs and grass in upper branches of tall trees

Grosbeak

Grosbeaks are plump, slow-moving birds with powerful cone-shaped bills for cracking seeds. Males have seven- to eight-inch-long bodies; females are somewhat smaller. Their early mornings are often spent whistling rapid territorial songs from tall treetops. The females' song often mirrors that of the males. During breeding season grosbeaks spend most of their time in high treetops. They are very social birds that travel and even nest in flocks. Evening grosbeaks and rose-breasted grosbeaks are both familiar in the Midwest.

Evening grosbeak males have yellow bodies, yellow foreheads, gray necks, black caps and tails, and wings with white patches. Females are dusky with white marks on wings and tails. Evening grosbeaks mate and raise young in Canada and winter in the Midwest.

Rose-breasted grosbeak males have white underbellies and red chests with black heads, backs, tails, and wings. Wings are white barred. Females look like large sparrows with gray underbellies. This grosbeak mates and raises young in the Midwest and migrates in winter to the tropics. Females lay three to five pale blue eggs with brown spots for one to two broods per year; males feed fledglings while females incubate a second clutch. These birds often sing on the nests.

MIDWEST SPECIES: Evening Grosbeak; *Hesperiphona vespertina* or *Coccothraustes vespertinus*
Rose-breasted Grosbeak; *Pheucticus ludovicianus*

FOOD SOURCES: insects, fruit, conifer seeds, cherry and apple blossoms

FEEDERS: hanging and post feeders—set out safflower and sunflower seed, fruits, peanuts

DRINKING AND BATHING: birdbaths

PLACES TO HIDE: conifers and deciduous woodlands near grassy lawns

PLACES TO RAISE YOUNG: saucers of loose twigs 5 to 15 feet off the ground in forks of deciduous trees

Indigo Bunting

In summer, indigo bunting males are an unbelievably dark blue with bright black eyes and black markings on wings and tail. These are shy birds just a little bit bigger than goldfinches. Arriving in early summer from the West Indies and Mexico, they establish large territories along streams, lakes, and open woodlands. Males are the last singers of summer, singing from perches in high treetops until fall, when they migrate south. In winter, the males turn a mottled blue-brown. Females are dark brown on top with soft beige-streaked underbellies and black markings on wings and tail. Female indigo buntings lay three to four white eggs in each of two broods each year. Fledglings leave the nest early, and the male parent will continue feeding them until they can take care of themselves while the female builds a second nest for the next brood. Their nests are often parasitized by brown-headed cowbirds.

SCIENTIFIC NAME: *Passerina cyanea*

FOOD SOURCES: grass and weed seeds

FEEDERS: these ground feeders like peanuts, pecans, niger thistle; they tend to visit feeders early before nest-building season

DRINKING AND BATHING: streams and lakes

PLACES TO HIDE: open woodlands, orchards, parks

PLACES TO RAISE YOUNG: shallow nest-cups of leaves, twigs, down, and recycled tissue in shrubs or brush piles

Northern Cardinal

Cardinals love backyards, parks, and farmlands. They are immediately identifiable with their all-red nine-inch-long bodies, black masks, head tufts, and powerful seed-cracking bills. Females are buff-brown with red areas. Females lay three to four gray eggs with spots and raise two to three broods a year. These are very social, nonmigratory, beloved backyard birds. All year-round both males and females sing loud, clear songs that brighten winter days and summer evenings. Cardinals will even answer whistles from people. They are the state bird of Illinois, Indiana, and Ohio.

SCIENTIFIC NAME: *Cardinalis cardinalis*

FOOD SOURCES: berries, sunflower seeds, pinecones, insects

FEEDERS: ground or low tray feeder—set out sunflower and safflower seed, peanuts, corn, fruit; mated pairs are territorial at feeders

DRINKING AND BATHING: birdbaths

PLACES TO HIDE: dense shrubs and thickets near grassy areas

PLACES TO RAISE YOUNG: loose cups of twigs in dense shrubs, small trees, low evergreen conifers, or vines

Pine Siskin

Similar to the goldfinch in appearance, pine siskins are friendly birds that travel in large groups with other finches. They have five-inch-long streaked brown upper bodies, white underbellies, and yellow splotches on wings and tail feathers. Females lay three to four eggs each season. Some pine siskins migrate with the weather and some spend winters in backyards with constant food supplies.

SCIENTIFIC NAME: *Carduelis pinus*

FOOD SOURCES: birches, pines, aspens, insects, weed and flower seeds

FEEDERS: hanging and window—set out thistle and sunflower seed

DRINKING AND BATHING: birdbaths

PLACES TO HIDE: mixed conifer and deciduous woodlands near lawns

PLACES TO RAISE YOUNG: shallow nest-cups of moss, grass, and feathers high up on evergreen branch tips

Rufous-sided Towhee

Also known as the eastern towhee, the male of this migratory species is a handsome, slender, eight-inch-long sparrow with black head, chest, and tail, black wings with white tips, white stomach, and rusty sides. Females share the same coloring but are more brown than black. Males sing their famous song "drink-your-tea" perched on the tips of tall trees. Mated pairs defend large territories. Four to five eggs are laid for each of two broods per year; brown-headed cowbirds tend to parasitize the nests.

SCIENTIFIC NAME: *Pipilo erythrophthalmus*

FOOD SOURCES: seeds and insects that they scratch up with both feet in a hopping motion

FEEDERS: low trays or ground—set out sunflower and thistle seed, millet, fruit, suet

DRINKING AND BATHING: birdbaths

PLACES TO HIDE: thickets and wooded areas

PLACES TO RAISE YOUNG: nests are holes in the ground lined with leaves, bark, pine needles, and grass under shrubs

Sparrow

Sparrows are small, five- to six-inch active birds with musical songs. They come in various shades of brown and beige with different patterns of brown streaks; some are touched by white, others by black, some by yellow, and others by rust. Sparrows usually travel in flocks of mixed types. Males sing in spring to attract mates. Females sing in winter to mark feeding territories and lay three to four pale blue-green eggs with dark spots in each of two broods per year. Those that migrate spend their winters in Central America.

MIDWEST SPECIES: Chipping Sparrow; *Spizella passerina*
Fox Sparrow; *Passerella iliaca*
Song Sparrow; *Melospiza melodia*
Tree Sparrow; *Spizella arborea*
White-crowned Sparrow; *Zonotrichia leucophrys*
White-throated Sparrow; *Zonotrichia albicollis*

FOOD SOURCES: grass and weed seeds, insects, spiders

FEEDERS: hanging or ground—set out sunflower seed, millet, corn

DRINKING AND BATHING: birdbaths

PLACES TO HIDE: conifers and thickets

PLACES TO RAISE YOUNG: nest-cups of grass, moss, and hair in shrubs, vines, or evergreens 1 to 10 feet off the ground

Blackbird, Meadowlark, and Oriole Family (Icteridae)

This family has nineteen native members in North America, including meadowlarks, bobolinks, and orioles. All are small to medium sized with powerful bills. Males tend to be larger and more colorful. They are social birds and can nest in groups.

Oriole

Both northern or Baltimore orioles and orchard orioles build nests and raise families in our suburban areas, migrating to southern Mexico and South America in winter. Males arrive in spring and sing songs of clear whistles and slurs from high treetops to attract mates. Females arrive in a separate group and take their time before choosing a mate. Males are aggressive during mating to both females and other males.

Formerly known as Baltimore orioles, the renamed northern orioles are a natural hybrid between Midwest bullocks and eastern Baltimore orioles. Males are eight inches long with distinctive orange and black bodies and two white wing patches. Females look like off-colored robins with white wing patches.

Orchard orioles are seven inches long. They are friendly, group-loving birds, nesting and living in loose colonies. Males have rusty bodies, black hoods and tails, and wings with white bars. Females are chartreuse with white-barred black wings and lay three to five mottled pale blue eggs in one brood per year. Females incubate the eggs, both parents feed the hatchlings, and the male rears the fledglings by himself. The female removes brown-headed cowbird eggs from the nest.

MIDWEST SPECIES: Northern Oriole; *Icterus galbula*
Orchard Oriole; *Icterus spurius*

FOOD SOURCES: insects and spiders in trees; fruit and seeds

FEEDERS: hanging or window—set out millet, fruit, grape jelly, or sugar water

DRINKING AND BATHING: streams and birdbaths are more attractive to these birds than food

PLACES TO HIDE: thick, deciduous woodlands and fruit orchards

PLACES TO RAISE YOUNG: hanging nests of twigs and grasses woven with string, fishing line, or yarn hanging 15 to 30 feet off the ground in apple, willow, cottonwood, maple, or other deciduous trees

Blackbird

These are our first birds of spring. Males arrive during the last vestiges of winter to sing and color brown marshes, ditches, fields, and wetlands while they lay claim to the best territories for attracting mates. Females arrive a week later and choose between males and sites. Males with large territories can often mate with more than one female. Kissing cousins, both the yellow-headed and red-winged blackbird migrate together and join together to attack common predators that enter nesting areas.

Yellow-headed blackbird males are eight to eleven inches long and black with yellow breasts and heads and black eye masks. Females are smaller and brown with yellow on their chests. They nest in Midwest wetlands and winter migrate to Mexico, only stopping by feeders on migratory routes. Their song is loud and rough.

Red-winged blackbird males are seven to nine inches long and all black with red and yellow shoulder patches. Females are brown streaked. They lay three to four pale blue-green or white eggs with dark speckles in two broods per year. Redwings, with their liquid, loud songs, often form the center of huge migrating groups of mixed blackbirds.

MIDWEST SPECIES: Yellow-headed Blackbird; *Xanthocephalus xanthocephalus*

Red-wingeded Blackbird; *Agelaius phoeniceus*

FOOD SOURCES: grain and insects from fields

FEEDERS: low tray—set out corn, millet, sunflower and safflower seed

DRINKING AND BATHING: natural sources

PLACES TO HIDE: marshes

PLACES TO RAISE YOUNG: 3 to 8 feet off the ground in willow and alder bushes

Mockingbird and Thrasher Family (Mimidae)

This family is composed of birds all native to the Americas. There are ten species in North America, all territorial and most mimics. Catbirds mimic a phrase one time, brown thrashers mimic twice, and mockingbirds repeat a phrase three times.

Brown Thrasher

Beautiful, rusty brown birds with white wing bars that are ten to twelve inches long including their very long tails. Their white breasts are heavily brown streaked and their bodies slender. Males arrive in our area from southern states in early spring just a few days ahead of the females to claim their territory. They are rather shy and sing hidden in treetops as females arrive. Together they choose a spot and build a nest to accommodate three to five pale blue eggs with brown spots.

SCIENTIFIC NAME: *Toxostoma rufum*

FOOD SOURCES: insects, worms, beetles, fruits, berries

FEEDERS: low trays—set out sunflower seeds, peanuts

DRINKING AND BATHING: birdbaths

PLACES TO HIDE: brush piles and thickets

PLACES TO RAISE YOUNG: nest-cups of grass and bark on a twig base

Gray Catbird

These dark gray, slender birds are eight to nine inches long with dark caps, a rusty spot on their rumps, and perky angled tails. Male and females look alike. Coming from Central America, males arrive in spring ahead of the females. Strutting males sing from the tops of shrubs to mark territory. Their songs often sound like a lost kitten mewing. Females lay three to five blue-green eggs in each of two broods per year and incubate the eggs until the nestlings leave; males look after the nestlings while females incubate the second batch. In the fall before migration, gray catbirds seem to sing for the joy of it. These fall songs are mixes of other birds' songs. These friendly birds will respond to people's whistles.

SCIENTIFIC NAME: *Dumetella carolinensis*

FOOD SOURCES: insects in leaves and summer berries

FEEDERS: hanging or low trays; also hummingbird feeders—set out suet, fruit, and peanuts

DRINKING AND BATHING: birdbaths

PLACES TO HIDE: thickets, woodlands

PLACES TO RAISE YOUNG: nest-cups of twigs and fine roots built in low bushes

Mockingbird

Gray birds nine to eleven inches long with white underbellies, white wing bars, and a flitting white-bordered tail, males show off with acrobatic flying feats, moving from high perch to perch, singing as they go. Once they find a garden that they like, mated pairs will aggressively defend their breeding area until the following spring, when the whole ritual begins again. Females lay and incubate three to six blue-green, brown-spotted eggs in each of two broods a year; males take a turn on the nest while their mates go out for food. Mockingbirds are famous mimics, barking like dogs or crowing like roosters. Some mockingbirds will even sing at night. They are often permanent residents in the Midwest.

SCIENTIFIC NAME: *Mimus polyglottos*

FOOD SOURCES: berries, bittersweet, and insects

FEEDERS: hanging or low trays—set out suet, fruit, and peanuts

DRINKING AND BATHING: birdbath

PLACES TO HIDE: woodland edges, conifer shrubs near grassy lawns

PLACES TO RAISE YOUNG: nests in low shrubs

Chickadee and Titmouse
Family (Paridae)

Twelve species are native to North America. These are small perching birds with short bills and wings.

Black-capped Chickadee

These are six-inch-long, small, round birds that are active, curious, and very friendly to people, other birds, and members of their flock. Patterned with black caps and bibs and white cheeks, they are agile and acrobatic; their songs are clear repeated notes. They summer in Canada and winter in our area. Females lay six to eight white eggs with brown spots and raise up to two broods per year.

SCIENTIFIC NAME: *Parus atricapillus*

FOOD SOURCES: pinecones, insects, berries

FEEDERS: ground, tray, hanging—set out sunflower, safflower, and thistle seed, suet, peanuts

DRINKING AND BATHING: birdbaths

PLACES TO HIDE: mixed woodlands, orchards

PLACES TO RAISE YOUNG: nests in old woodpecker holes, in cavities of trees, or in birdhouses 4 to 15 feet off the ground

Tufted Titmouse

Small, tufted, soft gray birds five inches long, with white faces, chests, and underbellies and rusty sides, titmice will mate for life, but will choose another mate if separated by death. In winter, family flocks group together with other small birds to defend huge neighborhood territories. In spring, they break up into smaller territories for nesting. Females lay five to six eggs in each of one to two broods per year; females incubate the eggs while both parents feed the nestlings. Young from the first brood will help feed the later brood. At the feeder, titmice will pick up a seed, fly to a tree, and use their feet to open the seed.

SCIENTIFIC NAME: *Parus bicolor*

FOOD SOURCES: insects, seeds, berries

FEEDERS: hanging; sometimes hummingbird feeders—set out sunflower seed, suet, nuts

DRINKING AND BATHING: birdbath

PLACES TO HIDE: woodlands

PLACES TO RAISE YOUNG: nests in old woodpecker holes

Woodpecker Family (Picidae)

There are twenty species of this family in North America, ranging from very small to very large perching birds with pointed tails, short legs, and claws for clinging. Males and females share the same coloring and marks. All eat insects and tree sap. They also like fruit and nuts, which they will store.

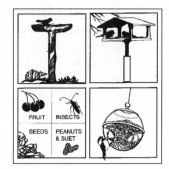

Northern Flicker

At twelve to fourteen inches long, with a soft brown head, black necklace, brown and black barred back, red crescent on the back of the head, white rump, and yellow wing linings, this is a very striking member of the woodpecker family. Also known as the yellow-shafted flicker, females and males look alike except that males have a black mustache. They mate for life and return to the same nesting tree each spring. Females lay five to ten eggs that both parents incubate, with the male taking the night shift. Both males and females will pick up a seed or corn kernel, wedge it in tree bark, and then crack it with their bills. At the end of summer, most flickers gather together in flocks to migrate south.

SCIENTIFIC NAME: *Colaptes auratus*

FOOD SOURCES: insects, fruit, berries, seeds; love ants

FEEDERS: hanging—set out suet, fruit, corn, peanuts

DRINKING AND BATHING: birdbaths

PLACES TO HIDE: open grassy lawn areas surrounded by trees

PLACES TO RAISE YOUNG: flickers gouge nesting holes in rotting trees 6 to 20 feet off the ground

Woodpecker

Only a few of the twenty woodpeckers in North America come to bird feeders and backyards. The best way to tell them apart is by their size. At six to seven inches, the downy woodpecker is the smallest of our woodpeckers. Males and females are mixed black and white with wing bars and short bills. Males have a patch of red on the back of their heads. Hairy woodpeckers look like the downy without the red head patch, but they are larger, at eight to ten inches, and have longer bills.

Red-bellied woodpecker males are eight inches long with full red caps; females have gray heads and red on the nape of the neck. Both have black and white zebra backs and white rumps with a red dusting on the underbelly. They move around according to food availability. Females lay four or five white eggs in each of two or three broods per year; both parents share incubation duties.

197

Woodpeckers make two different sounds with their bills. The first is an irregular pecking to search for food or excavate a nest hole. Rapid drumming is done by both males and females to claim territories and attract mates. If woodpeckers peck your house and remove wood chips, look for insect infestation. If they drum your house, cheer up—they'll stop soon. Woodpeckers are permanent residents of the Midwest.

MIDWEST SPECIES: Downy Woodpecker; *Picoides pubescens*
Hairy Woodpecker; *Picoides villosus*
Red-bellied Woodpecker; *Melanerpes carolinus*

FOOD SOURCES: sap, tree insects, worms, caterpillars, acorns

FEEDERS: hanging—set out suet, corn, peanuts, fruit

DRINKING AND BATHING: birdbath

PLACES TO HIDE: dead trees in dense tree areas

PLACES TO RAISE YOUNG: woodpeckers gouge nesting holes in evergreens 5 to 40 feet off the ground

Nuthatch Family (Sittidae)

There are four nuthatch species in North America. All have small bodies with short necks, short tails, powerful bills, and the ability to run up and down the trunk of a tree, seemingly defying gravity. Songs are flat whistles. Nuthatches will hoard food and migrate in groups when food supplies in an area run low.

The red-breasted nuthatch is a small charmer, very friendly and tame, four to five inches long, with blue-gray body, black cap, black and white eye stripe, and rusty breast and underbelly. Males have darker colors.

The white-breasted nuthatch is an acrobatic little bird five or six inches long, with plump gray body, short tail, white underbelly, black nape and cap, and white face. White-breasted nuthatches fly from feeder to feeder with chickadees in winter. Five to eight white eggs with brown spots are laid for one brood per year.

MIDWEST SPECIES: Red-breasted Nuthatch; *Sitta canadensis*
White-breasted Nuthatch; *Sitta carolinensis*

FOOD SOURCES: pine seeds and insects on bark

FEEDERS: hanging or low trays—set out sunflower seed, suet, peanuts

DRINKING AND BATHING: birdbaths

PLACES TO HIDE: dense woodlands and conifer trees

PLACES TO RAISE YOUNG: nests 10 to 15 feet off the ground in natural tree cavities or birdhouses

Gnatcatcher, Kinglet, and Warbler Family (Sylviidae)

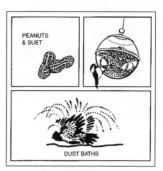

All are very small migrating birds with nervous wing movements and ferocious energy. They feed on insects in woodlands, wetlands, and marshes and tend to be very aggressive. Kinglets are tiny, lively, four-inch-long birds with dull olive uppers, white underbellies, and white wing bars. The golden-crowned kinglet has a tuft of gold feathers on the top of its head. The ruby-crowned kinglet's tuft is bright red. Both male and female kinglets use their feather tufts as embellishments during courtship and to intimidate rivals for their territory. The kinglet's song is high and thin, starting in several fast notes and ending in a series of long whistles. Females lay five to ten white eggs spotted with brown.

MIDWEST SPECIES: Golden-crowned Kinglet; *Regulus satrapa*
Ruby-crowned Kinglet; *Regulus calendula*

FOOD SOURCES: insects on conifers

FEEDERS: hanging, window or low tray—set out suet

DRINKING AND BATHING: dust baths

PLACES TO HIDE: wooded mix of conifers and deciduous trees

PLACES TO RAISE YOUNG: oblong nests suspended from conifer branches

Hummingbird Family (Trochilidae)

Among the tiniest and brightest of birds, fifteen species of hummingbird breed in North America. The hummingbirds' common name comes from the whirring sound its wings make while hovering and flying in every direction—up, down, sideways, and even upside down. They are among our fastest birds and can fly up to sixty miles per hour. These flying jewels quickly learn that red flowers are a consistent source of nectar and will explore any red object that looks promising, including clothing. Hummingbirds sip nectar from tubular flowers with their long tongues, which they draw in and out of a flower about thirteen times per second. Of these tiny wonders, only one is found in our area.

Ruby-throated Hummingbird

These small, charming flyers have long bills, green backs, and white underbellies. Males have a red, iridescent throat. Females are a quieter version, with green backs, white underbellies, and white throats. They lay two pea-sized white eggs in each of one or two broods per year. These small jewels migrate to Mexico in the fall and return in the spring. Very friendly and tame, they enjoy sugar water in special hummingbird feeders. Add one part sugar to four parts water, boil into syrup, and refrigerate; hummingbirds need a huge amount of nectar per day—equivalent to a human drinking twenty gallons of sugar water a day.

SCIENTIFIC NAME: *Archilochus colubris*

FOOD SOURCES: small insects and nectar from red flowers

FEEDERS: hanging and window—set out sugar water

DRINKING AND BATHING: leaf dew

PLACES TO HIDE: trees near grassy lawns

PLACES TO RAISE YOUNG: nests are jumbo thimbles of plant fuzz, spider silk, and lichens attached to small branches of deciduous or evergreen trees 10 to 20 feet above the ground

Bluebird and Thrush Family (Turdidae)

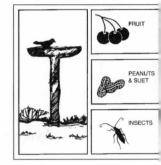

This family consists of small to large perching birds that favor open areas, have fledglings with spotted breasts, and feed on insects and fruit.

American Robin

Robins are the best known songbirds in America and have been chosen the state bird of Michigan and Wisconsin. These familiar birds are gray-brown, nine to eleven inches long, with orange breasts, white throats, long tails, and white-rimmed eyes. Most robins migrate south during the winter months and north during the summer months. All spring and summer their rich, flowing songs of up and down trills fill early mornings and late afternoons. Females lay four "robin's egg blue" eggs in each of two to three broods a year. Robins recognize brown-headed cowbird eggs and will remove them from their nests; fledglings gather with migrating flocks each fall—they're the ones trying to look like they know what they are doing.

SCIENTIFIC NAME: *Turdus migratorius*

FOOD SOURCES: insects and fruit

FEEDERS: low trays—set out fruit and nuts; some robins overwinter in areas where they can eat fruit all winter

DRINKING AND BATHING: love to bathe in water, play in lawn sprinklers, and fluff in dust and mud puddles

PLACES TO HIDE: shrubby areas and trees around grassy lawns

PLACES TO RAISE YOUNG: nesting platforms in the forks of trees 6 to 15 feet off the ground

Eastern Bluebird

Eastern bluebird males have beautiful blue tops, rusty middles, and white underbellies. They are six inches long. Females are duller. Males sing rich and varied songs consisting of a series of mellow warblings. In our area they are year-round residents when food and water are consistent. Females lay four or five pale blue eggs in each of two to three broods per year; young fledglings will help feed the newest brood. Males spend their nights in the nest with their mates and nestlings. Bluebird nesting boxes must have predator baffles to protect nestlings from starlings, sparrows, cats, snakes, raccoons, and chipmunks. This is the state bird of Missouri. Many feel that the bluebird trails established and monitored by midwesterners have saved this wonderful songbird from extinction.

SCIENTIFIC NAME: *Sialia sialis*

FOOD SOURCES: insects and fruits from cherry, chokecherry, dogwood, hackberry, highbush cranberry, grape, holly, inkberry, mountain ash, serviceberry, Virginia creeper, and winterberry

FEEDER: hanging or window—set out peanuts, suet, fruit

DRINKING AND BATHING: whole families will use birdbath

PLACES TO HIDE: large trees around edges of grassy lawns and meadows

PLACES TO RAISE YOUNG: special nesting boxes with 1.5-inch openings or natural tree cavities 4 to 20 feet off the ground

Wood Thrush

Eight-inch-long birds with beautiful rusty backs and white stomachs speckled with brown, wood thrushes overwinter in Panama and summer in the Midwest, where they claim territory, mate, and raise young. At dawn and sunset, the rich flutelike songs of these beautiful little singers fill the air. Females lay three to four eggs; nests are often decorated with white paper streamers collected from household trash.

SCIENTIFIC NAME: *Hylocichla mustelina*

FOOD SOURCES: insects, spiders, worms, berries

FEEDER: low trays—set out nuts and fruit

DRINKING AND BATHING: birdbaths

PLACES TO HIDE: shrubs and thickets

PLACE TO RAISE YOUNG: mud-lined cups of grass and paper 10 feet off the ground in shrubs

Problem Birds

Brown-headed Cowbird; *Molothrus ater*

Medium-sized black birds with brown heads, cowbirds originally followed herds of buffalo across Midwest plains, eating ticks and laying their eggs on the go. But things change. Today these nest parasites remove one egg from another bird's nest, replace it with one of their own, then go off to hang around telephone wires to gossip and mate again. Since their eggs hatch sooner, with larger nestlings, cowbird babies get fed first and resident nestlings starve to death. It is believed that this cowbird behavior is contributing to the decline of songbird populations.

Common Grackle; *Quiscalus quiscula*

These are large blackbirds with yellow eyes. They are very aggressive. Grackles will rob nests and eat anything—other birds, eggs, insects, grain—to satisfy their mineral and nutritional needs during mating and propagation. They live in large groups that migrate south into large colonies. One or two aren't overwhelming in the garden, but when the whole group stops by you know it. People who feed bread and food scraps are always on the grackles' food route.

Starling; *Sturnus vulgaris*

Starlings are eight-inch birds that have beautiful black iridescent feathers and yellow bills. In fall, when they migrate, their bills turn dark and their feathers are speckled. In 1890, a group of one hundred starlings were introduced into New York's Central Park. Their descendants can now be found in Mexico, Canada, Alaska, and all of our lower forty-eight states. While other birds are devastated by habitat loss, the introduced European starling thrives. These days adaptability is everything and starlings are tough, flexible competitors. Fighting in gangs, they are among the bullies of the songbird circuit. They even compete with woodpeckers for nesting sites. If starlings are not protected in your area and are a major pest, you might do as the French do—serve bacon-wrapped roasted starlings for dinner.

House Sparrow; *Passer domesticus*

This nonnative bird is not a sparrow but a finch. Also known as the English sparrow, this aggressive competitor overwhelms native songbirds at feeds and nesting sites, leaving native species without food or shelter. House sparrows compete one-on-one with eastern bluebirds. As bluebird populations decline, house sparrow populations explode. How to help? Monitor bluebird nesting houses to see that the correct bird is using the house and withhold millet and sunflower seeds at the feeder.

What to Plant for Songbirds

The following landscaping shrubs are mainstays of wildlife habitats. Our feathered friends seem to prefer fresh foods to dried seeds. They eat from perennial beds and flower gardens long before they eat seeds from the feeder. Natural landscapes will attract birds to your yard and provide excellent nesting sites.

American Highbush Cranberry

This native has deep green leaves, white flower clusters in late spring, and edible scarlet berries in the fall. It is easy to grow and trouble free.

BOTANICAL NAME: *Viburnum trilobum*

KNOWN TO ATTRACT: 28 species of birds

REQUIRES: average soil, sun to light shade, and room to stretch out

HEIGHT: 8 to 12 feet

WIDTH: 5 to 6 feet

IN BLOOM: May to June

IN FRUIT: September to May

Raspberry

Raspberry bushes form dense, prickly thickets that are excellent sources of food and cover. Everbearing hybrids have one large harvest and several smaller flushes through frost. Standard hybrids have one main crop of berries in July.

BOTANICAL NAME: *Rubus*

KNOWN TO ATTRACT: 97 species of birds

REQUIRES: poor to average soil, full sun, some varieties will spread by underground runners

HEIGHT: 3 to 5 feet

WIDTH: 2 to 3 feet

IN BLOOM: not noticeable

IN FRUIT: July to September

Dogwood

The Latin genus name, *Cornus,* covers a large group of shrub dogwoods with clustered red, blue, or white berries, bunched white flowers, and bright stems for winter color. Of this group, gray dogwood (*Cornus racemosa*) is a Midwest native. It has gray stems, spreads by underground runners, and is an excellent plant for woodland edges.

BOTANICAL NAME: *Cornus*

KNOWN TO ATTRACT: 47 species of birds

REQUIRES: average soil, sun to partial shade

HEIGHT: 5 to 8 feet

WIDTH: 3 to 4 feet across

IN BLOOM: April to June

IN FRUIT: August to February

Elderberry

A group of clump-forming shrubs with cream-colored flat-topped clusters of flowers. The American elder (*Sambucus canadensis*) produces dark berries that are often harvested for pies and wine. Birds love these berries and have been known to become intoxicated if berries ripen and ferment before they can be eaten.

BOTANICAL NAME: *Sambucus*

KNOWN TO ATTRACT: 50 species of birds

REQUIRES: average soil, sun to shade

HEIGHT: 5 to 8 feet

WIDTH: 3 to 4 feet across

IN BLOOM: May to June

IN FRUIT: July to October

Nanking Cherry

This is a beautiful shrub with white and pink flowers and abundant small fruit. Depending upon the hybrid, cherries can be either red or white and make excellent jelly. Birds love Nanking cherries so much that they will fight over them.

BOTANICAL NAME: *Prunus tomentosa*

KNOWN TO ATTRACT: 49 species of birds

REQUIRES: average soil, sun to partial shade

HEIGHT: 6 feet

WIDTH: 3 to 5 feet across

IN BLOOM: May

IN FRUIT: July

Here is a listing of other plants that provide food or cover for birds in Midwest gardens.

Trees

Alder (*Alnus*)

Conifers (*various*)

Crabapple (*Malus*)

Hackberry (*Celtis*)

Hawthorn (*Crataegus*)

Hickory (*Carya*)

Kentucky Coffee Tree (*Gymnocladus*)

Mountain Ash (*Sorbus*)

Mulberry (*Morus*)

Oak (*Quercus*)

Serviceberry (*Amelanchier*)

Sumac (*Rhus*)

Wild Plum (*Prunus*)

Shrubs

Barberry (*Berberis*)

Conifers (*various*)

Lilac (*Syringa*)

Ninebark (*Physocarpus*)

Viburnum (*Viburnum*)

Vines

Grape (*Vitis*)

Virginia Creeper (*Parthenocissus*)

Flowers

Aster (*Aster*)

Black-Eyed Susan (*Rudbeckia*)

Coneflower (*Echinacea*)

Sedum (*Sedum*)

Sunflower (*Helianthus*)

Iowa Songbird and Wildlife Habitat Packages

The Iowa State Forest Nursery offers landowners low-cost packets of tree and shrub seedlings for establishing garden habitats in Iowa. Songbird and wildlife packets contain groups of native plants priced very reasonably, often at the price of one larger shrub at a commercial nursery. For more information, call 1-800-865-2477 or 1-515-233-1161. Check with your state's department of natural resources to find out if these special packages are available in your state.

Foods for Feeders

Studies have shown that birds must eat vast amounts of high-energy food. In summer, they can go almost two days without food. In winter, they need food twice a day. During short winter days, they must eat about fifty percent of their body weight just to keep warm. That is equivalent to a 150-pound person eating seventy-five pounds of food per day.

Birds seem to establish a feeding route that they follow from food source to food source. It takes about two weeks for birds to discover that a new restaurant in the neighborhood is offering food and water.

To attract the most birds, place some feeders close to the house and some farther away. Try low tray feeders with a roof, hanging feeders, and feeders that stick by suction cups to your viewing windows.

Once a month all feeders should be washed in a mild dish soap and weak bleach solution and allowed to air-dry before being refilled. If you have problems with aggressive birds like house sparrows and starlings, remove the food sources or foods that attract them.

Seeds

During fall and winter, the majority of garden birds will be attracted to feeders. Food offered at various levels will attract different birds. Purchase only the birdseed that your favorite birds will eat. Birds toss aside unwanted seeds in mixes, which attract rabbits, raccoons, and squirrels. There is also the danger that unwanted seeds under the feeder will spread disease when mixed with bird droppings. Most feed stores, nurseries, and garden centers sell seed separately by the pound so that you can make your own mixes.

Special Feeding Note

If you have a past history of rodents in your area, use only hulled sunflower seeds. Spent shells dropped under feeders can attract mice, squirrels, and even rats. If squirrels are a problem, consider switching to shelled safflower seeds. In our yard, squirrels don't seem to like safflower.

Peanut Butter–Suet Cookies

Making suet cookies is fun. It's a little bit like making an annual batch of Christmas cookies. Here's a basic formula that is popular in hanging suet feeders. If you feed this all year, you may see parents teaching their young fledglings how to eat suet.

Suet Cookies

1 cup vegetable shortening

1 cup peanut butter

2 tablespoons corn oil

1/2 cup whole wheat and/or soy flour

1/2 cup crushed eggshells

Cornmeal to firm up mixture

Optional (add according to bird preference any or all): cracked corn; shelled peanuts, walnuts, pecans, sunflower seeds; cranberries; raisins; mountain ash berries; rolled oats

Once everything is mixed together, form into individual patties, wrap each in waxed paper, and freeze group in a large plastic baggie.

Remember Grit

Birds have no teeth to chew so they eat sand or gravel—grit—to help grind up their food. In the winter, snow covers grit sources, forcing birds to hunt along roadsides, where they are often hit by cars.

Providing grit to the feeder area will guarantee guests of all types. Commercial fine chicken grit or ground oyster shells are available from feed stores for less than five dollars for a fifty-pound bag. An added benefit, grit is wonderful for spring-flowering bulbs—its sharp edges incorporated into the soil deter moles and squirrels.

Water—the Key to Attracting Birds

Water. You have it, they need it. Water attracts more birds than anything else you can do. Birdbaths need to be shallow and clean. Since birds are not potty-trained, they will forget themselves and dirty the water. Hose out the birdbath daily, and wash weekly with dish soap and a mild solution of liquid chlorine bleach. In the winter, use an Underwriters Laboratory-approved electric heater connect to a GFIC (ground-fault interrupt circuit) outdoor socket to keep water open. Contrary to some reports, glycerin and antifreeze will kill birds and pets.

Housing and Nesting Supplies

Bird boxes, nests, and houses can be fancy or simple. Birdhouses seem to please people more than birds, although twenty-four varieties of birds will consider human-inspired housing. Order a set of the inexpensive booklets mentioned below to find out what to do and what not to do when building or buying birdhouses. Your local Department of Natural Resources (DNR) also has free or low-cost pamphlets about bird housing. To help with home furnishings, a basketful of twine pieces, fabric, hair, and feathers can be placed next to birdfeeders.

Predators

In addition to natural predators—raccoons, snakes, hawks, owls, fox, cats, starlings, sparrows—a 1990 study of cats and wildlife revealed that free-roaming cats kill over seventy-eight million small mammals and birds annually. Responsible pet owners should keep their cats leashed or in the house and away from birdbaths, nests, and feeder areas. If there are no cats in your neighborhood and you notice a pile of feathers, look for hungry hawks, owls, or eagles. These natural predators are also protected by federal law. They are part of the natural food chain and it is illegal to poison or trap them.

Window Warriors

Each spring too many migrating birds fly full-speed into windows and are injured or killed. Silhouettes, balloons, and other gimmicks are not effective. To help, experiment by moving your feeders further away from the windows or closer to the windows. This will give migrating birds room to maneuver and gain speed away from reflective surfaces. If and when a bird does hit your window, gently place the bird into a sheltered outside location to allow it time to recoup. Keep pets inside while the bird is recovering.

Anting, Mothballing, and Flowering

Many birds pick up ants, beetles, mothballs, flowers, and even coffee grounds to rub over their bodies. It is thought that their strong odors help repel parasites and pests.

Bird Groups and Associations

Midwest Working Group on Neotropical Migrating Birds
Nongame Bird Coordinator
U.S. Fish and Wildlife Service
Federal Building, 1 Federal Drive
Fort Snelling, MN 55111-4056

Write to learn more about neotropical migrating birds and conservation groups.

Migratory Songbirds
National Fish and Wildlife Foundation
1120 Connecticut Avenue, NW
Suite 900
Washington, DC 20036

Over two hundred species of birds migrate to winter homes in Mexico, Central and South America, and the Caribbean. They fly south by the millions and return each spring to breeding areas in the Midwest. This organization offers a free *Partners in Flight* newsletter about neotropical migrating bird conservation activities.

National Audubon Society
Membership Data Center
PO Box 51001
Boulder, CO 80322-1001

An introductory $20 annual membership includes 6 issues of their award-winning magazine, *Audubon;* membership in a local chapter; and many other membership benefits.

National Wildlife Federation Backyard Wildlife Habitat Program
PO Box 50281
Hampden Station
Baltimore, MD 21211

The National Wildlife Federation provides information on how to plant for wildlife, guides to attracting birds, and a journal for keeping notes. Informational and registration packets are $12.95 plus tax. Registration is $15. Over twenty thousand American backyards have qualified for certification under this program. The purpose of the program is to counteract the habitat destruction of suburban and urban development.

U.S. Consumer Information Center, 7C
PO Box 100
Pueblo, CO 81002

This organization will send you a free booklet from the Department of the Interior U.S. Fish and Wildlife Service called *Backyard Bird Problems* (576D), and for fifty cents, they'll include three booklets on how to attract, feed, and house different birds, packaged together as *For the Birds* (362D). Also ask for *National Wildlife Refuges: A Visitor's Guide* (132D, $1.25).

National Wildlife Refuges

In 1903, President Theodore Roosevelt issued an executive order to protect the egrets, herons, and other birds on Florida's Pelican Island. Before he left office in 1909, he created fifty-two additional refuges. In 1929, Congress passed the Migratory Bird Conservation Act, which created migratory bird refuges. Today there are over four hundred refuges on millions of acres in the United States. For a listing of refuges located in the Midwest, please see Section Six.

Lists and Other Resources

The Weather and Your Garden

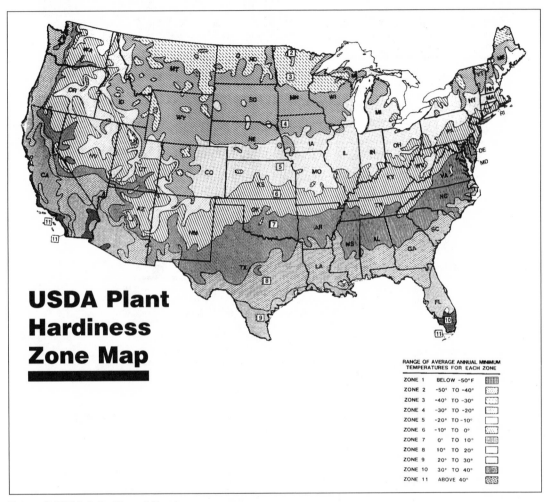

USDA Plant Hardiness Zone Map

RANGE OF AVERAGE ANNUAL MINIMUM TEMPERATURES FOR EACH ZONE

ZONE 1	BELOW −50°F	
ZONE 2	−50° TO −40°	
ZONE 3	−40° TO −30°	
ZONE 4	−30° TO −20°	
ZONE 5	−20° TO −10°	
ZONE 6	−10° TO 0°	
ZONE 7	0° TO 10°	
ZONE 8	10° TO 20°	
ZONE 9	20° TO 30°	
ZONE 10	30° TO 40°	
ZONE 11	ABOVE 40°	

Photo credit: USDA Agricultural Research Magazine

Hardiness in the Midwest

Hardiness is determined by a plant's resistance to freezing. Soil conditions can be an important factor. Soils with clay, which retain water, and sandy soils, which do not hold water at all, will influence survival at extreme temperatures. Hardiness is different in every garden, depending on local conditions and the gardener.

AVERAGE LAST SPRING FROSTS AND FIRST AUTUMN FROSTS BY REGION

Illinois

Chicago	190 days	4–10/10–26
Peoria	196 days	4–08/11–03
Springfield	201 days	4–04/10–29

Indiana

Evansville	213 days	3–25/11–09
Fort Wayne	189 days	4–12/10–29
Indianapolis	199 days	4–07/11–03

Iowa

Des Moines	191 days	4–06/10–28
Sioux City	183 days	4–10/10–22

Kansas

Topeka	195 days	4–09/10–27
Wichita	219 days	3–31/11–10

Michigan

Detroit	187 days	4–15/10–29
Grand Rapids	172 days	4–26/10–19
Marquette	125 days	5–22/10–03

Minnesota

Duluth	144 days	5–10/10–05
Minneapolis	175 days	4–19/10–19
St. Paul	182 days	4–13/10–26

Missouri

Kansas City	218 days	3–29/11–09
St. Louis	215 days	3–25/11–07
Springfield	204 days	4–03/11–07

Nebraska

North Platte	152 days	4–25/10–05
Omaha	190 days	4–08/10–23

North Dakota

Bismark	136 days	5–11/9–24
Fargo	137 days	5–13/9–27

Ohio

Cincinnati	203 days	4–05/11–04
Cleveland	189 days	4–19/11–07
Columbus	190 days	4–13/11–04

Pennsylvania, western

Pittsburgh	187 days	4–20/10–23

South Dakota

Rapid City	150	5–07/10–04
Sioux Falls	152	5–05/10–03

Wisconsin

Green Bay	165 days	4–26/10–16
La Crosse	186 days	4–10/10–26
Milwaukee	192 days	4–13/11–01

The above numbers have been collected at regional airport weather stations by the Midwestern Climate Center. When using this chart, remember that houses, bodies of water, rainfall, and trees will all affect air temperature. An Indian summer can extend the growing season by weeks, allowing that perfect mum to bloom on and on. An early killing frost can bring the season to a sudden halt.

Parts of the same garden will have different microclimates. A north-sloping garden will have warmer temperatures at the top of the slope than at the bottom. A south-sloping garden will have warmer temperatures and a longer growing season. The heat from the south side of a brick house can easily add three weeks to the growing season. A raised bed with a plastic cover added as a temporary greenhouse can add two weeks.

Taking all these variances into consideration, gardeners in areas with less than 180 days' growing time should consider starting seeds indoors or outside in cold frames six weeks before the last spring frost date, or plan to purchase seedlings.

Gardeners in areas with more 180 days' growing time can safely direct-sow seeds as soon as the correct soil temperature is reached. A sheet of black plastic will help warm the soil and temporary floating row covers can be used in cold snaps.

If a late spring frost does get to seedlings, sprinkling lukewarm water over the leaves before the sun shines directly on them will offset permanent damage. Tulips, iris, peonies, daffodils, bluebells, crocus, and other spring bloomers all seem to have a natural antifreeze built into their systems. Flower petals may be ruined by frosts, but early-season plants will not be damaged by cold snaps.

Gardening by the Moon

We have all seen books at the checkout counter of our favorite nurseries proclaiming the virtues of planting by phases of the moon. Many of us even know gardeners who attribute their success to moon gardening.

There is enough truth in moon–gardening folklore that scientists have been studying the moon's effect on plants. At the USDA-Agricultural Research Service National Soil Tilth Laboratory in Ames, Iowa, studies have shown that farmers who till their soil on moonless nights have less weed-seed germination in their fields than others. At other universities, researchers have found that the gravitational pull of the moon affects not only ocean tides, but all water on the earth, including the dew that surrounds seedlings. On another campus, researchers charting the electrodynamic fields, or life fields, in trees found cycles that related to moon activity. Who knows what these researchers will find out about the moon and its influence on your garden?

Moon gardening—fact or fiction? If you would like to find out for yourself, here are some general guidelines for gardening by the moon:

The Decreasing Moon

The period from the full moon through the last quarter is said to be the best for weeding, cultivating, harvesting, and planting anything that bears its crop below the ground.

The New Moon

Pruning and propagation is said to be best done when the moon is just starting to grow. Late evenings during the dark of the new moon are the best time to turn over the soil.

The Increasing Moon

The first quarter though the full moon as the light grows is said to be the best time to transplant and to plant anything that bears its crop above the ground.

The Full Moon

This is the time to enjoy night-blooming flowers and to sow seeds that need light to germinate.

What's in a Name?
Gardener's Latin

In ordinary language, the word "flower" identifies the brightest part of the plant. In biology, flower is the term used to describe a plant's reproductive parts.

Although many flowers are recognized nationally by their common names, many other such names vary from region to region. There are currently four different plant types labeled "bluebell" for sale in popular plant catalogs. Only the difference in botanical names gives a clue as to which bluebell will work in your garden.

People who love plants have classified them in many ways. In A.D. 50 a Roman scholar known as Pliny the Elder set up a system using size and form to group plants into three major categories—herbs, shrubs, and trees. Practical naturalists of the Middle Ages divided plants once more into groups of medicinal, poisonous, or edible.

Swedish botanist Carl von Linné (1707–1778), creator of modern botanical labeling, tried to improve upon previous systems by classifying plants into general biological families. These families were divided into major subdivisions of plants with closely related sexual parts. Latin, the universal language of science, was selected to formalize plant identification. Von Linné, who Latinized his own name to Carolus Linnaeus, categorized over 7,000 plants and assigned each plant two names. These names and the labels he used—genus, species, variety—are still used today in nurseries, in garden books, and even on seed packets.

Genus, the first name of each plant, describes major plant subdivisions and is always capitalized. Each genus is divided into species, smaller groups of closely related plants that reproduce naturally from seed with minimal variation. Species names are always lowercase and either describe the plant's flowers and leaves, are taken from a person's name, or signify where the plant was discovered.

A third set of words is sometimes attached after the genus and species. These words specify either variety, plants that share an identifying characteristic occurring naturally, or hybrid, plants with specific traits engineered by growers or geneticists. A strain is a group of plants that differs in a minor way, such as in color, from the majority of its species. Seeds of strains and hybrids will not reproduce their parent plant. A cultivar, or "cultivated variety," is a variety whose identifying characteristics arose under cultivation and whose seeds will reproduce the parent plant. Cultivar names appear in English after the Latin botanical names and are usually put in single quotation marks: *Rudbeckia fulgida* 'Goldsturm'.

While botanical names are difficult to pronounce and sometimes make people's eyes glaze over, they are useful tools when planning gardens.

Some Species Names to Look For

Latin clues to plant colors, characteristics, and origin are often found in the second part of a botanical name. Botanical names have Latin gender endings—masculine, feminine, and neuter. The masculine ending is "us," the feminine is "a," and neuter is denoted by "um." While the last few letters of a name will change according to gender, the meaning of the words stays the same. Here are some of the Latin words you will find in the profiles in this book.

Explaining characteristics

acaulis   stemless

acuminata, acuminatus   pointed

angustifolius   sharp-leaved

aquila, aquilinus   eaglelike

barbatus   bearded

blanda, blandus   pleasant

botryoides   grapelike

calycinum, calycinus, calycosus   with a calyx

campanulatus   like a little bell

canalicula, canaliculatum   grooved

comosus, comosum   tufted

cordata, cordatus   heart-shaped

coronaria, coronatus   crowned

crista, cristatus   crested

dentata, dentosus   toothed

didyma, didymus   in pairs

dipterocarpus, dipterocarpum   two-winged

ensifolia, ensifolius   sword-leaved

floreplena   with a double flower

foetidissima, foetidissimus   stinking

folia, folius   a leaf

fulgida, fulgidus   shining

grandifloria, grandiflorus   large-flowered

grandifolia, grandifolius   large-leaved

helianthoides   sunflowerlike

involucrata, involucratus   with flower bracts

laenis   smooth

laetus   bright

laevis   smooth

lancifolium, lancifolius   lance-leaved

latifolius, latifolium   broad-leaved

linifolius, linifolia   flax-leaved

macrophylla, macrophyllus   large-leaved

maculata, maculatus   spotted

margaritus   pearly

matronalis   matronly

maximus, maximum   largest

media, medius   intermediate

meleagris   spotted

minor, minus   smaller

mollis   with flexible hairs

moscheutos, moschatus   musky

multiflorus   many-flowered

nummularius, nummularium   like a coin

ocymoides   like basil

odoratus, odoratum   fragrant

officinalis   medicinal

paniculata, paniculatus   in bunched clusters

patens   spreading

pedatus, pedatum   bird-footed

perenne, perennis   perennial

persicifolia   like a peach leaf

plantaginea, plantagineus   plantain

plenus   full

plumosus   feathery

podagraria   gouty (swollen)

poeticus   pertaining to poets

procumbens   prostrate

pulmo   a lung

pumila, pumilus   dwarf

punctata, punctatus   dotted

quinquefolia, quinquefolius   five-leaved

radicans rooting

recta, rectus erect

reptans, repens creeping

reticulata, reticulatus netted

rotundifolia, rotundifolius round-leaved

rugosa, rugosus wrinkled

saccharata, saccharum sugary

saponarius soapy

scorpioides scorpion-tailed

sempervirens evergreen

sensibilis sensitive

septemfida, septemfidus seven

serpyllum, serpyllifolius thymelike

simplex simple

speciosus, speciosum showy

spectabilis spectacular

squamigera, squamatus with small scales

sublata, sublatus sharp, pointed

superba, superbus, superbum superb

terminalis at the end (of a twig, etc.)

ternata in threes

tetragona four-sided

tinctoria, tinctorius for dyes

tomentosus downy

tuberosa, tuberosus tuberous

tulipa a turban

umbellatum, umbellatus umbrella-like

uvaria bearing grapes

varia variable

vitis grapevine

vulgaris usual, ordinary

Explaining origin

aestivus, aestivum of summer

alpina, alpinus, alpinum of the mountains

americana, americanus of America

ancyrensis of Ankara, Turkey

autumnale, autumnalis of autumn

byzantina of Byzantium

canadensis of Canada

carolina of Carolina

carpatica, carpaticus of the Carpathians

caucasica, caucasicus of the Caucasus

chalcedonica, chalcedonicus of Chalcedon

chinensis of China

dalmaticus, dalmaticum of Dalmatia

europaeus, europaeum of Europe

germanica, germanicus of Germany

hispanicus of Spain

hyemalis of winter

idaea of Mt. Ida

indica, indicus of India

japonica, japonicus of Japan

majalis of May

maritima, maritimus of the sea

montana, montanus of the mountains

neapolitanus, neapolitanum of Naples, Italy

nivalis of the snow

novi-angliae of New England

novi-belgii of New York

orientalis of the East

palustris of bogs

ritro of Eurasia

saxatilis of the rocks

sibirica, sibiricus of Siberia

sinensis of China

vernus, vernalis of spring

virginica, virginianus of Virginia

Explaining colors of leaves and flowers

amethystinum, amethystinus violet

azureus sky blue

caerulea, caeruleus deep blue

candidus, candidum white

cardinalis red

chrysos gold

coccineus scarlet

incana, incanus light gray

lacteus milk white

leukos white

nigra, niger black

plumbaginoides lead blue

purpureus purple

rubens, rubra red

sanguinea, sanguineus blood red

Latin names close to home

illinoensis	of Illinois	*michiganensis*	of Michigan
ioensis	of Iowa	*missouriensis*	of Missouri
mentorensis	of Mentor, Ohio		

Cross–Referenced Listing of Scientific and Common Names in This Book

Plants by Botanical Name

A	A
Abies	Fir
Acer	Maple
Acer griseum	Paperback Maple
Acer rubrum	Red Maple
Acer saccharum	Sugar Maple
Achillea	Yarrow
Actinidia kolomikta	Hardy Kiwi
Adiantum pedatum	Maidenhair Fern
Aegopodium podagraria	Goutweed
Aesculus parviflora	Bottlebrush Buckeye
Agastache	Anise Hyssop
Ajuga reptans	Carpet Bugle
Alcea	Hollyhock
Allium	Allium
Allium schoenoprasum	Chives
Allium tuberosum	Garlic Chives
Alnus	Alder
Amelanchier	Serviceberry
Amorpha canescens	Leadplant
Ampelopsis	Pepper Vine
Andropogon gerardi	Big Bluestem
Andropogon scoparius	Little Bluestem
Andropogon ternarius	Splitbeard Bluestem
Anemone patens	Pasque Flower

Anethum graveolens	Dill
Anthriscus cerefolium	Chervil
Apium graveolens	Celery
Aquilegia	Columbine
Arabis	Rock Cress
Arctostaphylos	Kinnikinick
Arctostaphylos uva-ursi	Bearberry
Arenaria montana	Sandwort
Aristolochia durior	Dutchman's Pipe
Artemisia	Wormwood
Artemisia dracunculus	Tarragon
Artemisia schmidtiana	Silver Mound
Asarum	Wild Ginger
Asclepias	Milkweed
Asclepias tuberosa	Butterfly Weed
Asperula	Sweet Woodruff
Aster	Aster
Aster novae-angliae	New England Aster
Astilbe	Perennial Spirea
Athyrium goeringianum	Japanese Painted Fern
Aubrieta	Purple Rock Cress
Aurinia saxatilis	Basket of Gold

B

Baptisia	Indigo; Wild Indigo
Berberis	Barberry
Berberis thunbergii	Japanese Barberry
Bergenia	Heartleaf
Betula nigra	River Birch
Borago officinalis	Borage
Bouteloua curtipendula	Blue Grama
Bouteloua gracilis	Buffalo Grass
Buchloe dactyloides	Sideoats Grama

C

Calendula officinalis	Calendula
Camassia scilloides	Camass
Campanula	Bluebell
Campanula carpatica	Bellflower
Campsis	Trumpet Vine
Carpinus caroliniana	American Hornbeam

Carum carvi	Caraway
Carya	Hickory
Castilleja coccinea	Indian Paintbrush
Ceanothus americanus	New Jersey Tea
Celastrus	Bittersweet
Celtis	Hackberry
Centaurea cyanus	Bachelor's Button
Cerastium tomentosum	Snow in Summer
Ceratostigma	Plumbago
Chamaecyparis	False Cypress
Chelone glabra	Turtlehead
Chrysanthemum	Chrysanthemum; Mum
Chrysanthemum maximum	May Daisy
Cichorium intybus	Chicory
Cimicifuga	Fairy Candle
Cladrastis kentukea	Yellowwood
Clematis	Clematis
Clematis recta	Ground Clematis
Cobaea	Mountain Glory
Convallaria majalis	Lily of the Valley
Coreopsis	Coreopis; Tickseed
Coreopsis verticillata	Golden Daisy
Coriandrum sativum	Cilantro; Coriander
Cornus	Dogwood
Cornus alba	Dogwood
Cornus alternifolia	Pagoda Dogwood
Cornus canadensis	Bunchberry
Coronilla varia	Crown Vetch
Cosmos	Cosmos
Cotinus coggygria	Smokebush
Crataegus	Hawthorn
Crataegus crus-galli	Thornless Hawthorn
Crocus	Crocus

D | **D**
Daucus	Queen Anne's Lace
Delphinium	Rocket Larkspur
Dianthus	Pink
Dodekatheon meadia	Shooting Star
Dolichos	Hyacinth Bean
Duchesnea indica	Mock Strawberry

E

Echinacea	Coneflower
Echinops	Globe Thistle
Epimedium alpina	Barrenwort
Erigeron	Fleabane
Eryngium	Sea Holly
Eryngium yuccifolium	Rattlesnake Master
Erythronium mesochoreum	Dog-tooth Violet
Euonymus	Burning Bush
Euonymus fortunei	Wintercreeper
Eupatorium	Joe-Pye Weed
Euphorbia corollata	Flowering Spurge

F

Festuca	Blue Fescue
Festuca rubra	Red Fescue
Foeniculum vulgare	Fennel
Fothergilla major	Large Fothergilla
Fragaria	Strawberry
Fragaria virginiana	Wild Strawberry
Fraxinus	Ash

G

Gaillardia	Blanket Flower; Gaillardia
Gaultheria procumbens	Wintergreen
Gentiana puberulenta	Downy Gentian
Geranium	Cranesbill
Geum triflorum	Prairie Smoke
Ginkgo biloba	Ginkgo; Maidenhair Tree
Gymnocladus dioicus	Kentucky Coffee Tree
Gypsophila	Baby's Breath

H

Hamamelis	Witch Hazel
Hedera helix	Ivy
Helenium	Helen's Flower
Helianthus	Sunflower
Hemerocallis	Daylily
Hesperis matronalis	Dame's Rocket
Heuchera	Coral Bell
Heuchera micrantha	Purple-leaf Coral Bell
Hibiscus	Rose Mallow

Hosta	Hosta
Hydrangea anomala	Climbing Hydrangea
Hydrangea macrophylla	Hydrangea
Hydrangea paniculata	Hydrangea Tree
Hypericum calycinum	Rose of Sharon
Hypoxis hirsuta	Yellow-star Grass

I

Iberis sempervirens	Candytuft
Ilex	Holly
Ilex glabra	Inkberry
Ilex verticillata	Winterberry
Ipomoea	Cardinal Climber; Moonflower; Morning Glory
Iris ensata	Oriental Iris
Iris germanica	German Iris
Iris kaempferi	Japanese Iris
Iris sibirica	Siberian Iris

J

Juniperus	Juniper

K

Kalmia	Mountain Laurel
Kolkwitzia amabilis	Beautybush

L

Lamiastrum galeobdolon	Yellow Archangel
Lamium maculatum	Spotted Dead Nettle
Larix	Larch
Lathyrus	Everlasting Pea
Leguminosae	Sweet Pea
Liatris	Blazing Star; Gayfeather; Liatris
Lilium	Lily
Lilium longiflorum	Easter Lily
Limonium	Statice
Linaria	Wild Snapdragon
Linum lewisii	Blue Flax
Linum rubrum	Scarlet Flax
Lolium perenne	Perennial Ryegrass
Lonicera	Honeysuckle
Luffa acutangula	Luffa
Lupinus	Lupine

M

Magnolia x *loebneri*	Magnolia
Malus	Apple; Crabapple
Matteuccia pensylvanica	Fiddlehead Fern
Matteuccia struthiopteris	Fiddlehead Fern
Mentha	Mint
Monarda	Bee Balm
Morus	Mulberry
Myrica pensylvanica	Bayberry

N

Narcissus	Daffodil
Narcissus jonquilla	Jonquil
Nepeta	Catmint

O

Ocimum basilicum	Basil
Oenothera	Evening Primrose; Sundrop
Origanum majorana	Marjoram
Origanum vulgare	Oregano
Oxalis violacea	Sheep Sorrel

P

Pachysandra terminalis	Japanese Spurge
Paeonia	Peony
Paeonia lactiflora	Peony
Panicum virgatum	Switchgrass
Papaver rhoeas	Corn Poppy
Parthenocissus	Boston Ivy; Virginia Creeper
Pedicularis canadensis	Wood Betony
Penstemon digitalis	Beard Tongue
Perovskia atriplicifolia	Russian Sage
Petalostemum	Prairie Clover
Petroselinum crispum	Parsley
Phellodendron amurense	Corktree
Phlox	Creeping Phlox; Phlox
Phlox divericata	Woodland Phlox
Phlox pilosa	Western Phlox
Physocarpus	Ninebark
Physostegia	Obedient Plant
Picea	Spruce
Pimpinella ansium	Anise

Pinus	Pine
Poa pratensis	Kentucky Bluegrass
Polygonum	Fleeceflower
Polygonum aubertii	Silver Lace Vine
Populus	Aspen; Cottonwood; Poplar
Populus tremula	Quaking Aspen
Potentilla	Cinquefoil
Potentilla fruticosa	Potentilla; Cinquefoil
Prunella grandiflora	Self-heal
Prunella vulgaris	Heal-all
Prunus	Cherry; Wild Plum
Prunus x *cistena*	Sand Cherry
Prunus tomentosa	Nanking Cherry
Prunus virginiana	Canadian Cherry

Q

Quercus	Oak
Quercus bicolor	Swamp White Oak
Quercus macrocarpa	Bur Oak
Quercus palustris	Pin Oak
Quercus rubra	Red Oak

R

Ratibida	Mexican Hat
Rheum	Rhubarb
Rhododendron	Azalea; Rhododendron
Rhus	Sumac
Ribes	Currant; Gooseberry; Jostaberry
Rosa	Climbing Rose; Rose; Shrub Rose
Rosmarinus officinalis	Rosemary
Rubus	Raspberry
Rudbeckia	Black-eyed Susan

S

Sagina subulata	Pearlwort
Salix	Willow
Salvia	Sage; Summer Sage
Salvia officinalis	Sage
Sambucus	Elderberry
Saponaria ocymoides	Rock Soapwort
Satureja hortensis	Savory
Scabiosa	Pincushion Flower

Sedum	Low Stonecrop; Stonecrop
Sempervivum	Hen and Chickens
Silene armeria	Catchfly
Silphium integrifolium	Rosinweed
Silphium laciniatum	Compass Plant
Silphium terebinthinaceum	Prairie Dock
Sisyrinchium campestre	Blue-eyed Grass
Solanaceae	Petunia
Solidago	Goldenrod
Solidago gigantea	Late Goldenrod
Sorbusaucuparia	Mountain Ash
Sorghastrum nutans	Indian Grass
Sporobolus heterolepis	Prairie Dropseed
Syringa	Lilac
Syringa reticulata	Japanese Lilac Tree

T

Tagetes	Marigold
Tagetes signata pumila	Marigold
Taxus	Yew
Thuja occidentalis	Arbor Vitae
Thunbergia	Black-eyed Susan
Thymus serpyllum	Creeping Thyme
Thymus vulgaris	Thyme
Tiarella cordifolia	Foamflower
Tilia	Basswood
Tripsacum dactyloides	Eastern Gama
Tropaeolum canariense	Canary-bird
Tropaeolum majus	Nasturtium
Tsuga canadensis	Hemlock
Tulipa	Tulip

U

Ulmus	Elm

V

Vaccinium	Blueberry
Vaccinium macrocarpon	Cranberry
Vaccinium vitis-idaea	Cowberry
Vernonia	Ironweed
Veronica	Speedwell; Summer Speedwell
Veronica incana	Speedwell

Veronicastrum virginicum	Culver's Root
Viburnum	Viburnum
Viburnum trilobum	American Highbush Cranberry
Vinca minor	Periwinkle
Viola	Violet
Viola pedata	Bird's-foot Violet
Viola tricolor	Johnny-jump-up
Vitis	Grape
W	**W**
Waldsteinia ternata	Barren Strawberry
Weigela	Weigela
Wisteria floribunda	Japanese Wisteria
Z	**Z**
Zinnia	Zinnia

Birds by Scientific Name

A

| *Agelaius phoeniceus* | Red-winged Blackbird |
| *Archilochus colubris* | Ruby-throated Hummingbird |

B

| *Bombycilla cedrorum* | Cedar Waxwing |
| Bombycillidae | Waxwing Family |

C

Cardinalis cardinalis	Northern Cardinal
Carduelis flammea	Common Redpoll
Carduelis pinus	Pine Siskin
Carduelis tristis	American Goldfinch
Carpodacus mexicanus	House Finch
Carpodacus purpureus	Purple Finch
Coccothraustes vespertinus	Evening Grosbeak
Colaptes auratus	Northern Flicker
Columbidae	Pigeon Family
Corvidae	Crow and Jay Family
Corvus brachyrhynchos	Crow
Cyanocitta cristata	Blue Jay

D

| *Dumetella carolinensis* | Catbird; Gray Catbird |

F

| Fringillidae | Bunting, Finch, Grosbeak, and Sparrow Family |

H

| *Hesperiphona vespertina* | Evening Grosbeak |
| *Hylocichla mustelina* | Wood Thrush |

I

Icteridae	Blackbird, Meadowlark, and Oriole Family
Icterus galbula	Baltimore Oriole; Northern Oriole
Icterus spurius	Orchard Oriole

J

| *Junco hyemalis* | Dark-eyed Junco |

M

Melanerpes carolinus	Red-bellied Woodpecker
Melospiza melodia	Song Sparrow
Mimidae	Mockingbird and Thrasher Family

Mimus polyglottos	Mockingbird
Molothrus ater	Brown-headed Cowbird

P

Papilio polyxenes	Eastern Black Swallowtail
Paridae	Chickadee and Titmice Family
Parus atricapillus	Black-capped Chickadee
Parus bicolor	Tufted Titmouse
Passer domesticus	House Sparrow
Passerella iliaca	Fox Sparrow
Passerina cyanea	Indigo Bunting
Pheucticus ludovicianus	Rose-breasted Grosbeak
Picidae	Woodpecker Family
Picoides pubescens	Downy Woodpecker
Picoides villosus	Hairy Woodpecker
Pipilo erythrophthalmus	Rufous-sided Towhee

Q

Quiscalus quiscula	Common Grackle

R

Regulus calendula	Ruby-crowned Kinglet
Regulus satrapa	Golden-crowned Kinglet

S

Sialia sialis	Eastern Bluebird
Sitta canadensis	Red-breasted Nuthatch
Sitta carolinensis	White-breasted Nuthatch
Sittidae	Nuthatch Family
Spiza americana	Dickcissel
Spizella arborea	Tree Sparrow
Spizella passerina	Chipping Sparrow
Sturnus vulgaris	Starling
Sylviidae	Gnatcatcher, Kinglet, and Warbler Family

T

Toxostoma rufum	Brown Thrasher
Trochilidae	Hummingbird Family
Turdidae	Bluebird and Thrush Family
Turdus migratorius	American Robin

X

Xanthocephalus xanthocephalus	Yellow-headed Blackbird

Z

Zenaidura macroura	Mourning Dove
Zonotrichia albicollis	White-throated Sparrow
Zonotrichia leucophrys	White-crowned Sparrow

Butterflies by Scientific Name

A

Achalarus lyciades	Hoary-edge Skipper
Artogeia rapae	Cabbage White
Asterocampa clyton	Tawny Emperor

B

Basilarchia archippus	Viceroy
Basilarchia astyanax	Red-spotted Purple

C

Celastrina argiolus	Spring Azure
Colias eurytheme	Orange Sulfur
Colias philodice	Common Sulfur

D

Danaus plexippus	Monarch

E

Everes comyntas	Eastern Tailed Blue Hairstreak

H

Heraclides cresphontes	Giant Swallowtail

J

Junonia coenia	Buckeye

L

Limenitis archippus	Viceroy
Limenitis arthemis astyanax	Red-Spotted Purple
Lycaena thoe	Bronze Copper Hairsteak

N

Nymphalis antiopa	Mourning Cloak

P

Papilio polyxenes	Eastern Black Swallowtail
Polygonia comma	Comma Anglewing
Polygonia interrogationis	Question Mark
Pterourus glaucus	Tiger Swallowtail
Pyrgus communis	Checkered Skipper

S

Satyrium calanus	Banded Hairstreak

V

Vanessa atalanta	Red Admiral
Vanessa cardui	Painted Lady
Vanessa virginiensis	American Painted Lady

Plants by Common Name

A	A
Alder	*Alnus*
Allium	*Allium*
American Highbush Cranberry	*Viburnum trilobum*
Anise	*Pimpinella ansium*
Anise Hyssop	*Agastache*
Apple	*Malus*
Arbor Vitae	*Thuja occidentalis*
Ash	*Fraxinus*
Aspen	*Populus*
Aster	*Aster*
Azalea	*Rhododendron*

B	B
Baby's Breath	*Gypsophila*
Bachelor's Button	*Centaurea cyanus*
Barberry	*Berberis*
Barren Strawberry	*Waldsteinia ternata*
Barrenwort	*Epimedium alpina*
Basil	*Ocimum basilicum*
Basket of Gold	*Aurinia saxatilis*
Basswood	*Tilia*
Bayberry	*Myrica pensylvanica*
Bearberry	*Arctostaphylos uva-ursi*
Beard Tongue	*Penstemon digitalis*
Beautybush	*Kolkwitzia amabilis*
Bee Balm	*Monarda*
Bellflower	*Campanula carpatica*
Big Bluestem	*Andropogon gerardii*
Birch, River	*Betula nigra*
Bird's-foot Violet	*Viola pedata*
Bittersweet	*Celastrus*
Black-eyed Susan	*Rudbeckia; Thunbergia*
Blanket Flower	*Gaillardia*
Blazing Star	*Liatris*
Blue Fescue	*Festuca*
Blue Flax	*Linum lewisii*
Blue Grama	*Bouteloua gracilis*
Blue-eyed Grass	*Sisyrinchium campestre*
Bluebell	*Campanula*

Blueberry	*Vaccinium*
Borage	*Borago officinalis*
Boston Ivy	*Parthenocissus*
Bottlebrush Buckeye	*Aesculus parviflora*
Buckeye	*Junonia coenia*
Buffalo Grass	*Buchloe dactyloides*
Bunchberry	*Cornus canadensis*
Bur Oak	*Quercus macrocarpa*
Burning Bush	*Euonymus*
Butterfly Weed	*Asclepias tuberosa*

C

Calendula	*Calendula officinalis*
Camass	*Camassia scilloides*
Canadian Cherry	*Prunus virginiana*
Canary-bird; Canary Creeper	*Tropaeolum canariense*
Candytuft	*Iberis sempervirens*
Caraway	*Carum carvi*
Cardinal Climber	*Ipomoea*
Carpet Bugle	*Ajuga reptans*
Catchfly	*Silene armeria*
Catmint	*Nepeta*
Celery	*Apium graveolens*
Cherry	*Prunus*
Chervil	*Anthriscus cerefolium*
Chicory	*Cichorium intybus*
Chives	*Allium schoenoprasum*
Chrysanthemum	*Chrysanthemum*
Cilantro	*Coriandrum sativum*
Cinquefoil	*Potentilla*
Clematis	*Clematis*
Climbing Hydrangea	*Hydrangea anomala*
Climbing Rose	*Rosa*
Columbine	*Aquilegia*
Compass Plant	*Silphium laciniatum*
Coneflower	*Echinacea*
Coral Bell	*Heuchera*
Coreopsis	*Coreopsis*
Coriander	*Coriandrum sativum*
Corktree	*Phellodendron amurense*
Corn Poppy	*Papaver rhoeas*

Cosmos	*Cosmos*
Cottonwood	*Populus*
Cowberry	*Vaccinium vitis-idaea*
Crabapple	*Malus*
Cranberry	*Vaccinium macrocarpon*
Cranesbill	*Geranium*
Creeping Phlox	*Phlox*
Creeping Thyme	*Thymus serpyllum*
Crocus	*Crocus*
Crown Vetch	*Coronilla varia*
Culver's Root	*Veronicastrum virginicum*
Currant	*Ribes*

D

Daffodil	*Narcissus*
Dame's Rocket	*Hesperis matronalis*
Daylily	*Hemerocallis*
Dianthus	*Dianthus*
Dill	*Anethum graveolens*
Dog-tooth Violet	*Erythronium mesochoreum*
Dogwood	*Cornus; Cornus alba*
Downy Gentian	*Gentiana puberulenta*
Dutchman's Pipe	*Aristolochia durior*

E

Easter Lily	*Lilium longiflorum*
Eastern Gama Grass	*Tripsacum dactyloides*
Elderberry	*Sambucus*
Elm	*Ulmus*
Evening Primrose	*Oenothera*
Everlasting Pea	*Lathyrus*

F

Fairy Candle	*Cimicifuga*
False Cypress	*Chamaecyparis*
Fennel	*Foeniculum vulgare*
Fiddlehead Fern	*Matteuccia pensylvanica; Matteuccia struthiopteris*
Fir	*Abies*
Fleabane	*Erigeron*
Fleeceflower	*Polygonum*
Flowering Spurge	*Euphorbia corollata*

Foamflower	*Tiarella cordifolia*

G

G

Gaillardia	*Gaillardia*
Garlic Chives	*Allium tuberosum*
Gayfeather	*Liatris*
German Iris	*Iris germanica*
Ginkgo	*Ginkgo biloba*
Globe Thistle	*Echinops*
Golden Daisy	*Coreopsis verticillata*
Goldenrod	*Solidago*
Gooseberry	*Ribes*
Goutweed	*Aegopodium podagraria*
Grape	*Vitis*
Ground Clematis	*Clematis recta*

H

H

Hackberry	*Celtis*
Hardy Kiwi	*Actinidia kolomikta*
Hawthorn	*Crataegus*
Heal-all	*Prunella vulgaris*
Heartleaf	*Bergenia*
Helen's Flower	*Helenium*
Hemlock	*Tsuga canadensis*
Hen and Chickens	*Sempervivum*
Hickory	*Carya*
Holly	*Ilex*
Hollyhock	*Alcea*
Honeysuckle	*Lonicera*
Hosta	*Hosta*
Hyacinth Bean	*Dolichos*
Hydrangea	*Hydrangea macrophylla*
Hydrangea Tree	*Hydrangea paniculata*

I

I

Indian Grass	*Sorghastrum nutans*
Indian Paintbrush	*Castilleja coccinea*
Indigo	*Baptisia*
Inkberry	*Ilex glabra*
Iris	*Iris*
Ironweed	*Vernonia*
Ivy	*Hedera helix*

J

Japanese Barberry	*Berberis thunbergii*
Japanese Iris	*Iris kaempferi*
Japanese Lilac Tree	*Syringa reticulata*
Japanese Painted Fern	*Athyrium goeringianum*
Japanese Spurge	*Pachysandra terminalis*
Japanese Wisteria	*Wisteria floribunda*
Joe-Pye Weed	*Eupatorium*
Johnny-jump-up	*Viola tricolor*
Jonquil	*Narcissus jonquilla*
Jostaberry	*Ribes*
Junco	*Junco hyemalis*
Juniper	*Juniperus*

K

Kentucky Bluegrass	*Poa pratensis*
Kentucky Coffee Tree	*Gymnocladus dioicus*
Kinnikinick	*Arctostaphylos*
Kiwi	*Actinidia kolomikta*

L

Larch	*Larix*
Large Fothergilla	*Fothergilla major*
Late Goldenrod	*Solidago gigantea*
Leadplant	*Amorpha canescens*
Liatris	*Liatris*
Lilac	*Syringa*
Lily	*Lilium*
Lily of the Valley	*Convallaria majalis*
Little Bluestem	*Andropogon scoparius*
Low Stonecrop	*Sedum*
Luffa	*Luffa acutangula*
Lupine	*Lupinus*

M

Magnolia	*Magnolia* x *loebneri*
Maidenhair Fern	*Adiantum pedatum*
Maidenhair Tree	*Ginkgo biloba*
Maple	*Acer*
Marigold	*Tagetes; T. signata pumila*
Marjoram	*Origanum majorana*
May Daisy	*Chrysanthemum maximum*

Mexican Hat	*Ratibida*
Milkweed	*Asclepias*
Mint	*Mentha*
Mock Strawberry	*Duchesnea indica*
Moonflower	*Ipomoea*
Morning Glory	*Ipomoea*
Mountain Ash	*Sorbus aucuparia*
Mountain Glory	*Cobaea*
Mountain Laurel	*Kalmia*
Mulberry	*Morus*
Mum	*Chrysanthemum*

N

Nanking Cherry	*Prunus tomentosa*
Nasturtium	*Tropaeolum majus*
New England Aster	*Aster novae-angliae*
New Jersey Tea	*Ceanothus americanus*
Ninebark	*Physocarpus*

O

Oak	*Quercus*
Obedient Plant	*Physostegia*
Oregano	*Origanum vulgare*
Oriental Iris	*Iris ensata*

P

Pagoda Dogwood	*Cornus alternifolia*
Paperbark Maple	*Acer griseum*
Parsley	*Petroselinum crispum*
Pasque Flower	*Anemone patens*
Pearlwort	*Sagina subulata*
Peony	*Paeonia; P. lactiflora*
Pepper Vine	*Ampelopsis*
Perennial Ryegrass	*Lolium perenne*
Perennial Spirea	*Astilbe*
Periwinkle	*Vinca minor*
Petunia	*Solanaceae*
Phlox	*Phlox*
Pin Oak	*Quercus palustris*
Pincushion Flower	*Scabiosa*
Pine	*Pinus*
Pink	*Dianthus*

Plumbago	*Ceratostigma*
Poplar	*Populus*
Potentilla	*Potentilla fruticosa*
Prairie Dock	*Silphium terebinthinaceum*
Prairie Clover	*Petalostemum*
Prairie Dropseed	*Sporobolus heterolepis*
Prairie Smoke	*Geum triflorum*
Purple Rock Cress	*Aubrieta*
Purple-leaf Coral Bell	*Heuchera micrantha*

Q | **Q**
| Quaking Aspen | *Populus tremula* |
| Queen Anne's Lace | *Daucus* |

R | **R**
Raspberry	*Rubus*
Rattlesnake Master	*Eryngium yuccifolium*
Red Fescue	*Festuca rubra*
Red Maple	*Acer rubrum*
Red Oak	*Quercus rubra*
Rhododendron	*Rhododendron*
Rhubarb	*Rheum*
River Birch	*Betula nigra*
Rock Cress	*Arabis*
Rock Soapwort	*Saponaria ocymoides*
Rocket Larkspur	*Delphinium*
Rose	*Rosa*
Rose of Sharon	*Hypericum calycinum*
Rose Mallow	*Hibiscus*
Rosemary	*Rosmarinus officinalis*
Rosinweed	*Silphium integrifolium*
Russian Sage	*Perovskia atriplicifolia*

S | **S**
Sage	*Salvia; S. officinalis*
Sand Cherry	*Prunus x cistena*
Sandwort	*Arenaria montana*
Savory	*Satureja hortensis*
Scarlet Flax	*Linum rubrum*
Sea Holly	*Eryngium*
Sedum	*Sedum*
Self-heal	*Prunella grandiflora*

Serviceberry	*Amelanchier*
Sheep Sorrel	*Oxalis violacea*
Shooting Star	*Dodekatheon meadia*
Shrub Rose	*Rosa*
Siberian Iris	*Iris sibirica*
Sideoats Grama	*Buoteloua curtipendula*
Silver Lace Vine	*Polygonum aubertii*
Silver Mound	*Artemisia schmidtiana*
Smokebush	*Cotinus coggygria*
Snow in Summer	*Cerastium tomentosum*
Speedwell	*Veronica; V. incana*
Spirea	*Spirea*
Splitbeard Bluestem	*Andropogon ternarius*
Spotted Dead Nettle	*Lamium maculatum*
Spruce	*Picea*
Statice	*Limonium*
Stonecrop	*Sedum*
Strawberry	*Fragaria*
Sugar Maple	*Acer saccharum*
Sumac	*Rhus*
Summer Sage	*Salvia*
Summer Speedwell	*Veronica*
Sundrop	*Oenothera*
Sunflower	*Helianthus*
Swamp White Oak	*Quercus bicolor*
Sweet Pea	*Leguminosae*
Sweet Woodruff	*Asperula*
Switchgrass	*Panicum virgatum*

T   **T**

Tarragon	*Artemisia dracunculus*
Thornless Hawthorn	*Crataegus crus-galli*
Thyme	*Thymus; T. vulgaris*
Tickseed	*Coreopsis*
Trumpet Vine	*Campsis*
Tulip	*Tulipa*
Turtlehead	*Chelone glabra*

V   **V**

Viburnum	*Viburnum*
Violet	*Viola*
Virginia Creeper	*Parthenocissus*

W

Weigela	*Weigela*
Western Phlox	*Phlox pilosa*
Wild Indigo	*Baptisia*
Wild Ginger	*Asarum*
Wild Plum	*Prunus*
Wild Snapdragon	*Linaria*
Wild Strawberry	*Fragaria virginiana*
Willow	*Salix*
Winterberry	*Ilex verticillata*
Wintercreeper	*Euonymus fortunei*
Wintergreen	*Gaultheria procumbens*
Witch Hazel	*Hamamelis*
Wood Betony	*Pedicularis canadensis*
Woodland Phlox	*Phlox divericata*
Wormwood	*Artemisia*

Y

Yarrow	*Achillea*
Yellow Archangel	*Lamiastrum galeobdolon*
Yellow-star Grass	*Hypoxis hirsuta*
Yellowwood	*Cladrastis kentukea*
Yew	*Taxus*

Z

Zinnia	*Zinnia*

Butterflies by Common Name

A
American Painted Lady

B
Banded Hairstreak
Bronze Copper Hairsteak

C
Cabbage White
Checkered Skipper
Comma Anglewing
Common Sulfur

E
Eastern Black Swallowtail
Eastern Tailed Blue Hairstreak

G
Giant Swallowtail

H
Hoary-edge Skipper

M
Monarch
Mourning Cloak

O
Orange Sulfur

P
Painted Lady

Q
Question Mark

R
Red Admiral
Red-spotted Purple

S
Spring Azure

T
Tawny Emperor
Tiger Swallowtail

V
Viceroy

A
Vanessa virginiensis

B
Satyrium calanus
Lycaena thoe

C
Artogeia rapae
Pyrgus communis
Polygonia comma
Colias philodice

E
Papilio polyxenes
Everes comyntas

G
Heraclides cresphontes

H
Achalarus lyciades

M
Danaus plexippus
Nymphalis antiopa

O
Colias eurytheme

P
Vanessa cardui

Q
Polygonia interrogationis

R
Vanessa atalanta
Basilarchia astyanax; Limenitis arthemis astyanax

S
Celastrina argiolus

T
Asterocampa clyton
Pterourus glaucus

V
Basilarchia archippus; Limenitis archippus

Birds by Common Name

A

American Goldfinch	*Carduelis tristis*
American Robin	*Turdus migratorius*

B

Baltimore Oriole	*Icterus galbula*
Blackbird, Meadowlark, and Oriole Family	Icteridae
Black-capped Chickadee	*Parus atricapillus*
Bluebird and Thrush Family	Turdidae
Blue Jay	*Cyanocitta cristata*
Brown-headed Cowbird	*Molothrus ater*
Brown Thrasher	*Toxostoma rufum*
Bunting, Finch, Grosbeak, and Sparrow Family	Fringillidae

C

Catbird	*Dumetella carolinensis*
Cedar Waxwing	*Bombycilla cedrorum*
Chickadee and Titmice Family	Paridae
Chipping Sparrow	*Spizella passerina*
Common Grackle	*Quiscalus quiscula*
Common Redpoll	*Carduelis flammea*
Crow	*Corvus brachyrhynchos*
Crow and Jay Family	Corvidae

D

Dark-eyed Junco	*Junco hyemalis*
Dickcissel	*Spiza americana*
Downy Woodpecker	*Picoides pubescens*

E

Eastern Bluebird	*Sialia sialis*
Evening Grosbeak	*Coccothraustes vespertinus; Hesperiphona vespertina*

F

Fox Sparrow	*Passerella iliaca*

G

Gnatcatcher, Kinglet, and Warbler Family	Sylviidae
Golden-crowned Kinglet	*Regulus satrapa*

Goldfinch	*Carduelis tristis*
Gray Catbird	*Dumetella carolinensis*

H

H

Hairy Woodpecker	*Picoides villosus*
House Finch	*Carpodacus mexicanus*
House Sparrow	*Passer domesticus*
Hummingbird Family	Trochilidae

I

I

Indigo Bunting	*Passerina cyanea*

M

M

Mockingbird	*Mimus polyglottos*
Mockingbird and Thrasher Family	Mimidae
Mourning Dove	*Zenaida macroura*

N

N

Northern Cardinal	*Cardinalis cardinalis*
Northern Flicker	*Colaptes auratus*
Northern Oriole	*Icterus galbula*
Nuthatch Family	Sittidae

O

O

Orchard Oriole	*Icterus spurius*

P

P

Pigeon Family	Columbidae
Pine Siskin	*Carduelis pinus*
Purple Finch	*Carpodacus purpureus*

R

R

Red-bellied Woodpecker	*Melanerpes carolinus*
Redpoll	*Carduelis flammea*
Red-breasted Nuthatch	*Agelaius phoeniceus*
Red-winged Blackbird	*Sitta canadensis*
Rose-breasted Grosbeak	*Pheucticus ludovicianus*
Ruby-crowned Kinglet	*Regulus calendula*
Ruby-throated Hummingbird	*Archilochus colubris*
Rufous-sided Towhee	*Pipilo erythrophthalmus*

S

S

Song Sparrow	*Melospiza melodia*
Starling	*Sturnus vulgaris*

T

Tree Sparrow	*Spizella arborea*
Tufted Titmouse	*Parus bicolor*

W

Waxwing Family	Bombycillidae
White-breasted Nuthatch	*Sitta carolinensis*
White-crowned Sparrow	*Zonotrichia leucophrys*
White-throated Sparrow	*Zonotrichia albicollis*
Woodpecker Family	Picidae
Wood Thrush	*Hylocichla mustelina*

Y

Yellow-headed Blackbird	*Xantheocephalus xanthocephalus*

National Wildlife Refuges in the Midwest

The following Midwest refuges are managed by the U.S. Department of Interior Fish and Wildlife Service. Those marked with a star welcome visitors with free informational brochures and/or special programs about migrating and residential wildlife.

Illinois National Wildlife Refuges
☆Chautauqua NWR, Havana
Mark Twain Complex, Quincy

Indiana National Wildlife Refuge
Muscatatuck NWR, Seymour

Iowa National Wildlife Refuges
☆DeSoto NWR, Missouri Valley
Union Slough NWR, Titonka
Walnut Creek NWR, Prairie City

Kansas National Wildlife Refuges
☆Flint Hills NWR, Hartford
☆Quivira NWR, Stafford

Michigan National Wildlife Refuges
Harbor Island NWR, Seney
☆Huron NWR, Seney
☆Shiawassee NWR, Saginaw

Minnesota National Wildlife Refuges
☆Agassiz NWR, Middle River
Big Stone NWR, Ortonville
Hamden Slough NWR, Audubon
☆Minnesota Valley NWR, Bloomington
Morris NWR, Morris
☆Rice Lake NWR, McGregor
☆Sherburne NWR, Zimmerman
☆Tamarac NWR, Rochert
Upper Mississippi River NWR, Winona

Missouri National Wildlife Refuges
Clarence Cannon NWR, Annada
☆Mingo NWR, Puxico
Squaw Creek NWR, Mound City
☆Swan Lake NWR, Sumner

Nebraska National Wildlife Refuges
☆Crescent Lake NWR, Ellsworth
Fort Niobrara NWR, Valentine
North Platte NWR, Minatare
Valentine NWR, Valentine

North Dakota National Wildlife Refuges
☆Arrowwood NWR, Pingree
☆Audubon NWR, Coleharbor
☆Chase Lake Prairie Project, Woodworth
Des Lacs NWR, Kenmare
J. Clark Salyer NWR, Upham
Kellys Slough NWR, Devils Lake
Lake Alice NWR, Devils Lake
Lake Ilo NWR, Dunn Center
Lake Zahl NWR, Crosby
☆Long Lake Complex, Moffitt
Lostwood NWR, Kenmare
☆Sullys Hill National Game Preserve, Fort Totten
Tewaukon NWR, Cayuga
Upper Souris NWR, Foxholm

Ohio National Wildlife Refuge
☆Ottawa NWR, Oak Harbor

Pennsylvania National Wildlife Refuge
☆Erie NWR, Guys Mills

South Dakota National Wildlife Refuge
☆LaCreek NWR, Martin
☆Lake Andes NWR, Lake Andes
Pocasse NWR, Columbia
Sand Lake NWR, Columbia
☆Waubay NWR, Waubay

Wisconsin National Wildlife Refuges
Horicon NWR, Mayville
☆Necedah NWR, Necedah
☆Trempealeau NWR, Trempealeau

For a free copy of a brochure filled with information on all of our National Wildlife Refuges, call 1–800/344-WILD.

Midwest Gardens to Visit

Midwest AARS Test Gardens (for Roses)

Illinois

Alton	Nan Elliot Memorial Rose Garden
Evanston	Merrick Park Rose Garden
Glencoe	Bruce Krasberg Rose Garden
Libertyville	Lynn J. Arthur Rose Garden
Peoria	George L. Luthy Memorial Botanical Garden
Rockford	Sinnissippi Rose Garden
Springfield	Washington Park Rose Garden
Wheaton	Cantigny Gardens

Indiana

Ft. Wayne	Lakeside Rose Garden

Iowa

Ames	Reiman Gardens, Iowa State University

In addition to its All-America Rose Selection display garden, Jones Rose Garden has a special display of eighty-five Midwest hardy tea and shrub rose hybrids developed by Dr. Griffith J. Buck, a professor of horticulture at ISU in the 1960s. You can request a list of commercial retailers that carry these hardy roses.

Bettendorf	Bettendorf Park Board Municipal Rose Garden
Cedar Rapids	Noelridge Park Rose Garden
Davenport	Vander Veer Park Municipal Rose Garden
Des Moines	Greenwood Park Rose Garden
Dubuque	Dubuque Arboretum Rose Garden
Muscatine	Weed Park Memorial Rose Garden
State Center	State Center Public Rose Garden

Kansas

Topeka	E.F.A. Reinisch Rose Garden

Michigan

East Lansing	Michigan State University Horticultural Gardens
Lansing	Frances Park Memorial Rose Garden

Minnesota

Minneapolis	Lyndale Park Municipal Rose Garden

Missouri

Cape Girardeau	Capaha Rose Display Garden
Kansas City	Laura Conyers Smith Municipal Rose Garden
St. Louis	Anne L. Lehmann Rose Garden; Gladney Rose Garden

Nebraska

Boys Town	AARS Constitution Rose Garden
Lincoln	Lincoln Municipal Rose Garden
Omaha	Memorial Park Rose Garden

Ohio

Akron	Stan Hywet Hall and Gardens
Bay Village	Cahoon Memorial Rose Garden
Columbus	Columbus Park of Roses
Mansfield	Charles Edwin Nail Memorial Rose Garden

Pennsylvania

Allentown	Malcolm W. Gross Memorial Rose Garden
Hershey	Hershey Gardens
Kennett Square	Longwood Gardens
Philadelphia	Morris Arboretum Rose Garden
West Grove	Robert Pyle Memorial Rose Garden

South Dakota

Rapid City	Rapid City Memorial Rose Garden

Wisconsin

Hales Corners	Boerner Botanical Garden
Madison	Olbrich Botanical Gardens; All-America Display Rose Garden

Midwest AAS (All-America Selection) Display Gardens

Illinois

Altamont	Alwerdt's Gardens
Belleville	Belleville Area College
East Peoria	Illinois Central College
Glencoe	Chicago Botanic Garden
Mahomet	Mabery Gelvin Botanical Gardens
River Grove	Triton Botanical Garden
Springfield	Washington Park Botanical Garden
Wheaton	Cantigny Gardens

Indiana

Bloomington	Hilltop Garden and Nature Center
Fort Wayne	Foster Garden
Nobesville	Parson's Patch

Iowa

Ames	Iowa State University
Cedar Rapids	Noelridge Park
Davenport	Vander Veer Botanical Park and Center
Des Moines	Des Moines Botanical Center
Dubuque	Dubuque Arboretum and Botanical Gardens
South Amana	Amana Colonies Community Gardens

Kansas

Colby	NWK Research-Extension Center
Wichita	Botanica, The Wichita Gardens

Michigan

Frankenmuth	Frankenmuth Mutual Insurance Co.
Kalamazoo	Kalamazoo Mall
Midland	Dow Gardens
Niles	Fernwood Botanic Gardens
Rochester Hills	Bordine's Better Blooms
Tipton	Hidden Lake Gardens

Minnesota

Chanhassen	Minnesota Landscape Arboretum
Grand Rapids	North Central Experiment Station
Minneapolis	Lyndale Park Gardens
Morris	West Central Experiment Station
St. Paul	University of Minnesota, St. Paul

Missouri

Cape Girardeau	SE Missouri State University
Charleston	Danforth FFA Garden
Clayton	St. Louis County Government Center
Columbia	University of Missouri
Jefferson City	Lincoln University Gardens
Kingsville	Powell Gardens
St. Louis	Missouri Botanical Gardens

Nebraska

Lincoln	State Fair Park Arboretum

North Dakota

Dunseith	International Peace Garden
Fargo	North Dakota State University

Ohio

Ashland	Ashland High School
Cincinnati	Ault Park
Cincinnati	Delhi Flower and Garden Centers
Cincinnati	Spring Grove Cemetery and Arboretum
Cleveland	Rockerfeller Park Gardens
Columbus	Schmidt Nursery Company
Dayton	Cox Arboretum
Mansfield	Kingwood Center
New Albany	Schmidt Nursery, Front Porch II
Newark	Wilson's Hillview Display Garden
Strongsville	Gardenview Horticultural Park
Toledo	Toledo Botanic Gardens
Wooster	Ohio State University
Youngstown	Fellows Riverside Gardens

Pennsylvania

Kennett Square	Longwood Gardens
Lahaska	Peddlers Village

Wisconsin

Eau Claire	University of Wisconsin
Hancock	Hancock Agricultural Research Station
Madison	West Madison Research Farm
Milwaukee	ANR Garden Plots, Vincent High School
Randolph	Jung Seed Company

Other Public Gardens by State and City

Illinois

Flower: Violet

Bird: Cardinal

Tree: White Oak

Insect: Monarch Butterfly

Rockhome Gardens

Route 2

Arcola, IL 61910

800-549-ROCK

Butterflies, grasses, herbs, perennials, prairies, roses, spring bulbs, trees, shrubs, vegetables, wildflowers

Illinois Wesleyan University

PO Box 2900

Bloomington, IL 61702-2900

309-556-3034

Trees, shrubs

Brookfield Zoo
3300 Golf Road
Brookfield, IL 60513
708-485-0263
Butterflies, grasses, perennials, spring bulbs, trees, shrubs

Garfield Park Conservatory
300 N. Central Park Blvd.
Chicago, IL 60624
312-746-5100
Butterflies, grasses, herbs, perennials, spring bulbs, trees, shrubs, vegetables, wildflowers

Lincoln Park Conservatory
2400 N. Stockton Drive
Stockton Drive, Fullerton Parkway
Chicago, IL 60614
312-742-7737
Perennials, spring bulbs

Dr. Fithian Herb Garden
Vermilion County Museum
116 North Gilbert Street
Danville, IL 61832-8506
Butterflies, herbs, perennials, trees, shrubs, vegetables, wildflowers

Illinois Central College
Horticulture Department
East Peoria, IL 61635
309-694-8446
Butterflies, grasses, herbs, perennials, trees, shrubs, vegetables

Shakespeare Garden
Garden Club of Evanston
2703 Euclid Place
Northwestern University, Chapel Garden
Evanston, IL 60201

Bald Eagle Nursery
18510 Sand Road
Fulton, IL 61252
815-589-4121
Grasses, perennials

Linmar Gardens
504 S. Prospect
Galena, IL 61036
Perennials

Chicago Botanic Garden

1000 Lake Cook Road
Glencoe, IL 60022
847-835-5440

Fruits, grasses, herbs, perennials, prairies, roses, spring bulbs, trees, shrubs, vegetables, wildflowers

Garfield Farm Museum

3 North 016 Garfield Rd
Box 403
LaFox, IL 60147
630-584-8485

Herbs, prairies, roses, vegetables, wildflowers

The Morton Arboretum

4100 Illinois Route 53
Lisle, IL 60532-1293
630-719-2400

Herbs, prairies, trees, shrubs

Lilacia Park

Lombard Park District
150 South Park Avenue
Lombard, IL 60148

Herbs, perennials, prairies, spring bulbs, trees, shrubs

Botanic Garden

PO Box 1040
Mahomet, IL 61853
217-586-4630

Grasses, herbs, perennials, prairies, roses, spring bulbs, trees, shrubs, vegetables, wildflowers

Robert Allerton Park and Conference Center

University of Illinois at Urbana-Champaign
515 Old Timber Road
Monticello, IL 61856
217-762-7011

Butterflies, perennials, prairies, spring bulbs, wildflowers

Naper Settlement

523 South Webster Street
Naperville, IL 60540
630-420-6010

Herbs, perennials, spring bulbs, trees, shrubs, wildflowers

Fell Arboretum

Illinois State University
Campus Box 3200
Normal, IL 61790-3200
309-438-7337

Butterflies, grasses, perennials, prairies, trees, shrubs, wildflowers

Oak Park Conservatory

Parks, Recreation Department of Oak Park
1 Village Hall Plaza
Oak Park, IL 60302
708-386-4700

Butterflies, grasses, herbs, perennials, prairies, wildflowers

George L. Luthy Memorial Botanical Garden

2218 North Prospect Road
Peoria, IL 61603
309-686-3362

Butterflies, grasses, herbs, perennials, roses, spring bulbs, trees, shrubs, wildflowers

Forest Park Nature Center

5809 Forest Park Drive
Peoria Heights, IL 61614
309-686-3360

Butterflies, prairies, trees, shrubs, wildflowers

American Hemerocallis Display Garden

Richard Ford
PO Box 55
Petersburg, IL 62675
217-632-3791

Perennials

American Hemerocallis Display Garden

Charles Branch
329 East Market Street
Piper City, IL 60959
815-686-2323

Perennials

Klehm Arboretum and Botanic Garden

2701 Clifton Avenue
Rockford, IL 61101
815-965-8146

Butterflies, grasses, perennials, trees, shrubs, vegetables

Lincoln Memorial Garden and Nature Center

2301 E. Lake Shore Drive

Springfield, IL 62707

Prairies, trees, shrubs

Washington Park Botanical Garden

Fayette, Chatham Road

PO Box 5052

Springfield, IL 62705

217-753-6228

Butterflies, grasses, herbs, perennials, roses, trees, shrubs

Cantigny Gardens

1 South 151 Winfield Road

Wheaton, IL 60187

708-260-8169

Grasses, herbs, perennials, prairies, roses, spring bulbs, trees, shrubs, vegetables, wildflowers

Indiana

Flower: Peony

Bird: Cardinal

Tree: Tulip Tree

Wesselman Park

551 North Boeke Road

Evansville, IN 47711-5994

812-479-0771

Butterflies, perennials, prairies, trees, shrubs, wildflowers

American Hemerocallis Display Garden

Bee's Garden

8207 Seiler Road

Fort Wayne, IN 48606

Perennials

Foelinger-Freiman Botanical Conservatory

Ft. Wayne Parks, Recreation

1100 South Calhoun Street

Fort Wayne, IN 46802-3007

219-427-6442

Perennials

Garfield Park Conservatory

2505 Garfield Plaza Drive

Indianapolis, IN 46203

317-327-7184

Butterflies, grasses, herbs, perennials, spring bulbs, trees, shrubs

Holliday Park

6349 Spring Mill Road
Indianapolis, IN 46260-4261
317-327-7180

Butterflies, herbs, perennials, prairies, trees, shrubs, wildflowers

The Gardens of the Indianapolis Museum of Art

1200 West 38th Street
Indianapolis, IN 46208-4196
317-923-1331

Grasses, herbs, perennials, roses, spring bulbs, trees, shrubs, wildflowers

Buckley Homestead

3606 Belshaw Road
Lowell, IN 46356
219-696-0769

Herbs, perennials, roses

Talbott-Hyatt Pioneer Garden

304 West Second Street
500 West Street (mailing address)
Madison, IN 47250
812-265-2967

Perennials, roses, wildflowers

Oakhurst Gardens

1200 North Minnestrista Parkway
Muncie, IN 47303-2925
765-741-5113

Butterflies, grasses, herbs, perennials, roses, spring bulbs, trees, shrubs, vegetables, wildflowers

American Hemerocallis Display Garden

The Daylily Farm
10732 West State Road 114
Rensselaer, IN 47978
219-866-8317

Perennials (daylilies)

Hayes Regional Arboretum

801 Elks Road
Richmond, IN 47374
765-962-3745

Spring bulbs, trees, shrubs, wildflowers

Billie Creek Village

RR 2, Box 27
Rockville, IN 47872
765-569-3430

Butterflies, herbs, perennials, trees, shrubs

Purdue University Horticultural Gardens

Horticulture Department
Purdue University
West Lafayette, IN 47907
765-496-2358

Grasses, herbs, perennials, spring bulbs, trees, shrubs

Merry Lea Environmental Learning Center

Goshen College
Box 263
Wolf Lake, IN 46796

Butterflies, herbs, perennials, prairies, wildflowers

Iowa

Flower: Wild Prairie Rose
Bird: Goldfinch
Tree: Oak

Reiman Gardens

Iowa State University
1407 Elwood Drive
Ames, IA 50011
515-294-2710

Grasses, herbs, perennials, roses, trees, shrubs, vegetables

South Bluff Nature Center

Bellevue State Park
24668 Highway 52
Bellevue, IA 52031

Butterflies, perennials, prairies, wildflowers

Cedar Heights School

Outdoor Classroom
2417 Rainbow Drive
Cedar Falls, IA 50613

Butterflies, wildflowers

Hearst Center for the Arts

304 W. Seerley Blvd.
Cedar Falls, IA 50613
319-273-8641

Perennials, spring bulbs, trees, shrubs, wildflowers

Brucemore
2160 Linden Drive SE
Cedar Rapids, IA 52403
319-362-7375

Butterflies, grasses, herbs, perennials, spring bulbs, vegetables

Bickelhaupt Arboretum
340 South 14th Street
Clinton, IA 52732-5432
319-242-4771

Grasses, herbs, perennials, prairies, roses, spring bulbs, trees, shrubs, wildflowers

Vander Veer Botanical Park
214 W. Central Park Avenue
2816 Eastern Avenue (mailing)
Davenport, IA 52803
319-326-7894

Butterflies, grasses, perennials, roses, spring bulbs, trees, shrubs, vegetables, wildflowers

Des Moines Botanical Center
909 East River Drive
Des Moines, IA 50316-2897
515-271-8727

Perennials, roses, trees, shrubs

Des Moines Water Works Crabapple Arboretum
408 Fleur Drive
Des Moines, IA 50321-1190

Trees, shrubs

Ewing Park Lilac Arboretum
5100 Southeast Indianola Drive
Des Moines, IA 50325-9695

Trees, shrubs

Dubuque Arboretum, Gardens
3800 Arboretum Drive
Dubuque, IA 52001
319-556-2100

Butterflies, grasses, herbs, perennials, prairies, roses, spring bulbs, trees, shrubs, vegetables, wildflowers

Iowa City Area Science Center
504 E. Bloomington Street
Iowa City, IA 52245
319-337-2007

Butterflies

257

Iowa Arboretum

1875 Peach Avenue
Madrid, IA 50156
515-795-3216

Butterflies, grasses, herbs, perennials, prairies, roses, spring bulbs, trees, shrubs, wildflowers

Prairie Pedlar

1677 270th Street
Odebolt, IA 51458
712-668-4840

Herbs

Cedar Valley Arboretum, Botanic Gardens

Hawkeye Community College
PO Box 1833
Waterloo, IA 50704
319-232-3397

Grasses, herbs, perennials, prairies, trees, shrubs

Kansas

Flower: Sunflower
Bird: Western Meadowlark
Tree: Cottonwood

Dyck Arboretum of the Plains

Hesston College
PO Box 3000
Hesston, KS 67062

Perennials, trees, shrubs, wildflowers

Kansas State University Gardens

Kansas State University
Manhattan, KS 66506

Grasses, herbs, perennials, roses, spring bulbs, vegetables

Overland Park Arboretum and Botanical Garden

8500 Santa Fe Street
Overland Park, KS 66212
913-685-3604

Butterflies, grasses, herbs, perennials, prairies, spring bulbs, trees, shrubs, wildflowers

Botanica, the Wichita Gardens

701 Amidon
Wichita, KS 67203
316-264-0448

Butterflies, grasses, perennials, prairies, roses, spring bulbs, trees, shrubs, wildflowers

Michigan

Flower: Apple Blossom
Bird: Robin
Tree: White Pine

Matthaei Botanical Gardens

University of Michigan
1800 N. Dixboro Road
Ann Arbor, MI 48105
313-998-7061

Butterflies, herbs, perennials, prairies, roses, spring bulbs, trees, shrubs, wildflowers

Nichols Arboretum

School of Natural Resources
University of Michigan
Ann Arbor, MI 48109
313-763-4033

Perennials, prairies, trees, shrubs, wildflowers

Grand Oak Herb Farm

2877 Miller Road
Bancroft, MI 48414

Herbs, perennials, wildflowers

Binder Park Zoo

7400 Division Street
Battle Creek, MI 49014-9500
616-979-1351

Butterflies, grasses, perennials, wildflowers

Leila Arboretum Society

928 West Michigan Avenue
Battle Creek, MI 49017

Perennials, spring bulbs, trees, shrubs

For-Mar Nature Preserve and Arboretum

Genessee County Parks & Recreation
2142 N. Genesee Road
Burton, MI 48509
810-789-8568

Butterflies, grasses, perennials, spring bulbs, trees, shrubs, wildflowers

Anna Scripps Whitcomb Conservatory

Belle Isle Park
Detroit, MI 48207
313-267-7133

Grasses, perennials, roses, spring bulbs

Seven Ponds Nature Center

3854 Crawford Road
Dryden, MI 48428-9776

Butterflies, herbs, prairies, wildflowers

Botany Greenhouse, Butterfly House

Michigan State University
North Campus, Department of Botany, Plant Pathology
East Lansing, MI 48824-1312
517-355-0229

Butterflies

Clarence E. Lewis Landscape Arboretum

University of Michigan
Bogue Street, Service Road
Plant, Soil Sciences Building
East Lansing, MI 48824-1325
517-355-0348

Perennials, spring bulbs, trees, shrubs

Horticultural Demonstration Gardens

Michigan State University
Wilson Road, Bogue Street
East Lansing, MI 48824-1325
517-355-0348

Grasses, roses, trees, shrubs, vegetables

W. J. Beal Botanical Garden

Michigan State University
412 Olds Hall
East Lansing, MI 48824-1047
517-355-9582

Herbs, trees, shrubs

Frederik Meijer Gardens
3411 Bradford NE
Grand Rapids, MI 49546
616-957-1580

Butterflies, grasses, perennials, spring bulbs, trees, shrubs, vegetables, wildflowers

Slayton Arboretum
Hillsdale College
Barber Drive
Hillsdale, MI 49242
517-437-7341

Butterflies, grasses, herbs, perennials, prairies, roses, spring bulbs, trees, shrubs, wildflowers

Kalamazoo Nature Center
7000 North Westnedge Avenue
PO Box 127
Kalamazoo, MI 49004
616-381-1574

Butterflies, grasses, perennials, prairies, trees, shrubs, wildflowers

Howard Christensen Nature Center
16160 Red Pine Drive
Kent City, MI 49330
616-887-1852

Butterflies, perennials, trees, shrubs

Cooley Gardens
South Capitol Avenue and Main Street
PO Box 14164
Lansing, MI 48901

Grasses, perennials, roses, spring bulbs, trees, shrubs

Grand Hotel
Mackinac Island, MI 49757
906-847-3331

Herbs, perennials, roses, spring bulbs, trees, shrubs, wildflowers

Dow Gardens
1018 West Main Street
Midland, MI 48640
517-631-2677

Herbs, perennials, spring bulbs, trees, shrubs, wildflowers

Fernwood Nature Center, Botanic Garden

13988 Range Line Road
Niles, MI 49120
616-683-8653

Butterflies, grasses, herbs, perennials, prairies, roses, spring bulbs, trees, shrubs, wildflowers

Hidden Lake Gardens

Michigan State University
6280 West Munger Road (M-50)
Tipton, MI 49287
517-431-2060

Grasses, perennials, spring bulbs, trees, shrubs, wildflowers

Minnesota

Flower: Lady's Slipper
Bird: Loon
Tree: Red Pine

Northland Arboretum

Paul Bunyan Conservation Area
PO Box 375
Brainerd, MN 54601
218-829-8770

Perennials, prairies, trees, shrubs, wildflowers

Minnesota Arboretum, Horticulture Research Center

3675 Arboretum Drive
PO Box 39
Chanhassen, MN 55317

Grasses, perennials, prairies, roses, spring bulbs, trees, shrubs, wildflowers

Eloise Butler Wildflower Garden

Theodore Wirth Park
3800 Bryant Avenue South
Minneapolis, MN 55409-1029

Butterflies, grasses, prairies, wildflowers

Como Park Conservatory

1325 Aida Place
Midway Parkway, Kaufman Drive
Saint Paul, MN 55103
612-487-8200

Herbs, perennials, roses, spring bulbs

Linnaeus Arboretum

Gustavus Adolphus College
Saint Peter, MN 56082
507-933-7003

Butterflies, grasses, herbs, perennials, prairies, roses, trees, shrubs, wildflowers

Dodge Nature Center

365 Marie Avenue West
West Saint Paul, MN 55118-3848
612-455-4531

Butterflies, prairies, vegetables, wildflowers

Missouri

Flower: Red Hawthorn Blossom
Bird: Bluebird
Tree: Flowering Dogwood

Chance House, Gardens

316 East Sneed
Centralia, MO 65240

Grasses, perennials, roses, spring bulbs, vegetables

Shaw Arboretum of the Missouri Botanical Gardens

PO Box 38
I-44, State Highway 100
Gray Summit, MO 63039
314-451-3512 / 451-0850

Butterflies, grasses, perennial, prairies, trees, shrubs, wildflowers

Jacob L. Loose Park

5200 Pennsylvania Avenue
Kansas City, MO 64112

Butterflies, grasses, herbs, perennials, roses, trees, shrubs

Kansas City Zoological Garden

6700 Zoo Drive
Kansas City, MO 64132-4200
816-871-5700

Butterflies, grasses, herbs, perennials, prairies, vegetables, wildflowers

Laura Conyers Smith Rose Municipal Garden

Kansas City Parks, Recreation
Loose Park Garden Center
5200 Pennsylvania
Kansas City, MO 64112
816-561-9710

Herbs, perennials, roses, trees, shrubs

Nelson-Atkins Museum of Art Sculpture Garden

4525 Oak Street
Kansas City, MO 64111-1873
816-221-0660

Perennials, spring bulbs

Powell Gardens

1609 NW US Highway 50
Kingsville, MO 64061
816-697-2600

Butterflies, grasses, herbs, perennials, prairies, spring bulbs, trees, shrubs, vegetables, wildflowers

Horticulture and Agroforestry Research Center

10 Research Center Road
New Franklin, MO 65274
660-848-2268

Grasses, prairies, trees, shrubs

Missouri Botanical Garden

4344 Shaw Boulevard
PO Box 299
Saint Louis, MO 63166-0299
314-577-9400 or 1-800-642-8842

Butterflies, grasses, herbs, perennials, roses, spring bulbs, trees, shrubs, vegetables, wildflowers

St. Louis Zoo

Forest Park
Saint Louis, MO 63110

Grasses, trees, shrubs

Tower Grove Park

4255 Arsenal Avenue
Saint Louis, MO 63116-1901
314-771-2679

Butterflies, grasses, herbs, perennials, roses, spring bulbs, trees, shrubs

Springfield Conservation Nature Center

4600 South Chrisman
Springfield, MO 65804-4931

Butterflies, prairies, wildflowers

Nebraska

Flower: Goldenrod
Bird: Western Meadowlark
Tree: Cottonwood

Sallows Conservatory, Arboretum

PO Drawer D
City of Alliance
Alliance, NE 69301
308-762-5400, ext. 288

Perennials, spring bulbs, trees, shrubs

Folsom Children's Zoo, Botanical Garden

1222 South 27th
Lincoln, NE 68502
402-475-6741

Butterflies, grasses, herbs, perennials, trees, shrubs, wildflowers

Alice Abel Arboretum

NE Wesleyan University
5000 Saint Paul Avenue
Lincoln, NE 68504-2796
402-465-2324

Grasses, perennials, roses, trees, shrubs, wildflowers

Antelope Park Rose Garden, Sunken Garden

27th and C Street
Lincoln, NE 68502

Hazel Abel Park

18th and E Street
Lincoln, NE 68508

Dept of Parks and Recreation

2740 A Street
Lincoln, NE 68502
402-441-7847

Grasses, herbs, perennials, roses, wildflowers

Botanical Garden, Arboretum

University of Nebraska, Lincoln
PO Box 880609
Lincoln, NE 68588-0609

Butterflies, grasses, perennials, prairies, roses, spring bulbs, trees, shrubs, wildflowers

Pioneers Park Nature Center

Lincoln Parks, Recreation
3201 South Coddington
Lincoln, NE 68502

Butterflies, herbs, prairies, trees, shrubs, wildflowers

Arbor Lodge State Historical Park

Second Avenue
Nebraska City, NE 68410
402-873-7222

Perennials, roses, spring bulbs, trees, shrubs

University of Nebraska, West Central Center

Route 4, Box 46A
North Platte, NE 69101

Grasses, perennials, prairies, roses, trees, shrubs, wildflowers

Doorly Zoo

3701 South 10th Street
Omaha, NE 68107
402-733-8401

Butterflies, grasses, perennials, prairies, roses, wildflowers

Gilman Park Arboretum

106 South First Street
Pierce, NE 68767
402-329-4873

Grasses, perennials, trees, shrubs, wildflowers

North Dakota

Flower: Wild Prairie Rose
Bird: Western Meadowlark
Tree: American Elm

International Peace Garden

PO Box 116, Route 1
Dunseith, ND 58329
701-263-4390

Herbs, perennials, prairies, spring bulbs, trees, shrubs, vegetables, wildflowers

Independence Park

Grand Forks Park District
Grand Forks, ND 58203

Herbs, perennials, roses, trees, shrubs

Ohio
Flower: Scarlet Carnation
Bird: Cardinal
Tree: Buckeye

Stan Hywet Hall, Gardens
714 N. Portage Path
Akron, OH 44303
330-836-5533
Perennials, roses, spring bulbs, trees, shrubs, wildflowers

Fellows Riverside Gardens on Price Road
Mill Creek Metro Park District
PO Box 596
7574 Columbiana Canfield Road
Canfield, OH 44406
330-702-3000
Grasses, herbs, perennials, roses, spring bulbs, trees, shrubs, vegetables

Adena State Memorial
Adena Road
PO Box 822
Chillicothe, OH 45601
Herbs, perennials, roses, spring bulbs, trees, shrubs

Cemetery of Spring Grove
4521 Spring Grove Avenue
Cincinnati, OH 45232
513-853-6865
Butterflies, grasses, perennials, roses, spring bulbs, trees, shrubs

Cincinnati Zoo, Botanical Garden
34400 Vine Street
Cincinnati, OH 45220-1399
Butterflies, grasses, perennials, spring bulbs, trees, shrubs, wildflowers

Civic Garden Center of Greater Cincinnati
2715 Reading Road
Cincinnati, OH 45206
513-221-0981
Butterflies, grasses, herbs, perennials, spring bulbs, trees, shrubs, wildflowers

Cleveland Botanical Garden
11030 E. Boulevard
Cleveland, OH 44106
216-721-1600
Grasses, herbs, perennials, roses, trees, shrubs, wildflowers

Cleveland Metroparks Zoo

3900 Wildlife Way

Cleveland, OH 44109

216-661-7511

Butterflies, grasses, herbs, perennials, prairies, roses, spring bulbs, trees, shrubs, vegetables, wildflowers

Rockefeller Park Greenhouse

750 East 88th Street

Cleveland, OH 44108-4100

216-664-3103

Butterflies, grasses, herbs, perennials, roses, spring bulbs, trees, shrubs, vegetables, wildflowers

Chadwick Arboretum

Ohio State University

2001 Fyffe Court

Columbus, OH 43210

614-292-3136

Grasses, perennials, roses, spring bulbs, trees, shrubs, wildflowers

Franklin Park Conservatory, Botanical Gardens

1777 East Broad Street

Columbus, OH 43203-2040

Butterflies, grasses, herbs, perennials, prairies, roses, spring bulbs, trees, shrubs, vegetables, wildflowers

Cox Arboretum

6733 Springboro Pike

Dayton, OH 45449

Butterflies, grasses, herbs, perennials, prairies, roses, spring bulbs, trees, shrubs, vegetables, wildflowers

Stillwater Gardens

Five Rivers MetroParks

1301 East Siebenthaler Avenue

Dayton, OH 45414

937-277-9028

Butterflies, grasses, perennials, prairies, roses, spring bulbs, trees, shrubs, vegetables, wildflowers

Schedel Foundation Arboretum, Garden

19255 W. Portage River Road South

Elmore, OH 43416

419-862-3182

Butterflies, grasses, herbs, perennials, roses, spring bulbs, trees, shrubs, wildflowers

Rowe Arboretum

4600 Muchmore Road
Indian Hill, OH 45243
513-561-5151

Grasses, spring bulbs, trees, shrubs, wildflowers

Holden Arboretum

9500 Sperry Road
Kirtland, OH 44094
440-946-4400

Herbs, perennials, trees, shrubs

Penitentiary Glen Nature Center

8668 Kirtland-Chardon Road
Kirtland, OH 44094

Butterflies, grasses, perennials

Schoepfle Garden

12882 Diagonal Road
LaGrange, OH 44050
440-965-7237

Butterflies, grasses, perennials, roses, spring bulbs, trees, shrubs, wildflowers

Kingwood Center

900 Park Avenue West
Mansfield, OH 44906
419-522-0211

Butterflies, grasses, herbs, perennials, prairies, roses, spring bulbs, trees, shrubs, wildflowers

Dawes Arboretum

7770 Jacksontown Road, SE
Newark, OH 43055
1-800-44-DAWES

Perennials, trees, shrubs, wildflowers

Columbus Zoological Gardens

9990 Riverside Drive
PO Box 400
Powell, OH 43065

Butterflies, grasses, herbs, perennials, prairies, spring bulbs, trees, shrubs, wildflowers

Toledo Botanical Garden

5403 Elmer Drive
Toledo, OH 43615
419-936-2986

Grasses, herbs, perennials, roses, spring bulbs, vegetables, wildflowers

Toledo Zoological Society
2700 Broadway PO Box 4010
Toledo, OH 43609
419-385-5721

Butterflies, grasses, herbs, perennials, roses, trees, shrubs, vegetables, wildflowers

Inniswood Metro Gardens
940 Hempstead Road
Westerville, OH 43081
614-891-0700

Grasses, herbs, perennials, roses, spring bulbs, trees, shrubs, wildflowers

Secrest Arboretum
Ohio Agricultural Research and Development Center
1680 Madison Avenue
Wooster, OH 44619

Herbs, perennials, roses, trees, shrubs

Pennsylvania
Flower: Mountain Laurel Blossom
Bird: Ruffled Grouse
Tree: Hemlock

The American College
270 South Bryn Mawr Avenue
Bryn Mawn, PA 19010
610-526-2500

Butterflies, grasses, perennials, prairies, spring bulbs, trees, shrubs, wildflowers

Brandywine River Museum
PO Box 141
US Route 1, South of PA Route 100
Chadds Ford, PA 19317
610-388-2700

Butterflies, grasses, perennials, prairies, wildflowers

Churchville Nature Center
501 Churchville Lane
Churchville, PA 18966

Butterflies, herbs, perennials, prairies, wildflowers

Jenkins Arboretum
631 Berwyn-Baptist Road
Devon, PA 19333
610-647-8870

Butterflies, grasses, trees, shrubs, wildflowers (ferns)

Henry Schmieder Arboretum

Delaware Valley College
700 East Butler Avenue
Doylestown, PA 18901-2697
215-489-2283

Butterflies, grasses, herbs, perennials, prairies, roses, spring bulbs, trees, shrubs, wildflowers

Erie Zoological Society

423 West 38th Street
PO Box 3268
Erie, PA 16508-0268
814-864-4091

Butterflies, grasses, herbs, perennials, roses, spring bulbs, trees, shrubs, wildflowers

Haverford College Arboretum

370 Lancaster Avenue
Haverford, PA 19041-1392

Grasses, herbs, perennials, spring bulbs, trees, shrubs

Hershey Gardens

170 Hotel Road
PO Box 416
Hershey, PA 17033
717-534-3439

Grasses, herbs, perennials, roses, spring bulbs, trees, shrubs

Bald Eagle State Park

RD #1, Box 56
Howard, PA 16841

Butterflies, perennials, wildflowers

Longwood Gardens

PO Box 501
Kennett Square, PA 19348-0501
610-388-1000

Butterflies, grasses, herbs, perennials, prairies, roses, spring bulbs, trees, shrubs, vegetables, wildflowers

Alloway Gardens, Herb Farm

456 Mud College Road
Littlestown, PA 17340

Herbs, perennials, roses

Tyler Arboretum

515 Painter Road
Media, PA 19063-4424
610-566-5431

Butterflies, grasses, herbs, perennials, trees, shrubs, wildflowers

Pennsbury Manor

400 Pennsbury Memorial Road
Morrisville, PA 19067
215-946-0400

Vegetables

Nicolette House of Herbs

725 Walnut Street
Mt. Pleasant, PA 15666
412-547-2195

Herbs

Awbury Arboretum

Francis Cope House
One Aubury Road
Philadelphia, PA 19138

Butterflies, trees, shrubs, wildflowers

Bantram's Gardens

54th Street, Lindbergh Blvd.
Philadelphia, PA 19143
215-729-5281

Herbs, perennials, trees, shrubs, wildflowers

Morris Arboretum

University of Pennsylvania
100 Northwestern Avenue
Philadelphia, PA 19118
215-247-5777

Butterflies, grasses, herbs, perennials, roses, spring bulbs, trees, shrubs, wildflowers (ferns)

Phipps Conservatory

City of Pittsburgh
Schenley Park
Pittsburgh, PA 15213
412-622-6914

Butterflies, herbs, perennials, spring bulbs

Pittsburgh Civic Center Garden

Mellon Park
1059 Shady Avenue
Pittsburgh, PA 15232
412-441-4442

Butterflies, grasses, herbs, perennials, spring bulbs, trees, shrubs

South Dakota

Flower: Pasque Flower
Bird: Ring-necked Pheasant
Tree: Black Hills Spruce

Great Plains Native Plant Society

PO Box 461
Hot Springs, SD 57747
605-642-9378

Prairies, wildflowers

McCrory Gardens

Horticulture, Forestry, Landscape, Parks Department
South Dakota State University
Brookings, SD 57007-0996
605-688-5136

Butterflies, grasses, herbs, perennials, prairies, roses, trees, shrubs

Shakespeare Garden

400 College Avenue
PO Box 489
Wessington Springs, SD 57382

Butterflies, herbs, perennials, antique roses, spring bulbs, wildflowers

Wisconsin

Flower: Wood Violet
Bird: Robin
Tree: Sugar Maple

International Crane Foundation

E. 11376 Shady Lane Road
PO Box 447
Baraboo, WI 539130447
608-356-9462

Prairies

Old World Wisconsin

Outdoor Ethnic Museum
S. 103 W. 37890 Highway 67
Eagle, WI 53119
414-594-6300

Vegetables

Wehr Nature Center

Witnall Park Zoo
9701 W. College Avenue
Franklin, WI 53132

Prairies, roses, wildflowers

Green Bay Botanical Garden

2600 Larsen Road
PO Box 12644
Green Bay, WI 54307-2644
414-490-9457

Grasses, perennials, roses, trees, shrubs, wildflowers

Boerner Botanical Gardens

Milwaukee County Department of Parks
5879 South 92nd Street
Hales Corner, WI 53130
414-425-1130

Grasses, herbs, perennials, roses, spring bulbs, trees, shrubs, wildflowers

Rotary Gardens

1455 Palmer Drive
Janesville, WI 53545
608-752-3885

Perennials, prairies, roses, trees, shrubs, vegetables

Gideon Hixon House, Garden

429 North 7th Street
La Crosse, WI 54601-3301

Butterflies, grasses, herbs, perennials, roses, spring bulbs

Madison Arboretum

University of Wisconsin
1207 Seminole Hwy
Madison, WI 53711
608-263-7888

Butterflies, perennials, prairies, roses, trees, shrubs, wildflowers

Olbrich Botanical Gardens

3330 Atwood Avenue
Madison, WI 53704
608-246-4716

Grasses, herbs, perennials, roses, spring bulbs, wildflowers

Milwaukee County Zoo

10001 West Blumound Road
Milwaukee, WI 53226
414-771-5500

Vegetables

Mitchell Park Horticultural Conservatory

524 South Layton Blvd.
Milwaukee, WI 53215
414-278-4384

Grasses, perennials, spring bulbs

Paine Art Center and Arboretum

1410 Algoma Blvd
Oshkosh, WI 54901
414-235-4530

Grasses, herbs, perennials, roses, spring bulbs, trees, shrubs, wildflowers

Arboretum, Natural Gardens

US 14
Readstown, WI 54652

Butterflies, grasses, perennials, prairies, roses, trees, shrubs, wildflowers

Marathon County Historical Museum and Grounds

403 McIndoe Avenue
Wausau, WI 54403-4746
715-848-6143

Butterflies, perennials, roses, spring bulbs, trees, shrubs, wildflowers

Midwest Mail-Order Plant and Seed Sources

Here are some suggestions for Midwest nurseries and specialty growers; all will be eager to work with you. However, since time changes gardeners and gardens, please note that this information is offered only as possible places to buy plant material, not as specific recommendations.

A

Adamgrove
Route 1, Box 1472
California, MO 65018
free catalog
Perennials (daylilies)

Adams County Nursery
PO Box 108 / 26 Nursery Lane
Aspers, PA 17304
free catalog
Fruit

Alpine Valley Gardens
12446 County F
Stitzer, WI 53825
608-822-6382
free catalog
Groundcovers, perennials

Ambergate Gardens
8730 County Road 43
Chaska, MN 55318-9358
612-443-2248
catalog: $2.00 / display garden
Ornamental grasses, groundcovers, perennials

Amberway Gardens
5803 Amberway Drive
St. Louis, MO 63128
314-842-6103
catalog: $1.00 / display garden
Perennials (iris)

American Daylily and Perennials
PO Box 210
Grain Valley, MO 64029
800-770-2777
catalog: $5.00
Perennials (daylilies)

Anderson Iris Gardens
22179 Keather Avenue North
Forest Lake, MN 55025
612-433-5268
catalog: $1.00 / display gardens
Perennials (daylilies, iris, peonies)

Appalachian Gardens
PO Box 82
Waynesboro, PA 17268-0087
888-327-5483
free catalog
Butterflies, trees, shrubs

Arborvillage Farm Nursery
PO Box 227
Holt, MO 64048
catalog: $1.00 / display garden
Trees, shrubs

B

Bluestem Prairie Nursery
13197 East 13th Road
Hillsboro, IL 62049
217-532-6344
free catalog
Wildflowers

Bluestone Perennials
7211 Middle Ridge Road
Madison, OH 44057
800-852-5243
free catalog / display garden
*Ornamental grasses, groundcovers,
   herbs, perennials, bulbs, wildflowers*

Borbeleta Gardens
15980 Canby Avenue
Faribault, MN 55021-7652
507-334-2807
catalog: $3.00 / display garden
Perennials, bulbs

Bowman's Hill Wildflower
   Preserve
Washington Crossing Historic
   Park
PO Box 685
New Hope, PA 18938-0685
catalog: $1.00 / display garden
*Ornamental grasses, perennials, trees,
   shrubs, wildflowers*

Breck's Bulb Company
US Reservation Center
6523 North Galena Road
Peoria, IL 61632
800-722-9069
free catalog
Bulbs

Brookwood Garden
303 Fir Street
Michigan City, IN 46360
catalog: $2.98; includes a $5.00
   gift certificate / display garden
Perennials (daylilies, hosta)

Burpee Gardens
300 Park Avenue
Warminster, PA 18991-0001
800-888-1447
free catalog
*Fruit, ornamental grasses, groundcov-
   ers, herbs, perennials, prairies, roses,
   bulbs, trees, shrubs, vegetables*

Busse Gardens
5873 Oliver Avenue SW
Cokato, MN 55321-4229
800-544-3192
catalog: $2.00 / display garden
Perennials

C

Cape Iris Gardens
822 Rodney Vista Blvd
Cape Girardeau, MO 63701
573-334-3383
catalog: $1.00 / display garden
Bulbs, perennials (daylilies, iris)

Carino Nurseries
PO Box 538
Indiana, PA 15701
412-463-3350
free catalog
Fruit, trees, shrubs

Cascade Daffodils
PO Box 10626
White Bear Lake, MN 55110-
   0626
612-426-9616
catalog: $2.00 / display gardens
Bulbs

Cascade Forestry Nursery
22033 Fillmore Road
Cascade, IA 52033
319-852-3042
free catalog / display garden
Fruit, trees, shrubs (natives, conifers)

Charles Mueller
7091 N. River Road
New Hope, PA 18938
215-862-2033
free catalog / display gardens
Bulbs

Coburg Planting Fields
573 East 600 North
Valparaiso, IN 46383
219-462-4288
catalog: $2.00 / display garden
Perennials (daylilies)

Comanche Acres Iris Gardens
Route 1, Box 258
Gower, MO 64454
816-424-6436
catalog: $3.00 / display garden
Perennials (iris)

Companion Plants
7247 N. Coolville Ridge Road
Athens, OH 45701
614-592-4643
catalog: $3.00 / display garden
Herbs

CRM Ecosystems, Inc
Prairie Ridge Nursery
9738 Overland Road
Mt. Horeb, WI 53572
608-437-5245
catalog $3.00 / display garden
Butterflies, prairies, wildflowers

D

Davidson-Wilson Greenhouses
RR2, Box 168
Department 57
Crawfordsville, IN 47933-9426
catalog: $3.50 / display garden
Herbs

DeGiorgi Seed Company
6011 N Street
Omaha, NE 68117-1634
800-858-2580
free catalog / display garden
*Ornamental grasses, herbs, perennials,
    vegetables, wildflowers*

DeGrandchamp's Nursery
15575 77th Street
South Haven, MI 49090
616-637-3915
free catalog
Fruit

Down on the Farm Seed
PO Box 184
Hiram, OH 44234
catalog: $1.00, refundable with
    order
Herbs, vegetables (heirloom)

Dutchmill Gardens
1247 Union Street
Monroe, MI 48161
313-457-4326
free catalog / display garden
Perennials (daylilies)

E

Elixir Farm Botanicals
Brixey, MO 65618
417-261-2393
free catalog
Butterflies, herbs, perennials, wildflowers

Enchanted Valley Garden
9123 N. Terrorial Road
Evansville, WI 53536
608-882-4200
free catalog / display garden
Perennials (daylilies)

Enders Greenhouse
104 Enders Drive
Cherry Valley, IL 61016
815-332-5255
free catalog / display garden
Prairies, wildflowers

Englearth Gardens
2461 22nd Street
Hopkins, MI 49328
616-793-7196
free catalog / display garden
Perennials (daylilies, hosta)

F

Feder's Prairie Seed Company
12871 380th Avenue
Blue Earth, MN 56013-9608
507-526-3049
free catalog
Prairies, wildflowers

Fox Hollow Seed Company
PO Box 148
McGann, PA 16236
412-548-SEED
catalog: $1.00
Herbs, vegetables

G

Garden Perennials
Route 1, Box 164
Wayne, NE 68787-9801
402-375-3615
catalog: $1.00, refundable with
  first order / display garden
*Ornamental grasses, groundcovers,
  perennials, wildflowers*

Genesis Nursery
23200 Hurd Road
Tampico, IL 61283
catalog: $5.00
815-438-2220
Ornamental grasses, prairies

Gilberg Perennial Farms
2906 Ossenfort Road
Glencoe, MO 63038
314-458-2033
free catalog / display garden
*Ornamental grasses, groundcovers,
  herbs, perennials, bulbs, wildflowers*

Gilbert Wild and Son, Inc.
PO Box 338 / 112 Joplin St
Sarcoxie, MO 64862-0338
417-548-3514
catalog: $3.00 / display garden
Perennials (daylilies, iris, peonies)

Girard Nurseries
PO Box 428
Geneva, OH 44041
catalog: free / display garden
  located at 6839 N. Ridge E.,
  Route 20 in Saybrook
440-466-2881
*Groundcovers, ornamental grasses,
  trees, shrubs (conifers)*

Global Gardens
26820 Hwy. 169
Zimmerman, MN 55398
free catalog / display garden
612-856-3696
Perennials (daylilies, hosta)

Gourmet Gardener
8650 College Boulevard
Overland Park, KS 66210
913-345-0490
free catalog
Herbs, vegetables

Greenfield Herb Garden
PO Box 9
Depot and Harrison Street
Shipshewana, IN 46565
free catalog
800-831-0504
Herbs

H

Hamilton Seeds, Wildflowers
16786 Brown Road
Elk Creek, MO 65464
417-967-2190
free catalog / display garden
Prairies, wildflowers

Hartle-Gilman Gardens
4708 East Rose Street
Owatonna, MN 55060
507-451-3191
free catalog
Bulbs (lily)

Hartmann's Plantation
310 60th Street
Grand Junction, MI 49056
616-253-4281
free catalog
Fruit, groundcovers, trees, shrubs

Hauser's Superior View Farm
Route 1, Box 199
Bayfield, WI 54814
715-779-5404
free catalog / display garden
located 2.5 miles northwest of
Bayfield on County Trunk J
Perennials

Heard Gardens
5355 Merle Hay Road
Johnston, IA 50131
515-276-4533
catalog: $2.00 / display garden
Trees, shrubs (lilacs)

Heirloom Seed Project
Landis Valley Museum
2451 Kissel Hill Road
Lancaster, PA 17601
717-569-0401
catalog: $4.00
Fruit, herbs, vegetables

Heirloom Seeds
PO Box 245
W. Elizabeth, PA 15088-0245
412-384-0852
catalog: $1.00 - refundable with
first order
Herbs, vegetables

Henry Field Seed, Nursery
415 North Burnett
Shenandoah, IA 51602
605-665-4491
free catalog
*Butterflies, fruit, ornamental grasses,
groundcovers, herbs, perennials,
roses, bulbs, trees, shrubs, vegetables*

Hickory Hill Gardens
169 Ice Plant Road
PO Box 218
Loretto, PA 15940
814-886-2823
catalog: $2.75 / display garden
Perennials (daylilies)

Hildenbrandt's Garden
1710 Cleveland Street
Lexington, NE 68850-2721
308-324-4334
catalog: two first class stamps /
display garden
Perennials (daylilies, hosta, iris)

Historical Roses
1657 W. Jackson Street
Painesville, OH 44077
440-357-7270
free catalog with SASE
Roses

Hite Gardens

8255 Ratta Lee Lake Road
Clarkston, MI 48348
248-620-2629
catalog: two first class stamps
Perennials

Hobbycroft Gardens

Route 3, Box 219
Shelbyville, IL 62565
217-774-4509
free catalog / display garden
Perennials (daylilies)

Homestead Farms

Route 2, Box 31A
Owensville, MO 65066
573-437-4277
free catalog / display garden
Perennials (daylilies, hosta)

Huff's Garden Mums

710 Juniatta
Burlington, KS 66839
800-279-4675
free catalog / display garden
Perennials (chrysanthemums)

I

Indiana Berry and Plant Company

5218 West 500 South
Huntingburg, IN 47542
800-295-2226
free catalog / display garden
Fruit

Ion Exchange

1878 Old Mission Drive
Harpers Ferry, IA 52146-7533
800-291-2143
free catalog / display garden, all
natives
Butterflies, perennials, wildflowers

J

JB's Flower Garden

828 Comanche
Columbus, NE 68601
402-563-5438
free list / display gardens
Perennials (daylilies)

Josh's Daylilies

8787 North College Avenue
Indianapolis, IN 46240
317-848-7977
free catalog / display garden
Perennials (daylilies)

J.W. Jung Seed Company

335 S. High Street
Randolph, WI 53957-0001
800-297-3123
free catalog
*Butterflies, fruit, ornamental grasses,
groundcovers, herbs, perennials,
roses, bulbs, trees, shrubs, vegetables, wildflowers*

K

Klehm Nursery

4210 North Duncan Road
Champaign, IL 61821
800-553-3715
catalog: $4.00 refundable with
first order / display garden
*Ornamental grasses, perennials, trees,
shrubs*

Krohne Plant Farms

Route 6, Box 586
Dowagiac, MI 49057
616-424-5423
free catalog / display garden
Fruit

Kuk's Forest Nursery
10174 Barr Road
Brecksville, OH 44141-3302
216-546-2675
catalog: $2.00 / display garden
Perennials (hosta)

L

Lee's Gardens
PO Box 5
25986 Sauder Road
Tremont, IL 61568
catalog: $2.00 / display garden
Perennials, wildflowers

Lewis Mountain Herbs, Everlastings
2345 State Route 247
Manchester, OH 45144
catalog: $1.00 / display garden
Herbs

Liberty Seed Company
PO Box 806 / 128 -1st SE
New Philadelphia, OH 44663
800-541-6022
free catalog / display garden
Butterflies, fruit, ornamental grasses, groundcovers, herbs, perennials, prairies, roses, bulbs, trees, shrubs, vegetables, wildflowers

Limerock Ornamental Grasses, Inc.
70 Sawmill Road
Port Matilda, PA 16870
814-692-2272
catalog: $4.00 / display garden
Ornamental grasses

Little Valley Farm
5693 Snead Creek Road
Spring Green, WI 53588
608-935-3324
catalog: $1.00 / display garden
Prairies, ornamental grasses, trees, shrubs, wildflowers

M

Maple Tree Garden
PO Box 547
Ponca, NE 68770-0547
608-935-3324
catalog: $1.00 / display garden
Perennials (iris)

Majestic Gardens
2100 N. Preble County Line Road
West Alexandria, OH 45381
937-833-5100
catalog: two first class stamps / display garden
Perennials (daylilies)

Mari-Mann Herb Company
RR 4, Box 7
Saint Louis Bridge Road
Decatur, IL 62521-9404
217-429-1404
catalog: $2.00 / display garden
Herbs, perennials, wildflowers

Mary's Plant Farm
2410 Lanes Mill Road
Hamilton, OH 45013
513-894-0022
catalog: $1.00 / display gardens
Butterflies, ornamental grasses, groundcovers, herbs, perennials, roses, bulbs, trees, shrubs, wildflowers

McClure and Zimmerman
PO Box 368
108 W. Winnebago
Friesland, WI 53935
414-326-4220
free catalog
Bulbs

McGinnis Tree and Seed Company
309 East Florence
Glenwood, IA 51534
712-527-4308
free catalog
Prairies

Mellinger's, Inc.
2310 W. South Range Rd
Dept MWGB
North Lima, OH 44452
800-321-7444
free catalog / display garden
Fruit, ornamental grasses, groundcovers, herbs, perennials, prairies, bulbs, trees, shrubs, vegetables, wildflowers

Michigan Wildflower Farm
11770 Cutler Road
Portland, MI 48875-9452
517-647-6010
free catalog
Prairies, wildflowers

Midwest Wildflowers
PO Box 64
Rockton, IL 61072
catalog: $1.00
Wildflowers

Milaeger's Gardens
4838 Douglas Avenue
Racine, WI 53402-2498
800-669-9956
catalog: $1.00 / display garden
Ornamental grasses, perennials

Missouri Wildflowers Nursery
9814 Pleasant Hill Road
Jefferson City, MO 65109
573-496-3492
catalog: $1.00
Prairies, trees, shrubs, wildflowers

Mums by Paschke
12286 East Main Road
North East, PA 16428
814-725-9860
free catalog / display gardens
Perennials (chrysanthemum)

Musser Forests
PO Box 340, Dept. MW 97
Route 119 North
Indiana, PA 15701
412-465-5685
free catalog / display garden
Groundcovers, perennials, trees, shrubs

N

North Pine Iris Gardens
PO Box 595
308 North Pine
Norfolk, NE 68701
402-371-3895
catalog: $1.00 / display garden
Perennials (daylilies, hosta, iris)

Northern Grown Perennials
RR#1, Box 43
Ferryville, WI 54628
608-734-3178
catalog: $1.00 / display garden
Perennials (daylilies, hosta)

**Northwind Nursery and
  Orchards**
7910 335th NW
Princeton, MN 55371
612-389-4920
catalog: $1.00 / display garden
Fruit

O

Oikos Tree Crops
PO Box 19425
Kalamazoo, MI 49019-0425
616-624-6233
free catalog of natives
Fruit, trees, shrubs

Old House Gardens
536 Third Street
Ann Arbor, MI 48103-4957
catalog: $2.00
Bulbs (antique)

Otis Twilley Seed Company
PO Box 65
Trevose, PA 19053
800-622-7333
free catalog
Perennials, vegetables, wildflowers

P

PG Allen Farm Supply
Route 2, Box 8
Bristow, NE 68719
402-583-9924
free list with first class stamp
Prairies

Pinecliffe Daylily Gardens
6604 Scottsville Road
Floyds Knob, IN 47119
812-923-8113
catalog: $2.00 / display garden
Perennials (daylilies)

Prairie Moon Nursery
Route 3, Box 163
Winona, MN 55987
507-452-1362
catalog: $2.00 / display garden
Prairies

Prairie Nursery
PO Box 306
Westfield, WI 59364
608-296-3679
free catalog / display garden
*Ornamental grasses, prairies, wild-
  flowers*

Prairie Seed Source
PO Box 83
North Lake, WI 53064-0083
catalog: $1.00
Prairies, wildflowers

R

**Rocky Meadow Orchard and
  Nursery**
360 Rocky Meadow Road NW
New Salisbury, IN 47161
812-347-2213
catalog: $1.00 / display garden
Fruit

S

Sam Hill Gardens
9405 NW 112th Street
Malcolm, NE 68402
402-796-2191
catalog: $1.00, refundable with
  first order / annual open
  house
Perennials (daylilies)

Sam Kedem Nursery
Town and Country Roses
12414 191st Street East
Hasting, MN 55033
612-437-7516
catalog: $2.00, refundable with
  first order / display garden
*Perennials, roses (Dr. Griffith Buck
  roses), trees, shrubs*

Savory's Gardens
5300 Whiting Avenue
Edina, MN 55439-1249
612-941-8755
catalog: $2.00 / display garden
Perennials (hosta, daylilies)

Seed Savers Heritage Farm
3076 North Winn Road
Decorah, IA 52101
319-382-5990
free catalog
Perennials, vegetables (heirloom)

Sevald Nursery
4937 3rd Avenue S
Minneapolis, MN 55409
612-822-3279
catalog: $1.00—refundable with
  first order
Perennials (peonies)

Shady Oaks Nursery
112 10th Avenue SE
Waseca, MN 56093
800-504-8006
free catalog / display gardens
Perennials

Sharp Brothers Seed
396 SW Davis Street, Ladue
Clinton, MO 64735
800-451-3779
free list
*Ornamental grasses, prairies, wild-
  flowers*

Siegers Seed Company
8265 Felch Street
Zeeland, MI 49464
800-962-4999
free catalog
Vegetables (bulk seeds)

Smith Nursery
PO Box 516
Charles City, IA 50616
free catalog
Fruit, trees, shrubs

Soules Garden
5809 Rahke Road
Indianapolis, IN 46217
317-786-7839
catalog: $1.00, refundable with
  first order / display garden
Perennials (hosta, daylilies)

Spring Hill Nurseries
6523 North Galena Road
Peoria, IL 61632
800-582-8527
free catalog / display garden
Perennials, roses

Starhill Forest Arboretum
Route 1, Box 272
Petersburg, IL 62675
217-632-3685
catalog: $1.00 or SASE
Trees, shrubs (seeds)

Stark Bro's Nurseries, Orchards
PO Box 10
Source Code AB 1700A9
Louisiana, MO 63353-0010
800-325-4180
Fruit, groundcovers, trees, shrubs

Stock Seed Farms, Inc.
28008 Mill Road
Murdock, NE 68407-2350
402-867-3771
free catalog / native grass fields
Ornamental grasses, perennials, wild-
  flowers

Sunnybrook Farms Nursery
PO Box 6
9448 Mayfield Road
Chesterfield, OH 44026
440-729-7232
catalog: $1.00, deductible on first
  order / display garden
Herbs, groundcovers, perennials
  (hosta)

T

The Bulb Crate
2560 Deerfield Road
Riverwoods, IL 60015
847-317-1414
free catalog / display gardens
Bulbs, perennials

The Fragrant Path
PO Box 328
Ft. Calhoun, NE 68023
catalog: $2.00 / seeds only
Butterflies, ornamental grasses, herbs,
  perennials, trees, shrubs, wildflowers

The Natural Garden
38W443 Highway 64
St. Charles, IL 60175
630-584-0150
free catalog
Perennials

The Primrose Path
RD 2, Box 110
Scottsdale, PA 15683
412-887-6756
catalog: $2.00
Perennials, wildflowers

The Rosemary House
120 South Market Street
Mechanicsburg, PA 17055
717-697-5111
catalog: $3.00 / display garden
Herbs

The Waushara Gardens
N5491 5th Drive
Plainfield, WI 54966
715-335-4462
free catalog
Perennials (lily)

Tollgate Gardens, Nursery
20803 Junction Road
Bellevue, MI 49021
616-781-5887
free list / display garden
Fruit (papaw and nut seedlings)

V

Valley of the Daylilies
3507 Glengary Lane
Cincinnati, OH 45236
513-984-0124
Perennials (daylilies)

Vans Pines Nursery
7550 144th Avenue
West Olive, MI 49460-9707
free catalog
800-88-TREES
Groundcovers, trees, shrubs (bulk
  seedlings)

Varga's Nursery
2631 Pickertown Road
Warrington, PA 18976
215-343-0646
plant list: $1.00 / display garden
Perennials (ferns)

Veldherr Tulip Gardens
12755 Quincy Street and US 31
Holland, MI 49424
616-399-1900
free catalog / display garden
Bulbs

W

Walker's Green Space
2699 53rd Street
Vinton, IA 52349
800-837-3873
free catalog
Prairies, wildflowers

Watson Park Daylilies
8753 Westfield Blvd.
Indianapolis, IN 46240
catalog: $1.00 / display gardens
Perennials (daylilies, hosta)

**Wavecrest Nursery,
   Landscaping**
2509 Lakeshore Drive
Fennville, MI 49408
display garden
*Butterflies, ornamental grasses,
   groundcovers, trees, shrubs*

Wedge Nursery
Route 2, Box 114
Albert Lee, MN 56007
catalog: $1.00
Trees, shrubs

White Oak Nursery
6145 Oak Point Court
Peoria, IL 61614
309-693-1354
catalog: SASE / display garden
Perennials (hosta)

Wildflowers from Nature's Way
3162 Ray Street
Woodburn, IA 50275
515-342-6246
free catalog / display garden
Prairies, wildflowers

Wildlife Nurseries
PO Box 2724
Oshkosh, WI 54903-2724
414-231-3780
catalog: $3.00
*Ornamental grasses, prairies, wild-
   flowers*

Windrose Ltd.
1093 Mill Road
Pen Argyl, PA 18072-9670
610-588-1037
catalog: $3.00
Perennials, trees, shrubs

Index

Please note that the listings pp. 219–288 are not indexed.